TRIALS, TRIBULATIONS,
AND CELEBRATIONS

Trials, Tribulations, and Celebrations ঌ

African-American Perspectives on Health, Illness, Aging, and Loss

MARIAN GRAY SECUNDY

EDITOR

with the Literary Collaboration of

LOIS LaCIVITA NIXON

INTERCULTURAL PRESS

For information, contact:
Intercultural Press, Inc.
P.O. Box 700
Yarmouth, ME 04096, USA

Book design by Jacques Chazaud.
Cover design by LetterSpace.
Cover illustration: William H. Johnson, *Going to Church*
  c. 1932, serigraph, 33 × 26³/4.
  The Barnett-Aden Collection, Museum of African-American Art, Tampa, Florida.
Reproduced with permission.

Printed in the United States of America.

Library of Congress Cataloging-in-Publication Data

Trials, tribulations, and celebrations : African-American
  perspectives on health, illness, aging, and loss / (compiled) by
  Marian Gray Secundy with the literary collaboration of Lois LaCivita
  Nixon.
      p.   cm.
  Includes bibliographical references.
  ISBN 1-877864-00-5
  1. Afro-Americans—Health and hygiene—Literary collections.
  2. Afro-American aged—Health—Literary collections. 3. American
  literature—Afro-American authors. 4. Afro-Americans—Health and
  hygiene. 5. Afro-American aged—Health. I. Secundy, Marian Gray,
  1938– . II. Nixon, Lois LaCivita.
  PS509.N4T7   1991
  810.8'0354'08996073—dc20   91-37596

I dedicate this book to my mother,

Hazel Yates Gray,

who always provides encouragement
for continuing productivity.
I promise that I will
keep on "keepin' on."
MGS

This anthology records the stories
and celebrates the spirit and strength
of our culturally diverse society.
It is dedicated
to the human need for story
and to each of us as storytellers.
LLN

Contents

☙ ❧

SECTION II:
AGING

SECTION III:
LOSS AND GRIEF

Aunt Sue's Stories

LANGSTON HUGHES

Aunt Sue has a head full of stories.
Aunt Sue has a whole heart full of stories.
Summer nights on the front porch
Aunt Sue cuddles a brown-faced child to her bosom
And tells him stories.

Black slaves
Working in the hot sun,
And black slaves
Walking in the dewy night,
And black slaves
Singing sorrow songs on the banks of a mighty river
Mingle themselves softly
In the flow of old Aunt Sue's voice,
Mingle themselves softly
In the dark shadows that cross and recross
Aunt Sue's stories.

And the dark-faced child, listening,
Knows that Aunt Sue's stories are real stories.
He knows that Aunt Sue never got her stories
Out of any book at all,
But that they came
Right out of her own life.

The dark-faced child is quiet
Of a summer night
Listening to Aunt Sue's stories.

Acknowledgments

This anthology has been 'birthin' for a real long time, and Lord knows we are delighted to see it born. In 1982, I was fortunate enough to be selected to attend a seminar in Literature and Medicine at Hershey Medical College in Pennsylvania where, thanks to the National Endowment for the Humanities, I met Joanne Trautmann Banks and was exposed to her brilliance, charm, and most importantly, inspiration. Leaving there, I resolved to set about putting together an anthology which would present the poetry, novels, short stories, and essays of African-American writers on the subject of grief and loss. The research which was undertaken has resulted in the book which you are now holding. And of course it could not have been finalized without the support, literally and figuratively, of numerous people.

Thank you from the bottom of my heart to Lois LaCivita Nixon, who joined this effort late in its inception and who, with competence, energy, and patience, has assisted me in bringing this project to full fruition; to Kay Watson who voluntarily labored over messy manuscripts, encouraged me to keep going, and tried her

xiii

best to keep me organized and calm; Joanne Trautmann Banks and Edmund Pellegrino, who served as mentors, returned phone calls promptly, and lent their ultimate support to us; Ethelbert Miller for always having the information I needed and cheerfully producing detailed resources upon a moment's notice; and Vanessa Stroman and Ruth Matthews McPherson, who allowed me to add one more set of duties to their already full and overflowing plates.

Marian Gray Secundy, ACSW, Ph.D.
Professor, Howard University
College of Medicine
Washington, D.C.

This project initiated by Marian Secundy allows for new visits with writers whose works remain, too often, out of mainstream reading. Many of the selections evoked memories of my association with the Peace Corps—both the training at Howard University and my subsequent assignment in Togo, Africa. The writings recall currents and tensions of the sixties that stirred us to "do something"!

My thanks to Nick Cunningham, M.D., head of our team of health care volunteers in Togo; his idealism and dedication set me on a lifelong path of interests that eventually led to Marian Secundy. I also want to express appreciation and gratitude to Delese Wear, Ph.D. (NEOUCOM); Roy Behnke, M.D. (USF); Jack Moore, Ph.D. (USF); and Howard Carter, Ph.D. (Eckerd College), who all contributed in special ways as the project developed.

Lois LaCivita Nixon, Ph.D., M.P.H.
Assistant Professor
University of South Florida College of Medicine

Foreword

❧ ☙

We are driven, it seems, to distinguish ourselves, one from the other. A person says: "I am *A*, you are *B*, and that perceived difference allows me to know myself. Moreover, when you come too close to my defenses, I will fight you simply because you are not *A*." On the other hand, there are times—far less frequent, but probably even more intense—when *A* is lonely and says to *B*: "I want now to embrace you as my brother or sister. I yearn to make you one with my own soul, and I will mourn until we find our unity." So speak nation and nation, men and women, black and white.

Where does it come from, this deep bifurcation of human need? Most explanations are cultural. The cause may lie instead in our biology or, more likely, in some transcendent combination of the two. In any case, this fine anthology addresses the need for separateness as well as the need for union, and therein lies some of its power.

Crisis, of course, is universal. Illness, aging, death—everyone encounters them. In these treacherous spheres, no one's distaste or fear is any more significant than another's. No one's triumph is any less worthy. Put these classic tales of black suffering alongside such mainstream classics as "The Death of Ivan Ilych" or "Tell Me a Riddle," and potentially divisive questions of who A and B are melt away in the face of common human destiny. Therefore, it should be a great comfort to readers of every background to set black literary pieces into the mosaic of the larger community. Without them, in fact, the mosaic can never attain that wholeness and harmony of segments that since ancient times have been thought beautiful.

If this book engenders a feeling of oneness, it also offers to refine readers' identities, both personal and professional, by expertly tracing the impact of certain differences. A is not B. Blacks' experience of health and illness is not precisely the same as whites'. Placed, as it is here, within the context of shared human experience, the fact does not arouse defensiveness. On the contrary, understanding black perspectives liberates our knowledge, imagination, and skills.

For instance, the terror of early, violent death by drugs and murder in some urban black neighborhoods profoundly changes the behavior of a mother who seeks pediatric care for her growing son. But if we merely note that sociological observation, we have not done enough. After all, most intelligent educators and care givers have filed that and similar information somewhere in their brains. The point is, information cannot be activated until we deeply realize its truth—that is, until we imagine what that mother and her child endure. To achieve that goal, we need stories of all kinds to embody and dramatize the facts.

Nor is the study of contemporary black situations enough. History lives on in a people, sometimes unconsciously, rather in the manner of the embryological world wherein ontogeny recapitulates phylogeny. So if we want to know and imagine the lives of today's black patients, we must learn something of yesterday's. Langston Hughes, Claude McKay, Zora Neale Hurston, and many others, with their tales and poems of past racial struggles, provide this essential data.

This anthology will find its place in many educational settings. I am particularly grateful, however, for its contribution to the development of literature and medicine, an area of study that began its full-time academic life in medical schools in 1972 and that now supports a journal, provides the focus for conferences, and generally weaves itself into the humanistic education of physicians. In the summer of 1982 the field had the good fortune to attract Marian Secundy to an NEH-sponsored summer seminar at the Pennsylvania State University, at which time she realized that there were worrisome gaps in the reading lists. That the field has taken its insights mainly from white literature is due in part to the conventional education of most of its teachers and to the relative inaccessibility of some of the major black texts on medical matters. In part, too, the infrequent appearances of black writing can be traced to the initial problems faced by the mainly white students and clinicians, who were struggling to accept the literature of their *own* traditions as an integral part of medical education. Now that humanities courses in medical schools are no longer a radical presence, students are more likely to know that literature offers an important vehicle for hearing the depth of their patients' voices.

Those voices must also, of course, be heard in their breadth—that is, in their various philosophical dialects. In this respect the pieces collected here are bountiful. How in the world, for instance, is a white, middle-class, twenty-five-year-old male doctor, who wants to perform his role in the most intelligent and beneficent way, to approach a poor, aging, folk-educated, black, female patient? Suppose that her economic struggles and her attitudes toward such basic matters as family, health care, and death are mysteries to him. He may know that medical care, built on scientific generalizations, ultimately succeeds as an individual case history or story. But no facts from the patient's chart will stimulate his appreciation of her individuality like familiarity with some of the literature of her culture. Yes, his abstract understanding of the universality of medical crises will assist him. But without some concrete appreciation of that woman's differences from him, he may not make a healing connection with her. Substitute a twenty-five-year-old middle- or upper-class black doctor in the preceding formula and, given the narrow focus of most premedical education, he or she still may not understand what values the woman brings, along with her ailing body, to the clinic.

In fact, we need every bit of help possible when we attempt to handle medical turning points, whether as professionals or as patients. We are extraordinarily vulnerable when we face serious illness and loss from either end of the stethoscope. How fortunate we are, then, to live in a country where we have a multitude of ethnic and racial groups, each of which has spent generations trying to decipher the meaning of human tragedy. Perhaps one measure of wisdom is our willingness to listen to the tales of that man of a different color on our left and that woman of a different color on our right as we walk together toward life's inevitable crises.

Joanne Trautmann Banks, Ph.D.
The Pennsylvania State University
College of Medicine, 1990

Ethnicity and Healing

Ethnicity imprints every person, even those who think they have shaken off or rejected its embrace. It binds those with common roots and separates them from those with different origins. It suffuses body and oral language, as well as the way we take in, or distance ourselves, from the world and other people. Even the white, mainstream American male who labels others as "ethnics" is himself indelibly ethnic. His "Americanism," or the version of it he derives from his roots and locale, makes him as much ethnic as the most recently arrived immigrant.

Ethnic imprints may lie dormant or be overt, but they become most apparent in times of elemental challenge—in birth, marriage, illness, suffering, and dying. Ethnicity is a force in both the genesis and healing of illness. It contributes to the uniqueness of the experience of illness—the very uniqueness the physician must somehow penetrate, at least in part, if he or she is to heal effectively. It is, as a consequence, a moral obligation of the conscientious healer to comprehend and to empathize to some extent with the cultural identity of those he or she purports to heal.

This anthology is intended to help those who provide care for black Americans to understand something of the experience of illness as it is shaped by African-American culture. It is an invitation, as well, to appreciate the richness of the culture of the patients they see daily, but often really do not "see." Through the words and imagination of black writers, we can develop some feeling for the experiences of being a black physician, of the anguish and pain of discrimination, of the memory of lynchings, of the reality of drug addiction and poverty, of being black, of being old or infirm, or of dying.

The editors hope that these pieces will engender empathy, compassion, and some sense of the moral obligation we have to comprehend the special story of black people in America. These stories, poems, reminiscences, and reflections are far more effective teachers than didactic essays on the sociology, mores, or ethics of African-American life. Literature captures the imagination, evokes a vicarious experience, and reaches the person in a way no scholarly lecture could. These authors have experienced much of what they write about. They each have found a voice through which to communicate something of the predicament and suffering of black patients. Compassion means feeling what another person is feeling. This is a matter in which the heart responds first. Then the head follows.

Obviously, we can never get into the skin of another person. The pieces in this anthology can at best invite understanding for those who are sensitive enough to hear the message. Some, of course, will be so encased in their own ethnicity that even these powerful words will go unheard or unread, but no one with a sense of what it is to help and to heal can remain indifferent to the voices that sound through these pages, sometimes quietly, occasionally angrily, always poignantly.

These are not entreaties to pity. Through the strictures of the black experience in America we meet heroes and heroines, and victims—but not self-pitying victims. Even in their duress, they radiate the richness and strength of a culture closed to white people by obstacles—of language, lifestyle, and custom.

Paradoxically, as we learn more about the uniqueness of African-American culture, we are drawn closer to the common humanity we share with the subjects of these stories and poems. For in the end, as Dr. Marian Secundy so wisely says in her introduction, there is more we hold in common than we recognize. All humans become ill, suffer, and die and are fearful, anxious, and vulnerable in the face of disease, dying, or disability. All seek health, help, and healing. Our finitude and our vulnerability are the universal experiences that weld all humans to each other.

It is manifestly impossible to gain any depth of perception about all the ethnic groups a physician or nurse is apt to encounter. But surely there is an obligation to learn about whatever group figures prominently among our patients. Beyond that, there is a special obligation to African-Americans. Their numbers are significant, and their assimilation into American life has been slow. Their forebears were not willing immigrants, but slaves. There are also the special features of the black health experience—the prevalence of poverty, the higher incidence of certain diseases, the alarming infant mortality, the limited access to health care, and the paucity of black health care professionals. Moreover, until recently with the rapid increase of Asian immigrants, African-Americans and Native Americans were the only groups who did not at least share, as other ethnic groups did, the common ground of Western European culture.

Some physicians and nurses might argue that all of this is well and good, but they can practice good medicine or nursing without empathy. Medicine is, after all, an objective enterprise, and physiology is physiology. While no doubt some physicians and nurses are remarkably gifted with the attributes of compassion, the likelihood is that most overestimate their capacities for empathy. Moreover, it is precisely the canons of "good medicine" that make the effort to learn about the cultural milieu of our patients morally mandatory.

Ethnicity enters into every step of the healing relationship—from data collection to the implementation of the treatment. To be sure, some ethnic factors like the incidence of race-related diseases, drug sensitivity, or nutrition are objective. But at most stages ethnicity plays decisive roles that are more qualitative than statistical.

The first step in helping a sick person is to decide what is wrong. This we do by observing, recording, and interpreting signs and symptoms. Ethnic background often influences the way a patient perceives pain or reacts to it, describes symptoms or decides which are more important, and determines which to reveal and which to conceal.

The second step is to establish a list of probable diagnoses and possible treatments. Ethnicity here may give weight to certain diagnoses as more probable than others. Race-specific drug sensitivity or toxicity can materially alter the therapeutic regimen.

The third step is to arrive at a treatment which is not only technically "correct" but in the patient's best interests as perceived by the patient. The patient's values determine what constitutes health and the good life and the costs he or she is willing to sustain to achieve them. The values a patient chooses may be subtly or overtly shaped by ethnicity. Care givers must know and respect those values even if they contravene their own values or those of the dominant culture.

Finally, the treatment must be incorporated into the lives of the patients if they are to be healed, especially if the illness is chronic. This step depends upon educating the patient about what is to be done and why. Ethnicity may be an obstacle or an aid. The patient must in turn be convinced that the treatment is worthwhile; but what is worthwhile in one cultural milieu may not be in another.

Clearly, ethnicity shapes the way a patient and a physician see, interpret, and communicate the predicament of illness to each other. At the moment of their interaction, each is a unique person at a particular point in life. How each perceives the other may enhance or impede the healing purpose of their encounter. To ignore ethnicity is perilous not only in human terms but in terms of objective medicine as well. It is conceivable in overwhelmingly acute trauma or illness for a care giver to treat a patient with a minimum of compassion or empathy; yet, even this is illusory since most clinical choices are value-laden. When the patient's cooperation and compliance are needed, as they are in most illnesses, effective treatment without empathy is impossible.

When physician and patient share the same ethnic roots, many of the barriers to healing inherent in the experience of illness can be removed. Understanding the patient's reactions, values, choices, and style is crucial in arriving at mutually comprehensible clinical decisions. Trust is an essential and ineradicable ingredient in being healed, and it is far easier to generate among cultural compatriots than among those from diverse ethnic backgrounds. Some of the inequality in knowledge, if not power, is removed. Compassion, which entails experiencing something of the patient's experience, is deepened.

Simply sharing the same ethnic origins, however, is not sufficient. Sometimes physicians or nurses consciously want to distance themselves from their own ethnic group because of differences in socioeconomic status, the patient's lifestyle, or a desire to become assimilated into the dominant culture. Repudiation of one's own roots is too often necessary for success in American society. Under such circumstances a compassionate person alien to the patient's culture may be better suited to treat a patient whose ethnicity is overt.

* * *

This collection can be read profitably by anyone who provides care for African-American patients. It is especially suitable for medical students and residents who are beginning to form their attitudes toward the different kinds of patients they are called upon to treat. Read and then discussed in small groups under the guidance of an appropriately skilled teacher, the selections in this anthology will enlighten, move, and inspire.

While those outside the African-American experience will profit most, there is much here for black Americans as well. Some have drifted away from their roots. Some perhaps are even ashamed of them. These African-Americans will find here refreshment and a revitalization of pride in their own rich heritage as well as insight into the predicament of some of their less fortunate brothers and sisters.

This anthology is a model other ethnic groups might well emulate. Hispanic-Americans and Asians have their own unique experiences which shape the way they see health and illness, recovery, and death. What this collection (and similar ones for other ethnic groups) illustrates is that the more we probe into the ethnicity of our fellow humans, the more we will understand our own ethnicity. Most important, we will come to understand that under the differences of language, style, custom, and physiognomy, there is a common substratum of humanity that unites us.

Edmund Pellegrino, M.D.
Director, Center for the Advanced Study of Ethics
Georgetown University, 1990

The Nature of
African-American Literature

⋙ ⋘

Today the interest in African-American literature is flourishing. Across the United States scholars are providing us with a number of critical and provocative texts. The appearance of books like Houston A. Baker, Jr.'s *Blues, Ideology and Afro-American Literature*[1] and *Black Literature and Literary Theory,* edited by Henry Louis Gates, Jr.,[2] point us in a new and exciting direction.

These books follow the renaissance in African-American literature, which started in the sixties and continues to the present. For years now the shelves of bookstores, libraries, and homes have been filled with the writings of Amiri Baraka, Sonia Sanchez, June Jordan, James Alan McPherson, Ntozake Shange, Gloria Naylor, Charles Johnson, Rita Dove, August Wilson, and others.

The outpouring of novels, plays, and poetry does not necessarily address the material needs of the African-American community.

1. Houston Baker, *Blues, Ideology and Afro-American Literature* (Chicago: University of Chicago Press, 1984).
2. Henry Louis Gates, ed., *Black Literature and Literary Theory* (New York: Methuen Press, 1984).

We are still confronted with the task of determining how our literature can be used. The consideration of art as a resource and as a creative process to assist in social development is essential when taking into account the status of our people.

In the introduction to his anthology, *Understanding the New Black Poetry*,[3] critic Stephen Henderson concludes that the theme of liberation is a principal one in African-American literature, a quest that manifests itself in the public as well as the private worlds of the African-American. It is deeply woven into our search for identity and acceptance in America as well as in our own hearts and minds. As much as American history has been shaped by the peculiar institution of slavery, so too must American literature confront the quality and nature of culture created by the descendants of slaves. It is the responsibility of our writers to restore history to memory.

Today the audience for our literature is greater than ever before, despite the fact that educational levels in our communities do not support as large a literature-reading population as they should— a deficiency that needs to be remedied as rapidly as possible. The question of readers and audience is most important when we try to assess the impact or influence of our literature. For the African-American in the New World, the printed word was a gift to be used in the battle against enslavement and oppression. Frederick Douglass knew the power of his words as he composed the narrative of his life. His ability to write while others could not reinforced the preciousness of the gift. For truly, that which was given to Wheatley, Dunbar, Hughes, Cullen, Hurston, Brown, Wright, Ellison, Baldwin, and Morrison was a gift containing inspiration, power, and magic.

If the African-American writer restores history to memory, then our literature must be seen as pedagogy in process and not simply as an artistic navigation through language. The social function of our literature must not only be acknowledged, it must be put to use. For example, throughout our cities our youth are trapped, addicted, and disillusioned. The doors of opportunity have never been opened. There is no light at the end of the tunnel—or is there? Richard Wright's *Native Son*[4] remains a masterpiece, as well as a

3. Stephen Henderson, *Understanding the New Black Poetry* (New York: William Morrow and Company, 1973).
4. Richard Wright, *Native Son* (New York: Harper and Row, 1940).

text to be used in understanding our young people. We question the violence in our society without attempting to find its roots or causes. The African-American writer's ability to explore the various dimensions of the African-American personality can be helpful in the liberation of our people. What Wright understood, as would Chester Himes, John Oliver Killens, and James Baldwin who followed him, was the plight of the manchild.

What makes African-American literature of clinical importance to professionals today is the desire of writers to direct their work first to the African-American community. This decision comes after a tradition in which many writers of color first made their literary appeals to the white audience. Their art was not much different from some of the legal and political statements made by leaders within their community. The work was a moral objection and a protest against the living conditions of the African-American. It was a plea for others to acknowledge our humanity. It was a rejection of stereotypes and racial inferiority. At times the work seemed to be more concerned with politics and sociology than aesthetics. Critics were quick to agree or disagree with what the author said, without paying attention to how it was said. Others simply dismissed the work if they were offended by the politics. To be included in the mainstream, or to swim alongside on one's own, has always been a dilemma confronting African-Americans. The decision of writers in the late sixties to accept the need for a black aesthetic and new criteria for judging literature should not come as a surprise. These decisions caused an evolutionary transformation within our culture. The significance of this is the equivalent of a developing country first deciding to feed its own people before sending its wealth and resources overseas. The literature written during the sixties was "hot," and it leaped from the page in much the same manner as flames shooting from the inner cities that exploded with annual riots each summer. What one heard was angry voices and cries for redemption. Maulana Ron Karenga outlined the goals of the new art. Its purpose was to be functional, collective, and committing. Karenga's position pushed the writer into the struggle for social change. It was a demand that the artist recognize his or her social responsibility. Although Karenga, Amiri Baraka, Addison Gayle, Jr., and others called for all artists to speak the truth to the people, there was little critical explanation of how this was to be done. Our failure is now evident in how little the current generation of African-American youth know about the Black Arts Movement. Our failure is one of pedagogy as well as limited resources.

The recent literature written by African-American women illustrates how art can assist in empowerment. The power of sisterhood has been reinforced by the rediscovered work of Zora Neale Hurston and the contemporary work of Ntozake Shange, Gloria Naylor, Toni Morrison, and Alice Walker. The energy presently behind black studies stems from black women studies and the groundwork laid by Gloria Hull, Barbara Smith, Paula Giddings, Claudia Tate, and Johnetta Cole. What we witness happening across America is the lives of women being transformed and shaped by literature.

African-American literature has the power to teach our people values. The strength of imaginative fiction and good poetry is its tendency to elevate a community to a higher moral ground.

I have stood in front of young African-American children, trying to encourage them to read Gwendolyn Brooks and Sterling Brown. I have been patient, knowing that the teaching and healing will be a slow process. The poems and stories discussed today are just the beginning—and all beginnings are difficult.

We must teach our literature not as exercise or assignment but as something essential to life itself. James Baldwin once described the writer's battle with society as being a lover's war. African-American literature is a constant reminder, a testimony, that we have always loved. This is the eternal message for all our new generations to learn. Our poetry, novels, plays, and essays are expressions of love. When our teachers teach our children about their beauty, then the beautiful ones will again see themselves. On that day the killings will stop and the land will no longer drink our blood.

Ethelbert Miller
Director, Afro-American Resources Center
Howard University

Introduction

ঙ্গ ঌ

> Stories spring from the half-spoken words of . . . patients.
>
> WILLIAM CARLOS WILLIAMS, M.D.

> A note for physicians: if you listen carefully to what pa-
> tients say, they will often tell you not only what is wrong
> with them, but also what is wrong with you.
>
> WALKER PERCY, M.D.

In recent decades the university curriculum for many health-care professionals has been revised to include classes in medical humanities.[1] Practicing nurses and physicians have been surprised, and often pleased, to learn that students now have the opportunity—elective or required—to study literature, art, and sometimes music and dance during medical school and residency programs.[2]

Contemporary medical students continue to develop strong

1. According to the General Professional Education Report (GPER) by the Association of American Medical Colleges (Washington, D.C. 1984), medical education should be based on skills derived from "knowledge of the natural sciences, the social sciences, and the humanities." At many of the 127 colleges of medicine, courses have been introduced on an elective or required basis pertaining to history, literature and poetry, and medical ethics.

2. These areas are reviewed often in the *International Arts-Medicine Association Newsletter* (Philadelphia), which has included some references to the following articles: "The Sound of Healing: Music and Medicine" by Richard Ratzan, M.D.; "Music and Genetics: Art in the Laboratory"; and "Dance Medicine." In addition, Oliver Saks' story, "The Man Who Mistook His Wife for a Hat," has been transformed into an opera, and Rembrandt's "Dr. Tulp's Anatomy Lesson" has come to life in an impressive film made by the Netherlands Ballet.

analytical skills in lecture, laboratory, and clinical settings. They dissect, examine, observe, consult, measure, and conclude. But unlike laboratory specimens, patients are not easily pinned down and measured. While scientific tools prepare students for their work, the tools offered by the humanities encourage them to see the persistent and intangible variables within both the patient and the examining physician: elusiveness, ambiguity, and complexity. What may have been tidy and absolute in the textbook becomes uncertain and imprecise in the realm of practice. For example, in spite of everything learned about labor and delivery protocols in the classroom and clinic, Hemingway's short story, "Indian Camp," in which a doctor disastrously overlooks significant family emotions while competently carrying out a medical procedure, produces a powerful and unforgettable lesson about professional management and human unpredictability.

Storytellers like Ernest Hemingway, William Carlos Williams, and others have the ability to illuminate the shadowy outlines of life. According to Anne Hudson Jones, a teacher of medical humanities,

> compassion is a function of point of view, of seeing and experiencing vicariously through another person's eyes, of identifying with another person. Traditional narrative structures force the reader to identify with the main character (or characters) in a story. It's the literary device itself that allows us to achieve the purpose of increasing . . . empathy and compassion.[3]

Readers of literature and viewers of art move temporarily into a world of interpretive experience; if the work is good, the kaleidoscopic elements lead to expanded thoughts about human behaviors and sensitivities. When we review different values and perspectives, we learn about our own capacities for dealing with them.

The training of health-care professionals now includes medical humanities courses and employs such works as Trautmann and Pollard's *Literature and Medicine: An Annotated Bibliography,* Cousins' *Physicians and Literature,* Brody's *Stories and Sickness,* and recently, Mukand's *Sutured Words.* Many professors focus on materials created by physician-writers such as Rabelais, Doyle, Chekhov, and Williams. However, stories by Kafka, Hemingway,

3. Joanne Trautmann, ed., *Healing Art in Dialogue* (Carbondale, IL: Southern Illinois University Press, 1981).

Oates, Tan, Marquez, and Morrison; poetry by Frost and Dickinson; and art by Munch, Rockwell, Cassatt, and Dix are also helpful in discussions about the complexities of health and illness by those studying medicine.

Materials currently available are limited in their ability to expose readers to cultural diversity in general and to the black experience in particular, especially as captured in the imagination of other African-Americans. This is regrettable, considering that nonblack students have limited exposure even to middle- and upper-class African-Americans, and few are properly prepared for communicating competently with disadvantaged black patients.

Many who teach medical humanities in medical colleges, nursing schools, and other health-care settings have noted the inaccessibility of material reflecting black experiences. This is unfortunate. Nursing and medical students usually have clerkships or practical courses in public hospitals where unsponsored or indigent patients are treated, many of whom are black. Recognizing that no collection of readings about the black health experience was yet available, we began collecting stories and poems that would provide a beginning. We knew from experience what the power and value of an excerpt from Toni Morrison's *The Bluest Eye* was for students rounding in obstetrics, where care for indigent mothers might be different from those with more affluent backgrounds and payment sources. This excerpt, our students said, captured and conveyed feelings they could not forget.

Our plan, therefore, has been to gather our examples from the abundance of black writing that reveals the significance of color and social distinctions and to offer them as a starting point for exploration. As readers will see, in spite of the characters' many differences, the experiences of them all are influenced directly or indirectly by color.

Robert Coles, in *William Carlos Williams: The Knack of Survival in America,* speaks of "special observations."[4] Our stories deal with those special observations in that they reflect the full range of human rationality and emotion and the commonality of pain, suffering, and poverty. There is a very real difference, however, between the world of a privileged, educated reader and that of a poor black

---

4. Robert Coles, *William Carlos Williams: The Knack of Survival in America* (New Brunswick, NJ: Rutgers University Press, 1975), 39–40.

living in a rigidly defined white social system. We believe our readers, especially those who work daily with black patients, will benefit
from the perspectives offered in this book.

Our effort is a beginning, an attempt to provide a wide selection
of imaginative works describing the circumstances under which African-Americans live and the values that are important to them. Our
choices are but a sampling of the eloquent and poignant expressions of black people, their communities and customs. The short
stories and poems presented here expose readers to new experiences, offer them new insights, and, finally, draw them into a confrontation with new realities and unexpected truths.

At a recent Howard University writers' conference, Joyce Ladner commented that these "truths, ultimate realities of black life, are
difficult to capture in sociological disciplines. The texture of life, its
subtleties and nuances, are more complex than can be demon-
strated quantitatively."[5] Most of us understand the implications of
her remarks. We recognize the need for the physician to "listen to
me, to my story, if he/she is to succeed in treating my illness." The
blood tests, urine analyses, and vital signs deliver certain factual
information, but the real story of "my illness" is that of sadness and
loss. Truth eradicates error; so it is with black literature—old and
new truths are brought together to be examined, experienced, and
used in creative and compassionate ways.

The three divisions of the book represent familiar thematic
patterns for organizing medical discussions: illness and health-seek-
ing behavior, aging, and loss and grief. Occasional introductory
comments about biographical or historical matters are offered, and
each section ends with a number of discussion questions.

Our selections present black reactions to oppression, including
depictions of survival coping mechanisms, endurance, and destructive behaviors to which African-Americans have sometimes been
driven. They provide intimate insights into black families and communities, including the collisions within families that tap deep into
cultural realities and personal emotions. Since, as Geneva Smitherman once noted, "the lessons and precepts about life and survival
are handed down from generation to generation through story,
song, and folk singing,"[6] public education has not been a source of

5. Joyce Ladner, paper presented at the Black Writers Conference, Howard
University, Washington, DC, May 1983.

learning about the life of African-Americans and about their beliefs, values, and cultural perspectives. Here we offer readers an opportunity to discover what Ralph Ellison called "the complex ambiguity of black humanity versus the oversimplified clown, beast, anger represented in white literature."[7]

This anthology, then, is a framework for sharing in story and poem the joys and sadness that concern us all. We believe that literature and art are vital and engender pleasure, pain, and a hope that lingers in the mind of the reader long after the book is closed. In the end, our mission in this book is simple: "to inspire and communicate. It is not a linguistic event. It is an act of live, creative art destroying elitism ... expressing enthusiasm for freedom, love of people, benevolence, kindness."[8] The African-American writers presented here do what their counterparts have done in the past: help us come to terms with frailty, faith, and mortality ... and, finally, help us to know and appreciate the absolute wonder of the trials, tribulations, and celebrations of black people.

Marian Gray Secundy
Lois LaCivita Nixon

6. Geneva Smitherman, *Talkin' and Testifyin'* (New York: Houghton-Mifflin Brown, 1977).

7. Ralph Ellison, "Twentieth-Century Fiction and the Black Mask of Humanity," in *Images of the Negro in American Literature,* edited by Seyman Gross and John Edward Hardy (Chicago: University of Chicago Press, 1966), 116.

8. Joyce Joyce, paper presented at the English Department Seminar Series, Howard University, Washington D.C., Spring 1984.

SECTION I

❦ ❧

Illness and Health-Seeking Behavior

Poetry does not move us to be just or unjust in itself. It
moves us to thoughts in whose light justice and injustice
are seen in fearful sharpness of outline.   J. Bronowski

God made man because he loves stories.   Elie Wiesel

Introduction

In this chapter are selections that tell us about illness and health-
seeking behaviors in black settings. What, we might ask, is
unique to those settings and what do these differences mean to
health-care providers?

We know that while the number of black physicians is increasing, the percentage remains low. Nurses and ancillary-care workers
may be black or white, but the higher the employment status and
pay level, the greater the likelihood that whites will predominate.
In the health field, African-Americans, in spite of the social and
educational incentives and successes with integration, are prominent as patients, primarily indigent patients. Health-care administra-
tors who run hospitals and physicians' offices attempt to stress sys-

tematic, efficient patient management, yet most medical histories or charted records do not provide any cultural or environmental background or insights, many of which are crucial for good patient care.

How can literature counterbalance this deficiency? Joanne Trautmann Banks suggests that

> we come to a piece of fiction each of us with our own limitations, those necessarily imposed by our functioning in the real world. No matter how well-trained as observers—and certainly medical education hopes to train good observers—we normally do not see the full range of details in any given situation.[1]

The value of literature, Trautmann Banks feels, derives in part from its ability to explore "relationships of ideas to people." The diverse characters in this chapter demonstrate that value: fact and fiction work together to tell a more complete story about human behavior. A care giver who tends only to the factual needs is limited to an incomplete understanding of the patient and the care that ought to be provided. As readers glimpse the private literary worlds, they will store fictional material away for reuse in patient care in the same way that factual material will be recalled for similar use. In other words, fact and fiction work together to tell a more complete story about human behavior.

Our selections include fictional portrayals of the physiciwns, patients, and society by African-American writers and illustrate diversities and racial distinctions. If you, the reader, are black, you may feel very close to what is presented; if you are white, you may be stimulated to ask new questions and see new approaches to what may have previously seemed immutable.

If our assumptions about role distinctions are accurate, we believe that the anthologized stories will improve levels of understanding between predominantly white care providers and black and other minority patients. Definitions of what have been described as "black attitudes" will be challenged and reassessed. Readers are invited to open themselves to the experience of discovery in encountering people who are much like everybody else, except in

---

1. Joanne Trautmann, "The Wonders of Literature in Medical Education," *Mobius* 2, no. 3 (1982): 24.

their endless struggle with the sometimes subtle, but more often overt, impositions of oppression.

We begin with two separate accounts of the black physician. The first, a poem entitled "Parish Doctor" by Sterling A. Brown, evokes through dialogue and description the mystical traditions of rituals, incantation, and sacrifice. Because the highly revered folk practitioners are certain (by instinct and tradition) of the causes and cures of illness, the young, modern parish doctor's medical skills have little community regard. In spite of professional training, he is expected to be the dispenser of folk medicines and potions deriving their value from traditional mindsets and superstitions. "Bitter-bitter is the best," they say. The poem illustrates the tenacious grip of inherited beliefs and practices in preference to the distrusted authority of systematic sciences.

From Langston Hughes we have a very different portrayal: a physician exhibiting the sin of pride, uppityness, and racial denial. Though these two pictures of the black physician represent extremes, there is nothing to suggest that the practices and attitudes are particular to those who have black skin: folk practices are common at all levels of society, and unattractive personality transformations associated with the acquisition of a medical degree or the donning of a white hospital jacket easily cross color lines.

We tend to equate birth with springtime and renewal, joy and promise. But as health workers know, dark shadows of pain, suffering, and disappointment are frequently cast over these occasions. Although many writers, ranging from Ernest Hemingway to Toni Morrison, have focused on the mechanics and emotions of labor and delivery, few have produced the personally sharpened focus of Toi Derricotte in the two poems entitled "Delivery" and "The Presentation." The narrative technique is stream of consciousness, so that the reader is enveloped in visual, emotional, and intellectual swirlings. The observations and feelings of the mother will linger in readers' minds, and health workers, who may have formed rigid and judgmental impressions of unwed mothers, may be startled into new awarenesses and sensitivities.

A thread of white oppression and mean-spiritedness based on skin color is woven through many of the subsequent stories in this section. "My Most Humiliating Jim Crow Experience" by Zora Neale Hurston, for example, is a direct confrontation with discrimination. Humiliation has many faces, as poignantly illustrated by other authors: physical examinations are rude and disrespectful (Jones); a black physician is abused for aiding a severely injured white girl (Edwards); a mother reveals a touching nobleness in her efforts to seek help for her young son's painful toothache (Gaines); a pubescent girl experiences fear, shame and uncertainty about what is happening at menarche (Bambara); and a rural mother, desperate for help from the white doctor who never arrives, resorts to unorthodox medicine for her dying baby (Walker).

Audre Lorde's personal chronicle of the effects of cancer on women in general, and on black women in particular, is a powerful account of struggle and determination. Cancer does not follow racial lines, and fears elicited by this nondiscriminating disease intrude from time to time into all of our lives. Lorde articulates our worst fears about the insidious disease and the metaphorical impact it has on others. She voices her "feelings and thoughts about the travesty of prostheses, the pain of amputation, the function of cancer in a profit economy, the confrontation with mortality, the strength of women loving, and the power and rewards of self-conscious living."[2] As a black lesbian, she has come to understand isolation; nevertheless, she was not prepared for the additional dimensions of isolation shared by all women with breast cancer. The increased awareness of being separate served ironically to intensify her sensual acuities, her awareness of others: "The terrible thing is that nothing goes past me these days, nothing." Later, she adds, that there

> is no room around me in which to be still, to examine and explore what pain is mine alone—no device to separate my struggle within from my fury at the outside world's viciousness, the stupid brutal lack of consciousness or concern that passes for the way things are. The arrogant blindness of comfortable white women.

The section concludes with a story and a poem about abortion from the maternal point of view. In a time when politicians and others relentlessly oversimplify the issue, these pieces illustrate the deeper intellectual soul-searching and emotional tribulations women go through in making their decisions.

The questions that follow this and each of the other two sections are intended for personal reflection and group discussion.

2. Audre Lorde, *The Cancer Journals*, 2nd ed. (San Francisco: Spinsters/Aunt Lute, 1980), 9.

4

Joyce Carol Oates recently observed that contrary impulses shape storytelling: one toward brevity, compactness, artful omission; the other toward expansion, amplification, enrichment. Our questions consider both impulses. Some refer to specific characters, settings, and events; others stretch beyond the confines of the page.

Parish Doctor

₰ STERLING A. BROWN

They come to him for subscriptions
They resent examination, investigation
They tell *him* what is wrong with them,
  They *know.*

It is pus on de heart, hole in de head
The maul is open, they got stummatache,
Somebody let some night air in the battens.
They want him only to subscribe,
The *medcins:* bitter-bitter is the best.

"Docteur, I doan b'leeve you can do nottin
  fuh me

I got a snake in me. I know, me, I been
  spelled.

You laugh, mon? I tell you son, a snake he in
  my inside."

He tells them he's the best conjuh doctor, best
  for roots and herbs,

North of New Orleans. They pop their eyes;

"You tink he know dose ting for true?"

They drink the boiled juices of a jit black hen
For diarrhea, for consumption
They kill a jit black dog, bury him three days,
  then cook him

And oil the ailing person with the grease;
For rheumatism they kill a turkey buzzard,

7

Dry him up; rub the stiff jints with the mess.
But jit black dogs and *caranchos* are none
        too plentiful.
They come to see their docteur, when these fail.

They like him; young, good-looking, easy laugher,
As brown as they and one of theirs forever.
The women call him *cher*: tender but embarrassed.
Their good men pass sly glances at his
        clipped moustache.

They think he lies about the conjuh knowledge
But still he got sharp eyes, you never know.
They pay him off with garden truck and cane
        juice.

One auntie brought him six hens tied together
Squawking and screaming enough to wake a
        graveyard.

One hen was jit-black to help him fix his
        medcins.

One night, past midnight, we jolted twelve miles to
        a cabin

It seemed as if the Lord would never make it.
"Tank Gawd, you'se here. I tole'em you would
        get here.

He's hurted bad. He caught a bullet in his laig.
Tank Gawd, you'se come." In the dull light of
        the lamp.

I watched his skillful probing for the slug.
Outside the ring of light, dark faces watched us,
His fingers were deft and gentle. The woman's
        sobbing

Quieted; the man on the table lay there
    sweating

Breathing heavily, but trusting; his eyes rolled
Following the hands.

Dr. Sidesaddle
ᡶ LANGSTON HUGHES

Dear Dr. Sidesaddle:

I, Jesse B. Semple, better known as Simple, take pen in hand to write you this letter. I have just read your article in *See-Saw Magazine* in which you writ about how you and your family have completely integrated, and that you-all have no problems whatsoever with your white neighbors and your white friends in your white house in your white neighborhood in the sideskirts of White Manors. First, Dr. Sidesaddle, I want to ask you how you can say yours is a white neighborhood if you are there? If one drop of black blood makes a white man black, you *colored* being in a white neighborhood must do something to that neighborhood that is not white.

Anyhow, dear Dr. Sidesaddle, your office is here in Harlem where I live. All of your patients is colored. You know that Harlem is not integrated and neither am I. But if you was to invite me up to your house in the suburbans, it would give me a chance to see what integration is like. But, of course, if I was to come up there, I expect no sooner had I arrived than somebody would say there was one Negro too many in the neighborhood. Of all the pictures I saw of you and your surroundings in that colored magazine last week, you and your wife and your children was the only colored in the pictures. All your friends and next-door neighbors are white.

The church you are going to in the pictures is white. I saw you and your wife setting in this pew. In front of you was white and behind you was white, and the minister was white. I did not even see a Negro in the choir—and you know Negroes can sing. Can't they have more than just two Negroes—you-all—in a integrated church? And when your children go to Sunday School do they ever see a black angel on their Sunday School cards? Do you-all ever sing any gospel songs? It looks like to me to be the kind of church in which a tambourine is never shook.

I went to a integrated church once with my wife, Joyce, down-

10

town in New York City, in which, Joyce said, the members are all looking for the higher things. The minister read his sermon off of a paper, and I must say it was all I could do to keep from going to sleep. Nobody in the congregation even said, "Amen!" When the songs were sung, nobody clapped a hand. Joyce said, "This is a dignified church."

I said, "It is dull to me."

Joyce said, "You do not appreciate thoughts in religion. You want emotions."

I said, "I want something to keep me awake."

Dear Dr. Sidesaddle, in a integrated church does a minister *have* to *read* his sermon? Or do all white ministers read from a paper? How come they are not so full of the spirit that they can just spill out God's word without first writing it down and reading it from a paper? They just drone along and never raise their voices, even to say, "Hallelujah!" I do not see how they ever make converts. Was you converted in that white church, or did you just integrate on general principles? I bet you do not even dare to pat your foot during a song.

In the pictures in that magazine, it shows you and your family being served your dinner by a Japanese butler. Now, dear Dr. Sidesaddle, I has nothing against the Japanese. But as bad as Negroes need work, why not me for your butler? And, since I expect you grew up on collard greens and ham, I do not think you was eating Japanese food. But what I am trying to get at—and to which I expects from you an answer—is this: As you roll down here to Harlem every day to your office in your white Thunderbird to give out prescriptions to black patients and operate on black appendages, then drive home every night to your white house in your white neighborhood in the suburbans, do you draw the color line yourself? Or is it your intention to integrate me along with you up there in White Manors someday? Dear Dr. Saddleside—I mean, Sidesaddle—that is all I wants to know as I sign off—

Yours sincerely truly,
Jesse B. Semple

11

Delivery

❧ TOI DERRICOTTE

i was in the delivery room. PUT YOUR
FEET UP IN THE STIRRUPS. i put them up, obedient
still humbled, though the spirit was growing larger
in me, that black woman was in my throat, her thin
song, high pitched like a lark, and all the muscles
were starting to constrict around her.
i tried to push just a little. it
didn't hurt. i tried a little more.

ROLL UP, guzzo said. he wanted to give me
a spinal. NO. I DON'T WANT A SPINAL. (same
doctor as ax handle up my butt, same as shaft
of split wood, doctor spike, driving the
head home where my soft animal cowed and prayed and
cried for his mother.)

or was the baby
part of this
whole damn
conspiracy,
in on it with
guzzo,
the two of them
wanting to shoot
the wood
up me for
nothing,
for playing
music to him
in the dark
for singing
to my round
clasped
belly
for filling

up with
pizza on a cold
night, dough
warm.

maybe
he
wanted
out,
was saying
give her
a needle
and let me/the hell/
out of here
who cares
what she
wants
put her
to sleep.

(my baby
pushing off
with his black
feet
from the dark
shore, heading
out, not
knowing
which way and trusting,
oarless and eyeless, so
hopeless
it didn't matter.)

no. not
my baby.
this
loved
thing
in/and of
myself

so i balled up
and let him
try to
stick it in.
    maybe
something was
wrong

    ROLL UP
he said
    ROLL UP
but i don't want it
    ROLL UP ROLL UP
but it doesn't hurt

we all stood,
nurses, round the white
light
hands
hanging
empty at our sides
    ROLL UP IN A BALL
all of us not
knowing
how
or if
in such a world without
false promises
we could say
anything
but, *yes,*
yes.
come take it
and be quick.

i put my belly in my hand
gave him that
thin side
of my back
the bones

intruding on the air
in little knobs
in joints
he might
crack
down my spine
his knuckles
rap
each twisted
symmetry
put me on
the rack,
each
nerve
bright
and stretched
like canvas.

he couldn't get it in!
three times, he tried
ROLL UP, he cried, ROLL UP
three times
he couldn't get it in!

dr. y (the head obstetrician)
came in

"what are you
doing, guzzo,
i thought she
wanted
natural . . .

(to me) do
you want
a shot . . . no? well,

PUT YOUR LEGS UP,
GIRL, AND
PUSH!"

and suddenly, the light
went out
the nurses
laughed
and nothing
mattered
in this 10
a.m. sun
shiny morning
we were well
the nurses and the
doctors cheering
that girl
combing hair
all in one
direction
shining
bright as water.

   i
grew deep
in me
like fist and i
grew deep
in me
like death
  and i
grew deep
in me
like hiding in the sea and
i was
over me
like
sun and i
was under
me
like sky and i
could look
into myself

like one
dark eye.

    i was her
and she was me
and we were
scattered round
like light
    nurses
      doctors
cheering

    such waves

my face
contorted,
never
wore
such mask, so
rigid
and so dark
    so
bright, un-
compromising
brave
no turning
back/no
no's.

i was so
beautiful. i
could look
up in the
light and
see my huge-
ness,
arc,
electric,
heavy, fleshy, living
light.

no wonder they
praised me,
a gesture
one makes
helpless and
urgent, praising
what goes on
without our praise.

when there
was nowhere
i could go, when i
was so deep
in myself
so large
i had to
let it out
they said
    drop back. i

dropped back
on the table
panting,
they moved
the head, swiveled
it correctly

    but i

       i

was
loosing
her. something
   a head
coming through
the door.
NAME PLEASE/
PLEASE /NAME /whose

head /i
don't know /some /
    disconnection

NAME PLEASE /

and i
am not ready:
the sudden visibility
his body,
his curly wet hair,
his arms
abandoned in that air,
an arching, squiggling thing,
his skin must be
so cold,
but there is nothing
i can do
to warm him,
his body clutches
in a wretched
spineless way.

they expect me
to sing
joy joy
a son is born,
child is given.
tongue
curled in my head
tears, cheeks
stringy with
damp hair.

this lump
of flesh,
lump of steamy
viscera.

who

is this
child

who

is his father

    a child
    never having
    been seen
    before,
    without
    credentials
    credit cards without
    employee
    reference or
    high school grades or
    anything
    to make him
    human make
    him mine but
    skein of
    pain to
    chop off
    at the navel.

    while they could
    they held him down and
    chopped him, held him up
    my little fish, my blueness
    swallowed in the air
    turned pink
    and wailed.

        no more. enough.
        i lay back, speechless, looking
        for something

20

to say to myself.

after you have
touched the brain,
that squirmy
lust of maggots,
after you have
pumped the heart,
that thief,
that comic, you
throw her in the trash.
and the little one
in a case
of glass . . .

he is not i
i am not him
he is not i

. . . the stranger . . .

blue
air
protects us from each other.

here.
here is the note he brings.
it says, *"mother."*

but i do not even know
this man.

The Presentation

ॐ TOI DERRICOTTE

they wheeled her out of the delivery room on a silver cart,
a piece of limp meat without a soul. when she woke the
day was fine crystal filaments shaking itself around
her.

she waited for something wrapped like a package, something
that knew its name better than she knew it; a thing she
had to discover, to unwrap and count, slowly, parting the
visible.

under her gown, the body of a stranger fed itself, sucked
moisture into her breasts, collapsed her womb like dried
eggplant.

a new muscle shaped her, clamped itself over her being.
whatever was left, hung limp: a dumb creature, numbly
attending.

My Most Humiliating Jim Crow Experience

&. ZORA NEALE HURSTON

My most humiliating Jim Crow experience came in New York instead of the South as one would have expected. It was in 1931 when Mrs. R. Osgood Mason was financing my researches in anthropology. I returned to New York from the Bahama Islands ill with some disturbances of the digestive tract.

Godmother (Mrs. Mason liked for me to call her Godmother) became concerned about my condition and suggested a certain white specialist at her expense. His office was in Brooklyn.

Mr. Paul Chapin called up and made the appointment for me. The doctor told the wealthy and prominent Paul Chapin that I would get the best of care.

So two days later I journeyed to Brooklyn to submit myself to the care of the great specialist.

His reception room was more than swanky, with a magnificent hammered copper door and other decor on the same plane as the door.

But his receptionist was obviously embarrassed when I showed up. I mentioned the appointment and got inside the door. She went into the private office and stayed a few minutes, then the doctor appeared in the door all in white, looking very important, and also very unhappy from behind his rotund stomach.

He did not approach me at all, but told one of his nurses to take me into a private examination room.

The room was private all right, but I would not rate it highly as an examination room. Under any other circumstances, I would have sworn it was a closet where the soiled towels and uniforms were tossed until called for by the laundry. But I will say this for it, there was a chair in there wedged in between the wall and the pile of soiled linen.

The nurse took me in there, closed the door quickly and disappeared. The doctor came in immediately and began in a desultory manner to ask me about my symptoms. It was evident he meant to get me off the premises as quickly as possible. Being the sort of objective person I am, I did not get up and sweep out angrily as I was first disposed to do. I stayed to see just what would happen, and further to torture him more. He went through some motions, stuck a tube down my throat to extract some bile from my gall bladder, wrote a prescription and asked for twenty dollars as fee.

I got up, set my hat at a reckless angle and walked out, telling him that I would send him a check, which I never did. I went away feeling the pathos of Anglo-Saxon civilization.

And I still mean pathos, for I know that anything with such a false foundation cannot last. Whom the gods would destroy, they first made mad.

Asylum

࿔ GAYL JONES

When the doctor coming? When I'm getting examined? They don't say nothing all these white nurses. They walk around in cardboard shoes and grin in my face. They take me in this little room and sit me up on a table and tell me to take my clothes off. I tell them I won't take them off till the doctor come.

Then one of them says to the other, You want to go get the orderly?

She might hurt herself.

Not me, I won't get hurt.

Then they go out and this big black woman comes in to look after me. They sent her in because they think I will behave around her. I do. I just sit there and don't say nothing. She acts like she's scared. She stands next to the door.

You know, I don't belong here, I start to say, but don't. I just watch her standing up there.

The doctor will come in to see you in a few minutes, she says.

I nod my head. They're going to give me a physical examination first. I'm up on the table but I'm not going to take my clothes off. All I want them to do is examine my head. Ain't nothing wrong with my body.

The woman standing at the door looks like somebody I know. She thinks I'm crazy, so I don't tell her she looks like somebody I know. I don't say nothing. I know one thing. He ain't examining me down there. He can examine me anywhere else he wants to, but he ain't touching me down there.

The doctor's coming. You can go to the bathroom and empty your bladder and take your clothes off and put this on.

I already emptied my bladder. The reason they got me here is my little nephew's teacher come and I run and got the slop jar and put it in the middle of the floor. That's why my sister's daughter had me put in here.

I take my clothes off but I leave my bloomers on cause he ain't examining me down there.

The doctor sticks his head in the door.

I see we got a panty problem.

I say, Yes, and it's gonna stay.

He comes in and looks down in my mouth and up in my nose and looks in my ears. He feels my breasts and my belly to see if I got any lumps. He starts to take off my bloomers.

I ain't got nothing down there for you.

His nose turns red. I stare at the black woman who's trying not to laugh. He puts a leather thing on my arm and tightens it. He takes blood out of my arm.

I get dressed and the big nurse goes with me down the hall. She doesn't talk. She doesn't smile. Another white man is sitting behind a desk. He is skinny and about my age and he attaches some things to my head and tells me to lay down. I lay down and see all the crooked lines come out. I stare at circles and squares and numbers and move them around and look at little words and put them together anyway I want to, then they tell me to sit down and talk about anything I want to.

How I do?

I can't tell you that, but we can tell you're an intelligent person even though you didn't have a lot of formal education.

How can you tell?

He doesn't say nothing. Then he asks, Do you know why they brought you here?

I peed in front of Tony's teacher.

Did you have a reason?

I just wanted to.

You didn't have a reason?

I wanted to.

What grade is Tony in?

The first.

Did you do it in front of the little boy?

Yeah, he was there.

He doesn't comment. He just writes it all down. He says tomorrow they are going to have me write words down, but now they are going to let me go to bed early because I have had a long day.

It ain't as long as it could've been.

What do you mean?

26

I look at his blue eyes. I say nothing. He acts nervous. He tells the nurse to take me to my room. She takes me by the arm. I tell her I can walk. She lets my arm go and walks with me to some other room.

Why did you do it when the teacher came?
She just sit on her ass and fuck all day and it ain't with herself.
I write that down because I know they ain't going to know what I'm talking about. I write down whatever comes into my mind. I write down some things that after I get up I don't remember.
We think you're sociable and won't hurt anybody and so we're going to put you on this floor. You can walk around and go to the sun room without too much supervision. You'll have your sessions every week. You'll mostly talk to me, and I'll have you write things down everyday. We'll discuss that.
I'll be in school.
He says nothing. I watch him write something down in a book. He thinks I don't know what he put. He thinks I can't read upside down. He writes about my sexual amorality because I wouldn't let that other doctor see my pussy.

My niece comes to visit me. I have been here a week. She acts nervous and asks me how I'm feeling. I say I'm feeling real fine except everytime I go sit down on the toilet this long black rubbery thing comes out a my bowels. It looks like a snake and it scares me. I think it's something they give me in my food.
She screws up her face. She doesn't know what to say. I have scared her and she doesn't come back. It has been over a month and she ain't been back. She wrote me a letter though to tell me that Tony wanted to come and see me but they don't allow children in the building.
I don't bother nobody and they don't bother me. They put me up on the table a few more times but I still don't let him look at me down there. Last night I dreamed I got real slender and turned white like chalk and my hair got real long and the black woman she helped them strap me down because the doctor said he had to look at me down there and he pulled this big black rubbery thing look like a snake out of my pussy and I broke the stirrups and jumped right off the table and I look at the big black nurse and she done turned chalk white too and she tells me to come to her because

27

they are going to examine my head again. I'm scared of her because she looks like the devil, but I come anyway, holding my slop jar.

If the sounds fit put them here.
They don't fit.
How does this word sound?
What?
Dark? Warm? Soft?
Me?
He puts down: libido concentrated on herself.
What does this word make you feel?
Nothing.
You should tell me what you are thinking?
Is that the only way I can be freed?

From **If We Must Die**

⤷ JUNIUS EDWARDS

The day was still young, and Will had time enough to find another job. There was another factory a couple blocks away. He
went there.

"I'd like to apply for a job."

"You'd like to apply for a job?"

"Yes, sir."

"You come from this town?"

"Yes, sir."

"Where'd you work last?"

Will told the man where he had worked, and the man picked
up the telephone and dialed the factory. Will knew it would be no
use. The man hung up the phone.

"Get out of here," he said.

Will left.

He went to three other places, but it was no use. They would
all check with the factory and find that he had tried to register to
vote and that he had been fired. It was no use. It was going to go
right on being no use. Will knew that. Even so, he decided to try
again the next day. He had wished that he could tell Mom he had
been fired and then add that he had gone out and found another
job. Now he couldn't do that. He knew it was no use. He started
to hope that it really would go right on being no use. He wished
they would keep saying "Get out of here" and keep throwing him
out. It was the best excuse he could give Mom for leaving town.
And home. He needed an excuse for Mom. I think I really wanted
to escape from it all along, thought Will.

After he was thrown out of the last personnel office, Will
headed for the bus stop. He had to walk two blocks to get to it. He
came to a corner and waited for the traffic light to change before
he crossed the street. While he stood there waiting, a woman came
up. She was alone and she was blind. She had gray hair, but she
wasn't really old. The gray was scattered through her brown hair,
and it was really the brown that Will saw first.

She and Will stood there on the corner, side by side, and waited for the light to change. Her head was turned toward Will.

"Would you be so kind to help me across the street?" she asked.

Will heard her, looked quickly at her and around her and saw no other person there, and realized she was talking to him. She stood there smiling. She had on dark glasses, and her teeth were even and very white. She had a red and white cane in her right hand. Will looked up at the traffic light just as it changed. He stepped quickly into the street and crossed it. When he was a half block away, he turned and looked back and saw that the woman was still standing there, waiting for someone to help her across the street.

Will had wanted to help her across the street. He wanted very much to help her across the street. He was raised that way. It would have been a very easy thing to do. But not for me. No. Not for me. I have learned my lesson, thought Will.

He had learned long ago what kindness meant, and he had learned, too, that he had to think and think good before he did something to help women, even if they needed it desperately, even if it took but a minute of his time, even if it meant their life or death.

Will had learned while he was still in the Army. It was during the time when he was almost completely well from his wound. They had sent him away from Korea and to a hospital near his home town, but far enough away to keep him from going home, except on weekends.

He had been in the hospital one month when the doctors told him that he was well enough to go out for four hours each day. The hospital was near a very small town, so small, in fact, that half the people from that town worked on the Army camp and in the Army hospital. Will knew the town couldn't be exciting because it was so small, and even if there was excitement, four hours wouldn't be enough time to really enjoy it, but he decided to go there anyway, just to see what it was like and, mainly, because it was the only place he could go to in four short hours.

There was a different system there, for Will, with the bus. He had to stand there until the other people were in the bus; then he got on and paid his fare and got off again and went to the back door and got on again. Will had to have the exact fare because the driver was only allowed to give change to the other people.

Will got on and paid his fare, and then he got off and ran to the back door. He had to run because there were times the driver would close the back door and drive off. If that had happened, Will would lose his money and lose his time because he would have had to stand there and wait for another bus. One of his fellow patients, who had been wounded in a leg and used crutches, had tried for an hour one day to get a bus. He was never able to make it to the back door in time. Then there was another fellow who hadn't been successful until the third bus came along. That was bad. He was an enlisted man in the United States Army, and that meant he could afford to lose neither time nor money.

When Will came through the back door, there, sitting on the back seat, was a captain who had been his doctor in Korea. Will recognized him, but the captain didn't remember Will. He had had so many patients. The captain explained that he had recently been assigned to the hospital and he was going to town for the first time, as was Will.

Since it was the first time for both of them, the captain suggested they see the town together. Will agreed, and smiled to himself thinking of this. Up there it would be queer. Up there it is not done. Officers and enlisted men would not go out together up there. Overseas and up there and out there it is unheard of. But down home it is not queer at all. If these officers are down home and they want to go out, they have to be prepared to go to the same places that the naughty enlisted men go. There were only a few places they could go, officers or not. Just because they were officers and gentlemen, that meant nothing. Not down home. Just because the all-powerful United States Government said they were officers and gentlemen, that meant nothing. Not down home. When they left the Army post, that was the end of that officers and gentlemen business. Down home they were dirt. They were dirt anyway, down home, but the uniform made them even more dirt. War and in between wars, the uniform was dirt. There was no down-home hospitality for uniforms. Officers learned quickly that they had to go to a certain part of the towns—the part looked upon by the locals as dirt, and when they got to that certain part, they had to find the part looked upon by the locals of that certain part as dirt. Then they were home; and they had to stay in that part of the certain part and chase and play with the same women that the enlisted men chased and played. The morale of these officers must be very, very low, thought Will.

When they got off the bus, they had to do it fast, Will on the captain's heels, because sometimes the driver would drive away when people were halfway through the back door. Sometimes it was wise to sit there until the bus came to a stop where many people would be using the front door. That way, there was no fear of the bus moving off when people were halfway through the back door.

"It's great to be back in the good old U.S.A.," Will said.

"The U.S.A., yes," the captain said. "This is really insane. I don't see why the Army had to build a hospital here, or anyway why they had to send me here."

"Can't you see?" Will tried to be cheerful. "The sunshine and good old down-home hospitality. And think of your patients."

"Yes," the captain said. "Well, let's not stand here. Let's take a look at the town, and then I have to get back."

"Oh. You got the duty tonight, Captain?"

"No."

"Then what's your rush?"

"Do you know where we are?"

"Sure."

"I have no desire to be here at high noon, let alone at night."

"It's not that bad. Different rules from up there, but it's not that bad," said Will.

"Maybe not. I just don't like it, that's all. I felt better when I was in Korea."

Will doubted that. The captain was bitter, so Will thought that he would be quiet for a while. They walked in silence for a while.

"Not a bad-looking town," Will said presently.

"Clean."

"Say. Get load of that."

There was a golden-haired girl one half block in front of them. From that distance, she looked very pretty.

"Reminds me of Paris, or better still, Stockholm," said the captain.

Will had never been to either Paris or Stockholm.

"Boy," he said, more at the knowledge of the captain having been in Europe than at the sight of the girl.

"Don't stare so hard," said the captain. "Remember where we are."

"Okay, but it's not that bad."

The girl stopped at the corner and waited for a car to pass, and then she stepped off the curb into the street. There was another car coming around the corner, and she did not see it. Will and the captain saw it. They yelled to the girl. She did not hear them. The car kept coming toward her. It refused to stop. They yelled again and again to the girl. Then she saw the car, and she stopped, stood still, and screamed, her hands up to her face. The car pushed toward her. Will and the captain yelled, trying to tell her to run, get out of the way. They couldn't move either. They had stopped walking, and they stood there yelling at the top of their voices. It was no use. The sight and the sound of steel against flesh against concrete told them it was no use. The car sped on.

"Come on, Doc," Will said. "Looks like you go on duty right here."

Will started to run to the girl. The captain grabbed his right arm, stopping him.

"Hold it," he said.

"Come on, Captain."

"Wait."

"Wait? But, Captain, that girl. . . ."

"I know."

"Well, come on."

"Don't be stupid. Remember where we are."

"So what? You're a doctor. You going to—"

"I know," the captain put in.

". . .Let that girl lay in the gutter?"

"Yes."

"Why, Captain?"

"Those people there, now, they'll take care of her."

"But you're a doctor."

"They'll get one."

"Captain. Are you crazy? You're just standing there. You're a doctor, man."

"I know what I'm doing."

Will couldn't understand it. "You're killing that girl," he said.

"They'll take care of her."

"Doctors never say that. I'll bet you've even doctored on Red prisoners in Korea. That girl is American."

"Don't get heated up."

"What do you expect me to do? You're a captain and an officer. It's your duty to help that girl."

"Okay. Okay. I know all that, but I just can't."

"I don't care what you think of this town. This is no time to—"

"At ease. Listen to me," the captain ordered.

"Yes, sir," Will said quickly and remembered he was still Army.

"Listen. They would never let me lay a hand on that girl. They wouldn't let me near her."

"How do you know? I don't see you trying to help her."

"What are—just what are you trying to prove?" the captain asked, his face lined.

"I just expect to see you do your duty. That's all. You're standing there and that poor girl could be dying."

They stared at each other in silence for a moment, searching. Then they looked over to where the girl was. She lay still. Five men stood around. They all looked helpless. One of them took off his jacket and made a cushion for her head.

"I learned a little about first aid," Will said.

"Okay," said the captain. "Okay."

"You're going to help." Will smiled.

"Let's go over there. We'll see."

They started off, walking. Before they got there, another man ran up. "I called the ambulance," he said to the others. "Is she bad?"

"Don't know."

"Looks like it."

The girl was crying.

"Help me," she said. "Please."

"I don't think we should fool with moving her," one of the men said.

"She's bleeding," another said.

"My leg," the girl cried.

"Don't nobody know what to do for her?"

"Please," the girl said.

Six men stood around her with their mouths hanging open, lighting cigarettes, rubbing chins, scraping feet in the dirty street, kicking up dust from the concrete, putting hands in pockets, taking them out—helpless.

"Now, you just take it easy, Miss."

"The doctor's coming."

"She's bleeding bad."

"Please."

"Anybody got a car?"

"Don't think we ought to move her."

"Please. My leg. My leg."

"Now, you just take it slow, Miss."

"The ambulance is coming soon, now."

"Quiet now, Miss."

"Please. My God, please help me." She kept crying.

"Easy, Miss."

She screamed.

Will and the captain arrived. "Pardon me," Will said. He pushed past one of the men. The captain was at his heels.

"What the—" one of the men started. He grabbed Will's right arm and pushed him back against the captain.

"Where are you-all going?" he asked.

"What do you think you're doing?" another asked.

"Get out of here."

"But we want to help," Will said. "He's a doctor."

"What?"

"Get out of here."

"I'm a doctor," the captain said.

"My leg, my leg. Please," the girl said.

All the men turned toward Will and the captain.

The girl screamed.

"You know what's good for you, you'll start hightailing it," one of the men said.

The others mumbled agreement.

"But I want to help. I'm a doctor."

"Don't talk back."

"I'm not going to tell you-all any more," a man said.

"But he's a doctor," Will said.

"You-all hear what I say?" a man yelled.

"My God. Please. Please," the girl said.

The captain moved toward the girl. The men, who were between the captain and the girl, moved forward. The captain stopped.

"You-all just going to stand there? You-all going to stand there?" one of the men asked, shouting.

The girl screamed.

"The girl," Will said.

"Girl? You being smart?" One of the men used both hands on Will's chest and pushed him back.

"You better git."

"Smart ones. Let's get them," another man said and moved forward.

"The girl," another said.

The man stopped. "Move," he said.

"Please. Please help me," the girl cried.

"Come on, let's go," the captain said to Will.

The girl screamed.

"Start running," a man said.

"Come on," the captain said.

They started off, walking. Will looked back at the girl.

"You want to die?" the captain asked Will. "You want to die? Let's get out of here."

Will kept looking back. "That poor girl," he said.

"Take it easy, Miss," one of the men said. He took out his handkerchief and kneeled down beside her. "Easy," he said and wiped her face.

"Help me, please. Help me."

"The doc's coming pretty soon now, Miss."

"Please. Please. God."

"Easy, Miss. Easy, now."

Will kept looking back, walking away and thinking the captain was beside him. The captain was twenty feet ahead of him, not looking back.

"I said run," a man shouted to them.

"Get a move on," another yelled.

It was then that Will turned and saw that the captain was well in front of him and beginning to run. Will ran too.

One of the men picked up a stone, and he threw it at them. It did not hit them. Two other men threw stones that missed too.

"Run. I said run, you dirty. . . ."

The girl screamed.

Will caught up with the captain, and they ran side by side.

They ran to the bus stop and, since there was no bus in sight, they ran to the next bus stop. Will fell down just as he got in the bus because he had let the captain go in first, and the bus jerked off just as Will stepped in, tripping him. They rode back to the hospital in silence. It was the last time Will had seen the captain, but he remembered him well, and he had learned a lesson. Will had learned to think before helping women. That is why he had not helped the blind woman across the street. He could not know who would have seen him do it. He could not know what would happen, and he did not want to find out. He could not know how many angry men would throw stones at him.

He was tired of it all.

The Sky Is Gray

&& ERNEST J. GAINES

G o'n be coming in a few minutes. Coming 'round that bend down there full speed. And I'm go'n get out my hankercher and I'm go'n wave it down, and us go'n get on it and go.

I keep on looking for it, but Mama don't look that way no more. She looking down the road where us jest come from. It's a long old road, and far's you can see you don't see nothing but gravel. You got dry weeds on both sides, and you got trees on both sides, and fences on both sides, too. And you got cows in the pastures and they standing close together. And when us was coming out yer to catch the bus I seen the smoke coming out o' the cows' nose.

I look at my mama and I know what she thinking. I been with Mama so much, jest me and her, I know what she thinking all the time. Right now it's home—Auntie and them. She thinking if they got 'nough wood—if she left 'nough there to keep 'em warm till us get back. She thinking if it go'n rain and if any of 'em go'n have to go out in the rain. She thinking 'bout the hog—if he go'n get out, and if Ty and Val be able to get him back in. She always worry like that when she leave the house. She don't worry too much if she leave me there with the smaller ones 'cause she know I'm go'n look after 'em and look after Auntie and everything else. I'm the oldest and she say I'm the man.

I look at my mama and I love my mama. She wearing that black coat and that black hat and she looking sad. I love my mama and I want put my arm 'round her and tell her. But I'm not s'pose to do that. She says that's weakness and that's cry-baby stuff, and she don't want no cry-baby 'round her. She don't want you to be scared neither. 'Cause Ty scared of ghosts and she always whipping him. I'm scared of the dark, too. But I make 'tend I ain't. I make 'tend I ain't 'cause I'm the oldest, and I got to set a good sample for the rest. I can't ever be scared and I can't ever cry. And that's the reason I didn't never say nothing 'bout my teef. It been hurting me and hurting me close to a month now. But I didn't say it. I didn't say it 'cause I didn't want act like no cry-baby, and 'cause I know us didn't have 'nough money to have it pulled. But, Lord, it been hurting me. And look like it won't start till at night when you trying to get little sleep. Then soon's you shet your eyes—umm-umm, Lord, look like it go right down to your heart string.

"Hurting, hanh?" Ty'd say.

I'd shake my head, but I wouldn't open my mouth for nothing. You open your mouth and let that wind in, and it almost kill you.

I'd just lay there and listen to 'em snore. Ty, there, right 'side me, and Auntie and Val over by the fireplace. Val younger 'an me and Ty, and he sleep with Auntie. Mama sleep 'round the other side with Louis and Walker.

I'd just lay there and listen to 'em, and listen to that wind out there, and listen to that fire in the fireplace. Sometime it'd stop long enough to let me get little rest. Sometime it just hurt, hurt, hurt. Lord, have mercy.

2

Auntie knowed it was hurting me. I didn't tell nobody but Ty, cause us buddies and he ain't go'n tell nobody. But some kind o' way Auntie found out. When she asked me, I told her no, nothing was wrong. But she knowed it all the time. She told me to mash up a piece o' aspirin and wrap it in some cotton and jugg it down in that hole. I did it, but it didn't do no good. It stopped for a little while, and started right back again. She wanted to tell Mama, but I told her Uh-uh. 'Cause I knowed it didn't have no money, and it jest was go'n make her mad again. So she told Monsieur Bayonne, and Monsieur Bayonne came to the house and told me to kneel down 'side him on the fireplace. He put his finger in his mouth and made the Sign of the Cross on my jaw. The tip of Monsieur Bayonne finger is some hard, 'cause he always playing on that guitar. If us sit outside at night us can always hear Monsieur Bayonne playing on his guitar. Sometime us leave him out there playing on the guitar.

He made the Sign of the Cross over and over on my jaw, but that didn't do no good. Even when he prayed and told me to pray some, too, that teef still hurt.

"How you feeling?" he say.

"Same," I say.

39

He kept on praying and making the Sign of the Cross and I kept on praying, too.

"Still hurting?" he say.

"Yes, sir."

Monsieur Bayonne mashed harder and harder on my jaw. He mashed so hard he almost pushed me on Ty. But then he stopped.

"What kind o' prayers you praying, boy?" he say.

"Baptist," I say.

"Well, I'll be—no wonder that teef still killing him. I'm going one way and he going the other. Boy, don't you know any Catholic prayers?"

"Hail Mary," I say.

"Then you better start saying it."

"Yes, sir."

He started mashing again, and I could hear him praying at the same time. And, sure 'nough, afterwhile it stopped.

Me and Ty went outside where Monsieur Bayonne two hounds was, and us started playing with 'em. "Let's go hunting," Ty say. "All right," I say; and us went on back in the pasture. Soon the hounds got on a trail, and me and Ty followed 'em all cross the pasture and then back in the woods, too. And then they cornered this little old rabbit and killed him, and me and Ty made 'em get back, and us picked up the rabbit and started on back home. But it had started hurting me again. It was hurting me plenty now, but I wouldn't tell Monsieur Bayonne. That night I didn't sleep a bit, and first thing in the morning Auntie told me to go back and let Monsieur Bayonne pray over me some more. Monsieur Bayonne was in his kitchen making coffee when I got there. Soon's he seen me, he knowed what was wrong.

"All right, kneel down there 'side that stove," he say. "And this time pray Catholic. I don't know nothing 'bout Baptist, and don't want know nothing 'bout him."

3

Last night Mama say: "Tomorrow us going to town."

"It ain't hurting me no more," I say. "I can eat anything on it."

"Tomorrow us going to town," she say.

And after she finished eating, she got up and went to bed. She always got to bed early now. 'Fore Daddy went in the Army, she used to stay up late. All o' us sitting out on the gallery or 'round the fire. But now, look like soon's she finish eating she go to bed.

This morning when I woke up, her and Auntie was standing 'fore the fireplace. She say: " 'Nough to get there and back. Dollar and a half to have it pulled. Twenty-five for me to go, twenty-five for him. Twenty-five for me to come back, twenty-five for him. Fifty cents left. Guess I get a little piece o' salt meat with that."

"Sure can use a piece," Auntie say. "White beans and no salt meat ain't white beans."

"I do the best I can," Mama say.

They was quiet after that, and I made 'tend I was still asleep.

"James, hit the floor," Auntie say.

I still made 'tend I was asleep. I didn't want 'em to know I was listening.

"All right," Auntie say, shaking me by the shoulder. "Come on. Today's the day."

I pushed the cover down to get out, and Ty grabbed it and pulled it back.

"You, too, Ty," Auntie say.

"I ain't getting no teef pulled," Ty say.

"Don't mean it ain't time to get up," Auntie say. "Hit it, Ty."

Ty got up grumbling.

"James, you hurry up and get in your clothes and eat your food," Auntie say. "What time yall coming back?" she say to Mama.

"That 'leven o'clock bus," Mama say. "Got to get back in that field this evening."

"Get a move on you, James," Auntie say.

I went in the kitchen and washed my face, then I ate my breakfast. I was having bread and syrup. The bread was warm and hard and tasted good. And I tried to make it last a long time.

Ty came back there grumbling and mad at me.

"Got to get up," he say. "I ain't having no teef pulled. What I got to be getting up for."

Ty poured some syrup in his pan and got a piece of bread. He didn't wash his hands, neither his face, and I could see that white stuff in his eyes.

"You the one getting a teef pulled," he say. "What I got to get up for. I bet you if I was getting a teef pulled, you wouldn't be getting up. Shucks; syrup again. I'm getting tired of this old syrup. Syrup, syrup, syrup. I want me some bacon sometime."

"Go out in the field and work and you can have bacon," Auntie say. She stood in the middle door looking at Ty. "You better be glad you got syrup. Some people ain't got that—hard's time is."

"Shucks," Ty say. "How can I be strong."

"I don't know too much 'bout your strength," Auntie say; "but I know where you go'n be hot, you keep that grumbling up. James, get a move on you; your mama waiting."

I ate my last piece of bread and went in the front room. Mama was standing 'fore the fireplace warming her hands. I put on my coat and my cap, and us left the house.

4

I look down there again, but it still ain't coming. I almost say, "It ain't coming, yet," but I keep my mouth shet. 'Cause that's something else she don't like. She don't like for you to say something just for nothing. She can see it ain't coming, I can see it ain't coming, so why say it ain't coming. I don't say it, and I turn and look at the river that's back o' us. It so cold the smoke just raising up from the water. I see a bunch of pull-doos not too far out—jest on the other side the lilies. I'm wondering if you can eat pull-doos. I ain't too sure, 'cause I ain't never ate none. But I done ate owls and black birds, and I done ate red birds, too. I didn't want kill the red birds, but she made me kill 'em. They had two of 'em back there. One in my trap, one in Ty trap. Me and Ty was go'n play with 'em and let 'em go. But she made me kill 'em 'cause us needed the food.

"I can't," I say. "I can't."

"Here," she say. "Take it."

"I can't," I say. "I can't. I can't kill him, Mama. Please."

"Here," she say. "Take this fork, James."

"Please, Mama, I can't kill him," I say.

I could tell she was go'n hit me. And I jecked back, but I didn't jeck back soon enough.

"Take it," she say.

I took it and reached in for him, but he kept hopping to the back.

"I can't, Mama," I say. The water just kept running down my face. "I can't."

"Get him out o' there," she say.

I reached in for him and he kept hopping to the back. Then I reached in farther, and he pecked me on the hand.

"I can't, Mama," I say.

She slapped me again.

I reached in again, but he kept hopping out my way. Then he hopped to one side, and I reached there. The fork got him on the leg and I heard his leg pop. I pulled my hand out 'cause I had hurt him.

"Give it here," she say, and jecked the fork out my hand.

She reached and got the little bird right in the neck. I heard the fork go in his neck, and I heard it go in the ground. She brought him out and helt him right in front o' me.

"That's one," she say. She shook him off and gived me the fork. "Get the other one."

"I can't, Mama. I do anything. But I can't do that."

She went to the corner o' the fence and broke the biggest switch over there. I knelt 'side the trap crying.

"Get him out o' there," she say.

"I can't, Mama."

She started hitting me across the back. I went down on the ground crying.

"Get him," she say.

"Octavia," Auntie say.

'Cause she had come out o' the house and she was standing by the tree looking at us.

"Get him out o'there," Mama say.

"Octavia," Auntie say, "explain to him. Explain to him. Jest don't beat him. Explain to him."

But she hit me and hit me and hit me.

I'm still young. I ain't no more 'an eight. But I know now. I know why I had to. (They was so little, though. They was so little. I 'member how I picked the feathers off 'em and cleaned 'em and helt 'em over the fire. Then us all ate 'em. Ain't had but little bitty piece, but us all had little bitty piece, and ever'body jest looked at me, 'cause they was so proud.) S'pose she had to go away? That's why I had to do it. S'pose she had to go away like Daddy went away? Then who was go'n look after us? They had to be somebody left to carry on. I didn't know it then, but I know it now. Auntie and Monsieur Bayonne talked to me and made me see.

5

Time I see it, get out my hankercher and start waving. It still 'way down there, but I keep waving anyhow. Then it come closer and stop and me and Mama get on. Mama tell me go sit in the back while she pay. I do like she say, and the people look at me. When I pass the little sign that say White and Colored, I start looking for a seat. I jest see one of 'em back there, but I don't take it, 'cause I want my Mama to sit down herself. She come in the back and sit down, and I lean on the seat. They got seats in the front, but I know I can't sit there, 'cause I have to sit back o' the sign. Anyhow, I don't want sit there if my Mama go'n sit back here.

They got a lady sitting 'side my mama and she look at me and grin little bit. I grin back, but I don't open my mouth, 'cause the wind'll get in and make that teef hurt. The lady take out a pack o' gum and reach me a slice, but I shake my head. She reach Mama a slice, and Mama shake her head. The lady jest can't understand why a little boy'll turn down gum, and she reach me a slice again. This time I point to my jaw. The lady understand and grin little bit, and I grin little bit, but I don't open my mouth, though.

They got a girl sitting 'cross from me. She got on a red over-coat, and her hair plaited in one big plait. First, I make 'tend I don't even see her. But then I start looking at her little bit. She make 'tend she don't see me neither, but I catch her looking that way. She got a cold, and ever' now and then she hist that little hankercher to her nose. She ought to blow it, but she don't. Must think she too much a lady or something.

Ever' time she hist that little hankercher, the lady 'side her say something in her yer. She shake her head and lay her hands in her lap again. Then I catch her kind o' looking where I'm at. I grin at her. But think she'll grin back? No. She turn up her little old nose like I got some snot on my face or something. Well, I show her both o' us can turn us head. I turn mine, too, and look out at the river.

The river is gray. The sky is gray. They have pull-doos on the water. The water is wavy, and the pull-doos go up and down. The bus go 'round a turn, and you got plenty trees hiding the river. Then the bus go 'round another turn, and I can see the river again. I look to the front where all the white people sitting. Then I look at that little old gal again. I don't look right at her, 'cause I don't want all them people to know I love her. I jest look at her little bit, like I'm looking out that window over there. But she know I'm looking that way, and she kind o' look at me, too. The lady sitting 'side her catch her this time, and she lean over and say something in her yer.

"I don't love him nothing," that little old gal say out loud.

Ever'body back there yer her mouth, and all of 'em look at us and laugh.

"I don't love you, neither," I say. "So you don't have to turn up your nose, Miss."

"You the one looking," she say.

"I wasn't looking at you," I say. "I was looking out that window, there."

"Out that window, my foot," she say. "I seen you. Ever' time I turn 'round you look at me."

"You must o' been looking yourself if you seen me all them times," I say.

"Shucks," she say. "I got me all kind o' boyfriends."

"I got girlfriends, too," I say.

"Well, I just don't want you to get your hopes up," she say.

I don't say no more to that little old gal, 'cause I don't want have to bust her in the mouth. I lean on the seat where Mama sitting, and I don't even look that way no more. When us get to Bayonne, she jugg her little old tongue out at me. I make 'tend I'm go'n hit her, and she duck down side her Mama. And all the people laugh at us again.

6

Me and Mama get off and start walking in town. Bayonne is a little bitty town. Baton Rouge is a hundred times bigger 'an Bayonne. I went to Baton Rouge once—me, Ty, Mama and Daddy. But that was 'way back yonder—'fore he went in the Army. I wonder when us go'n see him again. I wonder when. Look like he ain't ever coming home. . . . Even the pavement all cracked in Bayonne. Got grass shooting right out the sidewalk. Got weeds in the ditch, too; jest like they got home.

It some cold in Bayonne. Look like it colder 'an it is home. The wind blow in my face, and I feel that stuff running down my nose. I sniff. Mama say use that hankercher. I blow my nose and put it back.

Us pass a school and I see them white children playing in the

yard. Big old red school, and them children jest running and playing. Then us pass a cafe, and I see a bunch of 'em in there eating.
I wish I was in there 'cause I'm cold. Mama tell me keep my eyes
in front where they blonks.

Us pass stores that got dummies, and us pass another cafe, and
then us pass a shoe shop, and the bald-head man in there fixing
on a shoe. I look at him and I butt into that white lady, and Mama
jeck me in front and tell me stay there.

Us come to the courthouse, and I see the flag waving there.
This one yer ain't like the one us got at school. This one yer ain't
got but a handful of stars. One at school got a big pile of stars—one
for ever' state. Us pass it and us turn and there it is—the dentist
office. Me and Mama go in, and they got people sitting ever' where
you look. They even got a little boy in there younger 'an me.

Me and Mama sit on that bench, and a white lady come in
there and ask me what my name. Mama tell her, and the white lady
go back. Then I yer somebody hollering in there. And soon's that
little boy hear him hollering, he start hollering, too. His mama pat
him and pat him, trying to make his hush up, but he ain't thinking
'bout her.

The man that was hollering in there come out holding his jaw.

"Got it, hanh?" another man say.

The man shake his head.

"Man, I thought they was killing you in there," the other man
say. "Hollering like a pig under a gate."

The man don't say nothing. He jest head for the door, and the
other man follow him.

"John Lee," the white lady say. "John Lee Williams."

The little boy jugged his head down in his mama lap and holler
more now. His mama tell him go with the nurse, but he ain't thinking 'bout her. His mama tell him again, but he don't even yer. His
mama pick him up and take him in there, and even when the white
lady shet the door I can still hear him hollering.

"I often wonder why the Lord let a child like that suffer," a lady
say to my mama. The lady's sitting right in front o' us on another
bench. She got on a white dress and a black sweater. She must be
a nurse or something herself, I reckond.

"Not us to question," a man say.

"Sometimes I don't know if we shouldn't" the lady say.

"I know definitely we shouldn't," the man say. The man look

46

like a preacher. He big and fat and he got on a black suit. He got a gold chain, too.

"Why?" the lady say.

"Why anything?" the preacher say.

"Yes," the lady say. "Why anything?"

"Not us to question," the preacher say.

The lady look at the preacher a little while and look at Mama again.

"And look like it's the poor who do most the suffering," she say. "I don't understand it."

"Best not to even try," the preacher say. "He works in mysterious way. Wonders to perform."

Right then Little John Lee bust out hollering, and ever'body turn they head.

"He's not a good dentist," the lady say. "Dr. Robillard is much better. But more expensive. That's why most of the Colored people come here. The White people go to Dr. Robillard. Yall from Bayonne?"

"Down the river," my mama say. And that's all she go'n say, 'cause she don't talk much. But the lady keep on looking at her, and so she say: "Near Morgan."

"I see," the lady say.

7

"That's the trouble with the black people in this country today," somebody else say. This one yer sitting on the same side me and Mama sitting, and he kind o' sitting in front of that preacher. He look like a teacher or somebody that go to college. He got on a suit, and he got a book that he been reading. "We don't question is exactly the trouble," he say. "We should question and question and question. Question everything."

The preacher jest look at him a long time. He done put a toothpick or something in his mouth, and he jest keep turning it and turning it. You can see he don't like that boy with that book.

"Maybe you can explain what you mean," he say.

"I said what I meant," the boy say. "Question everything. Every stripe, every star, every word spoken. Everything."

"It 'pears to me this young lady and I was talking 'bout God, young man," the preacher say.

"Question Him, too," the boy say.

"Wait," the preacher say. "Wait now."

"You heard me right," the boy say. "His existence as well as everything else. Everything."

The preacher jest look cross the room at the boy. You can see he getting madder and madder. But mad or no mad, the boy ain't thinking 'bout him. He look at the preacher jest's hard's the preacher look at him.

"Is this what they coming to?" the preacher say. "Is this what we educating them for?"

"You're not educating me," the boy say. "I wash dishes at night to go to school in the day. So even the words you spoke needs questioning."

The preacher jest look at him and shake his head.

"When I come in this room and seen you there with your book, I said to myself, There's an intelligent man. How wrong a person can be."

"Show me one reason to believe in the existence of a God," the boy say.

"My heart tell me," the preacher say.

"My heart tells me," the boy say. "My heart tells me. Sure, my heart tells me. And as long as you listen to what your heart tells you, you will have only what the white man gives you and nothing more. Me, I don't listen to my heart. The purpose of the heart is to pump blood throughout the body, and nothing else."

"Who's your paw, boy?" the preacher say.

"Why?"

"Who is he?"

"He's dead."

"And your mom?"

"She's in Charity Hospital with pneumonia. Half killed herself working for nothing."

"And 'cause he's dead and she sick, you mad at the world?"

"I'm not mad at the world. I'm questioning the world. I'm questioning it with cold logic, sir. What do words like Freedom, Liberty, God, White, Colored mean? I want to know. That's why you are sending us to school, to read and to ask questions. And because we ask these questions, you call us mad. No, sir, it is not us who are mad."

"You keep saying 'us'?"

" 'Us' . . . why not? I'm not alone."

The preacher jest shake his head. Then he look at ever'body in the room—ever'body. Some of the people look down at the floor, keep from looking at him. I kind o' look 'way myself, but soon's I know he done turn his head, I look that way again.

"I'm sorry for you," he say.

"Why?" the boy say. "Why not be sorry for yourself? Why are you so much better off than I am? Why aren't you sorry for these other people in here? Why not be sorry for the lady who had to drag her child into the dentist office? Why not be sorry for the lady sitting on that bench over there? Be sorry for them. Not for me. Some way or other I'm going to make it."

"No, I'm sorry for you," the preacher say.

"Of course. Of course," the boy say, shaking his head. "You're sorry for me because I rock that pillar you're leaning on."

"You can't ever rock the pillar I'm leaning on, young man. It's stronger than anything man can ever do."

"You believe in God because a man told you to believe in God. A white man told you to believe in God. And why? To keep you ignorant, so he can keep you under his feet."

"So now, we the ignorant?"

"Yes," the boy say. "Yes." And he open his book again.

The preacher jest look at him there. The boy done forgot all about him. Ever'body else make 'tend they done forgot 'bout the squabble, too.

Then I see that preacher getting up real slow. Preacher a great big old man, and he got to brace hisself to get up. He come 'cross the room where the boy is. He jest stand there looking at him, but the boy don't raise his head.

"Stand up, boy," preacher say.

The boy look up at him, then he shet his book real slow and stand up. Preacher jest draw back and hit him in the face. The boy fall 'gainst the wall, but he straighten hisself up and look right back at that preacher.

"You forgot the other cheek," he say.

The preacher hit him again on the other side. But this time the boy don't fall.

"That hasn't changed a thing," he say.

The preacher jest look at the boy. The preacher breathing real hard like he jest run up a hill. The boy sit down and open his book again.

"I feel sorry for you," the preacher say. "I never felt so sorry for a man before."

The boy make 'tend he don't even hear that preacher. He keep on reading his book. The preacher go back and get his hat off the chair.

"Excuse me," he say to us. "I'll come back some other time. Yall, please excuse me."

And he look at the boy and go out the room. The boy hist his hand up to his mouth one time, to wipe 'way some blood. All the rest o' the time he keep on reading.

8

The lady and her little boy come out the dentist, and the nurse call somebody else in. Then little bit later they come out, and the nurse call another name. But fast's she call somebody in there, somebody else come in the place where we at, and the room stay full.

The people coming in now, all of 'em wearing big coats. One of 'em say something 'bout sleeting, and another one say he hope not. Another one say he think it ain't nothing but rain. 'Cause, he say, rain can get awful cold this time o' year.

All 'cross the room they talking. Some of 'em talking to people right by 'em, some of 'em talking to people clare 'cross the room, some of 'em talking to anybody'll listen. It's a little bitty room, no bigger 'an us kitchen, and I can see ever'body in there. The little old room 's full of smoke, 'cause you got two old men smoking pipes. I think I feel my teef thumping me some, and I hold my breath and wait. I wait and wait, but it don't thump me no more. Thank God for that.

I feel like going to sleep, and I lean back 'gainst the wall. But I'm scared to go to sleep. Scared 'cause the nurse might call my name and I won't hear her. And Mama might go to sleep, too, and she be mad if neither us heard the nurse.

I look up at Mama. I love my mama. I love my mama. And when cotton come I'm go'n get her a newer coat. And I ain't go'n get a black one neither. I think I'm go'n get her a red one.

"They got some books over there," I say. "Want read one of 'em?"

Mama look at the books, but she don't answer me.

"You got yourself a little man there," the lady say.

Mama don't say nothing to the lady, but she must 'a' grin a little bit, 'cause I seen the lady grinning back. The lady look at me a little while, like she feeling sorry for me.

"You sure got that preacher out here in a hurry," she say to that other boy.

The boy look up at her and look in his book again. When I grow up I want be jest like him. I want clothes like that and I want keep a book with me, too.

"You really don't believe in God?" the lady say.

"No," he say.

"But why?" the lady say.

"Because the wind is pink," he say.

"What?" the lady say.

The boy don't answer her no more. He jest read in his book.

"Talking 'bout the wind is pink," that old lady say. She sitting on the same bench with the boy, and she trying to look in his face. The boy make 'tend the old lady ain't even there. He jest keep reading. "Wind is pink" she say again. "Eh, Lord, what children go'n be saying next?"

The lady 'cross from us bust out laughing.

"That's a good one," she say. "The wind is pink. Yes, sir, that's a good one."

"Don't you believe the wind is pink?" the boy say. He keep his head down in the book.

"Course I believe it, Honey," the lady say. "Course I do." She look at us and wink her eye. "And what color is grass, Honey?"

"Grass? Grass is black."

She bust out laughing again. The boy look at her.

"Don't you believe grass is black?" he say.

The lady quit laughing and look at him. Ever'body else look at him now. The place quiet, quiet.

"Grass is green. Honey," the lady say. "It was green yesterday, it's green today, and it's go'n be green tomorrow."

"How do you know it's green?"

"I know because I know."

"You don't know it's green. You believe it's green because

someone told you it was green. If someone had told you it was black you'd believe it was black."

"It's green," the lady say. "I know green when I see green."

"Prove it's green."

"Surely, now," the lady say. "Don't tell me it's coming to that?"

"It's coming to just that," the boy say. "Words mean nothing. One means no more than the other."

"That's what it all coming to?" that old lady say. That old lady got on a turban and she got on two sweaters. She got a green sweater under a black sweater. I can see the green sweater 'cause some of the buttons on the other sweater missing.

"Yes, ma'am," the boy say. "Words mean nothing. Action is the only thing. Doing. That's the only thing."

"Other words, you want the Lord to come down here and show Hisself to you?" she say.

"Exactly, ma'am."

"You don't mean that, I'm sure?"

"I do, ma'am."

"Done, Jesus," the old lady say, shaking her head.

"I didn't go 'long with that preacher at first," the other lady say; "but now—I don't know. When a person say the grass is black, he's either a lunatic or something wrong."

"Prove to me that it's green."

"It's green because the people say it's green."

"Those same people say we're citizens of the United States."

"I think I'm a citizen."

"Citizens have certain rights. Name me one right that you have. One right, granted by the Constitution, that you can exercise in Bayonne."

The lady don't answer him. She jest look at him like she don't know what he talking 'bout. I know I don't.

"Things changing," she say.

"Things are changing because some black men have begun to follow their brains instead of their hearts."

"You trying to say these people don't believe in God?"

"I'm sure some of them do. Maybe most of them do. But they don't believe that God is going to touch these White people's hearts and change them tomorrow. Things change through action. By no other way."

Ever'body sit quiet and look at the boy. Nobody say a thing. Then the lady 'cross from me and Mama jest shake her head.

"Let's hope that not all your generation feel the same way you do," she say.

"Think what you please, it doesn't matter," the boy say. "But it will be men who listen to their heads and not their hearts who will see that your children have a better chance than you had."

"Let's hope they ain't all like you, though," the old lady say. "Don't forgot the heart absolutely."

"Yes, ma'am, I hope they aren't all like me," the boy say. "Unfortunately I was born too late to believe in your God. Let's hope that the ones who come after will have your faith—if not in your God, then in something else, something definitely that they can lean on. I haven't anything. For me, the wind is pink; the grass is black."

9

The nurse come in the room where us all sitting and waiting and say the doctor won't take no more patients till one o'clock this evening. My mama jump up off the bench and go up to the white lady.

"Nurse, I have to go back in the field this evening," she say.

"The doctor is treating his last patient now," the nurse say. "One o'clock this evening."

"Can I at least speak to the doctor?" my mama say.

"I'm his nurse," the lady say.

"My little boy sick," my mama say. "Right now his teef almost killing him."

The nurse look at me. She trying to make up her mind if to let me come in. I look at her real pitiful. The teef ain't hurting me a tall, but Mama say it is, so I make 'tend for her sake.

"This evening," the nurse say, and go back in the office.

"Don't feel 'jected, Honey," the lady say to Mama. "I been 'round 'em a long time—they take you when they want to. If you was White, that's something else; but you the wrong shade."

Mama don't say nothing to the lady, and me and her go outside and stand 'gainst the wall. It's cold out there. I can feel that wind going through my coat. Some of the other people come out of the room and go up the street. Me and Mama stand there a little while and start to walking. I don't know where us going. When us come to the other street us jest stand there.

"You don't have to make water, do you?" Mama say.

"No, ma'am," I say.

Us go up the street. Walking real slow. I can tell Mama don't know where she going. When us come to a store us stand there and look at the dummies. I look at a little boy with a brown overcoat. He got on brown shoes, too. I look at my old shoes and look at his'n again. You wait till summer, I say.

Me and Mama walk away. Us come up to another store and us stop and look at them dummies, too. Then us go again. Us pass a cafe where the white people in there eating. Mama tell me keep my eyes in front where they blonks, but I can't help from seeing them people eat. My stomach start to growling 'cause I'm hungry. When I see people eating, I get hungry; when I see a coat, I get cold.

A man whistle at my mama when us go by a filling-station. She made 'tend she don't even see him. I look back and I feel like hitting him in the mouth. If I was bigger, I say. If I was bigger, you see.

Us keep on going. I'm getting colder and colder, but I don't say nothing. I feel that stuff running down my nose and I sniff.

"That rag," she say.

I get it out and wipe my nose. I'm getting cold all over now— my face, my hands, my feet, ever'thing. Us pass another little cafe, but this'n for white people, too, and us can't go in there neither. So us jest walk. I'm so cold now, I'm 'bout ready to say it. If I knowed where us was going, I wouldn't be so cold, but I don't know where us going. Us go, us go, us go. Us walk clean out o' Bayonne. Then us cross the street and us come back. Same thing I seen when I got off the bus. Same old trees, same old walk, same old weeds, same old cracked pave—same old ever'thing.

I sniff again.

"That rag," she say.

I wipe my nose real fast and jugg that hankercher back in my pocket 'fore my hand get too cold. I raise my head and I can see David hardware store. When us come up to it, us go in. I don't know why, but I'm glad.

It warm in there. So warm in there you don't want ever leave. I look for the heater, and I see it over by them ba'ls. Three white men standing 'round the heater talking in creole. One of 'em come to see what Mama want.

"Got an axe handle?" she say.

Me, Mama, and the white man start to the back, but Mama stop me when us come to the heater. Her and the white man go on. I hold my hand over the heater and look at 'em. They go all the way in the back, and I see the white man point to the axe handle 'gainst the wall. Mama take one of 'em and shake it like she trying to figure how much it weigh. Then she rub her hand over it from one end to the other end. She turn it over and look at the other side, then she shake it again, and shake her head and put it back. She get another one and she do it jest like she did the first one, then she shake her head. Then she get a brown one and do it that, too. But she don't like this one neither. Then she get another one, but 'fore she shake it or anything, she look at me. Look like she trying to say something to me, but I don't know what it is. All I know is I done got warm now and I'm feeling right smart better. Mama shake this axe handle jest like she done the others, and shake her head and say something to the white man. The white man jest look at his pile of axe handle, and when Mama pass by him to come to the front, the white man jest scratch his head and follow her. She tell me come on, and us go on out and start walking again.

Us walk and walk, and no time at all I'm cold again. Look like I'm colder now 'cause I can still remember how good it was back there. My stomach growl and I suck it in to keep Mama from yering it. She walking right 'side me, and it growl so loud you can yer it a mile. But Mama don't say a word.

10

When us come up to the courthouse, I look at the clock. It got quarter to twelve. Mean us got another hour and a quarter to be out yer in the cold. Us go and stand side a building. Something hit my cap and I look up at the sky. Sleet falling.

I look at Mama standing there. I want stand close 'side her, but she don't like that. She say that's cry-baby stuff. She say you got to stand for yourself, by yourself.

"Let's go back to that office," she say.

Us cross the street. When us get to the dentist I try to open the door, but I can't. Mama push me on the side and she twist the knob.

But she can't open it neither. She twist it some more, harder, but she can't open it. She turn 'way from the door. I look at her, but I don't move and I don't say nothing. I done seen her like this before and I'm scared.

"You hungry?" she say. She say it like she mad at me, like I'm the one cause of ever'thing.

"No, ma'am," I say.

"You want eat and walk back, or you rather don't eat and ride?"

"I ain't hungry," I say.

I ain't jest hungry, but I'm cold, too. I'm so hungry and I'm so cold I want cry. And look like I'm getting colder and colder. My feet done got numb. I try to work my toes, but I can't. Look like I'm go'n die. Look like I'm go'n stand right here and freeze to death. I think about home. I think about Val and Auntie and Ty and Louis and Walker. It 'bout twelve o'clock and I know they eating dinner. I can hear Ty making jokes. That's Ty. Always trying to make some kind 'o joke. I wish I was right there listening to him. Giving anything in the world if I was home 'round the fire.

"Come on," Mama say.

Us start walking again. My feet so numb I can't hardly feel 'em. Us turn the corner and go back up the street. The clock start hitting for twelve.

The sleet's coming down plenty now. They hit the pave and bounce like rice. Oh, Lord; oh, Lord, I pray. Don't let me die. Don't let me die. Don't let me die, Lord.

11

Now I know where us going. Us going back o' town where the Colored people eat. I don't care if I don't eat. I been hungry before. I can stand it. But I can't stand the cold.

I can see us go'n have a long walk. It 'bout a mile down there. But I don't mind. I know when I get there I'm go'n warm myself. I think I can hold out. I think I can hold out. My hands numb in my pockets and my feet numb, too, but if I keep moving I can hold out. Jest don't stop no more, that's all.

The sky's gray. The sleet keep falling. Falling like rain now—

plenty, plenty. You can hear it hitting the pave. You can see it bouncing. Sometime it bounce two times 'fore it settle.

Us keep going. Us don't say nothing. Us jest keep going, keep going.

I wonder what Mama thinking. I hope she ain't mad with me. When Summer come I'm go'n pick plenty cotton and get her a coat. I'm go'n get her a red one.

I hope they made it Summer all the time. I be glad if it was Summer all the time—but it ain't. Us got to have winter, too. Lord, I hate the winter. I guess ever'body hate the winter.

I don't sniff this time. I get out my hankercher and wipe my nose. My hand so cold I can hardly hold the hankercher.

I think us getting close, but us ain't there yet. I wonder where ever'body is. Can't see nobody but us. Look like us the only two people moving 'round today. Must be too cold for the rest of the people to move 'round.

I can hear my teefes. I hope they don't knock together too hard and make that bad one hurt. Lord, that's all I need, for that bad one to start off.

I hear a church bell somewhere. But today ain't Sunday. They must be ringing for a funeral or something.

I wonder what they doing at home. They must be eating. Monsieur Bayonne might be there with his guitar. One day Ty played with Monsieur Bayonne guitar and broke one o' the string. Monsieur Bayonne got some mad with Ty. He say Ty ain't go'n never 'mount to nothing. Ty can go jest like him when he ain't there. Ty can make ever'body laugh mocking Monsieur Bayonne.

I used to like to be with Mama and Daddy. Us used to be happy. But they took him in the Army. Now, nobody happy no more. . . . I be glad when he come back.

Monsieur Bayonne say it wasn't fair for 'em to take Daddy and give Mama nothing and give us nothing. Auntie say, Shhh, Etienne. Don't let 'em yer you talk like that. Monsieur Bayonne say, It's God truth. What they giving his children? They have to walk three and a half mile to school hot or cold. That's anything to give for a paw? She got to work in the field rain or shine jest to make ends meet. That's anything to give for a husband? Auntie say, Shhh, Etienne, shhh. Yes, you right, Monsieur Bayonne say. Best don't say it in front of 'em now. But one day they go'n find out. One day. Yes, s'pose so, Auntie say. Then what, Rose Mary? Monsieur Bayonne say. I don't know, Etienne, Auntie say. All us can do is us job, and leave ever'thing else in His hand. . . .

Us getting closer, now. Us getting closer. I can see the railroad tracks.

Us cross the tracks, and now I see the cafe. Jest to get in there, I say. Jest to get in there. All ready I'm starting to feel little better.

12

Us go in, Ahh, it good. I look for the heater; there 'gainst the wall. One of them little brown ones. I jest stand there and hold my hand over it. I can't open my hands too wide 'cause they almost froze.

Mama standing right 'side me. She done unbuttoned her coat. Smoke rise out the coat, and the coat smell like a wet dog.

I move to the side so Mama can have more room. She open out her hands and rub 'em together. I rub mine together, too, 'cause this keep 'em from hurting. If you let 'em warm too fast, they hurt you sure. But if you let 'em warm jest little bit at a time, and you keep rubbing 'em, they be all right ever' time.

They got jest two more people in the cafe. A lady back o' the counter, and a man on this side the counter. They been watching us ever since us come in.

Mama get out the hankercher and count the money. Both o' us know how much money she got there. Three dollars. No, she ain't got three dollars. 'Cause she had to pay us way up here. She ain't got but two dollars and a half left. Dollar and a half to get my teef pulled, and fifty cents for us to go back on, and fifty cents worse o' salt meat.

She stir the money 'round with her finger. Most o' the money is change 'cause I can hear it rubbing together. She stir it and stir it. Then she look at the door. It still sleeting. I can yer it hitting 'gainst the wall like rice.

"I ain't hungry, Mama," I say.

"Got to pay 'em something for they heat," she say.

She take a quarter out the hankercher and tie the hankercher up again. She look over her shoulder at the people, but she still don't move. I hope she don't spend the money. I don't want her spend it on me. I'm hungry, I'm almost starving I'm so hungry, but I don't want her spending the money on me.

She flip the quarter over like she thinking. She must be thinking 'bout us walking back home. Lord, I sure don't want walk home. If I thought it done any good to say something, I say it. But my mama make up her own mind.

She turn way from the heater right fast, like she better hurry up and do it 'fore she change her mind. I turn to look at her go to the counter. The man and the lady look at her, too. She tell the lady something and the lady walk away. The man keep on looking at her. Her back turn to the man, and Mama don't even know he standing there.

The lady put some cakes and a glass o' milk on the counter. Then she pour up a cup o' coffee and set it side the other stuff. Mama pay her for the things and come back where I'm at. She tell me sit down at that table 'gainst the wall.

The milk and the cakes for me. The coffee for my mama. I eat slow, and I look at her. She looking outside at the sleet. She looking real sad. I say to myself, I'm go'n make all this up one day. You see, one day, I'm go'n make all this up. I want to say it now. I want to tell how I feel right now. But Mama don't like for us to talk like that.

"I can't eat all this," I say.

They got just three little cakes there. And I'm so hungry right now, the Lord know I can eat a hundred times three. But I want her to have one.

She don't even look my way. She know I'm hungry. She know I want it. I let it stay there a while, then I get it and eat it. I eat jest on my front teefes, 'cause if it tech that back teef I know what'll happen. Thank God it ain't hurt me a tall today.

After I finish eating I see the man go to the juke box. He drop a nickel in it, then he jest stand there looking at the record. Mama tell me keep my eyes in front where they blonks. I turn my head like she say, but then I yer the man coming towards us.

"Dance, Pretty?" he say.

Mama got up to dance with him. But 'fore you know it, she done grabbed the little man and done throwed him 'side the wall. He hit the wall so hard he stop the juke box from playing.

"Some pimp," the lady back o' the counter say. "Some pimp."

The little man jump up off the floor and start towards my mama. 'Fore you know it, Mama done sprung open her knife and she waiting for him.

"Come on," she say. "Come on. I'll cut you from your neighbo to your throat. Come on."

I got up to the little man to hit him, but Mama make me come and stand 'side her. The little man look at me and Mama and go back to the counter.

"Some pimp," the lady back o' the counter say. "Some pimp." She start laughing and pointing at the little man. "Yes, sir, you a pimp, all right. Yes, sir."

13

"Fasten that coat. Let's go," Mama say.

"You don't have to leave," the lady say.

Mama don't answer the lady, and us right out in the cold again. I'm warm right now—my hands, my yers, my feet—but I know this ain't go'n last too long. It done sleet so much now you got ice ever'where.

Us cross the railroad tracks, and soon's us do, I get cold. That wind go through this little old coat like it ain't nothing. I got a shirt and a sweater under it, but that wind don't pay 'em no mind. I look up and I can see us got a long way to go. I wonder if us go'n make it 'fore I get too cold.

Us cross over to walk on the sidewalk. They got jest one sidewalk back here. It's over there.

After us go jest a little piece, I smell bread cooking. I look, then I see a baker shop. When us get closer, I can smell it more better. I shet my eyes and make 'tend I'm eating. But I keep 'em shet too long and I butt up 'gainst a telephone post. Mama grab me and see if I'm hurt. I ain't bleeding or nothing and she turn me loose.

I can feel I'm getting colder and colder, and I look up to see how far us still got to go. Uptown is 'way up yonder. A half mile, I reckond. I try to think of something. They say think and you won't get cold. I think of that poem, *Annabel Lee*. I ain't been to school in so long—this bad weather—reckond they done passed *Annabel Lee*. But passed it or not, I'm sure Miss Walker go'n make me recite it when I get there. That woman don't never forget nothing. I ain't never seen nobody like that.

I'm still getting cold. *Annabel Lee* or no *Annabel Lee,* I'm still getting cold. But I can see us getting closer. Us getting there gradually.

Soon's us turn the corner, I see a little old white lady up in front o' us. She the only lady on the street. She all in black and she got a long black rag over her head.

"Stop," she say.

Me and Mama stop and look at her. She must be crazy to be out in all this sleet. Ain't got but a few other people out there, and all of 'em men.

"Yall done ate?" she say.

"Jest finished," Mama say.

"Yall must be cold then?" she say.

"Us headed for the dentist," Mama say. "Us'll warm up when us get there."

"What dentist?" the old lady say. "Mr. Bassett?"

"Yes, ma'am," Mama say.

"Come on in," the old lady say. "I'll telephone him and tell him yall coming."

Me and Mama follow the old lady in the store. It's a little bitty store, and it don't have much in there. The old lady take off her head piece and fold it up.

"Helena?" somebody call from the back.

"Yes, Alnest?" the old lady say.

"Did you see them?"

"They're here. Standing beside me."

"Good. Now you can stay inside."

The old lady look at Mama. Mama waiting to hear what she brought us in here for. I'm waiting for that, too.

"I saw yall each time you went by," she say. "I came out to catch you, but you were gone."

"Us went back o' town," Mama say.

"Did you eat?"

"Yes, ma'am."

The old lady look at Mama a long time, like she thinking Mama might be jest saying that. Mama look right back at her. The old lady look at me to see what I got to say. I don't say nothing. I sure ain't going 'gainst my mama.

"There's food in the kitchen," she say to Mama. "I've been keeping it warm."

Mama turn right around and start for the door.

"Just a minute," the old lady say. Mama stop. "The boy'll have to work for it. It isn't free."

"Us don't take no handout," Mama say.

"I'm not handing out anything," the old lady say. "I need my garbage moved to the front. Ernest has a bad cold and can't go out there."

"Us don't take no handout," Mama say.

"Not unless you eat," the old lady say. "I'm old, but I have my pride too, you know."

Mama can see she ain't go'n beat this old lady down, so she jest shake her head.

"All right," the old lady say. "Come into the kitchen."

She lead the way with that rag in her hand. The kitchen is a little bitty little thing, too. The table and the stove jest about fill it up. They got a little room to the side. Somebody in there laying cross the bed. Must be the person she was talking with: Alnest or Ernest—I forget what she call him.

"Sit down," the old lady say to Mama. "Not you," she say to me. "You have to move the cans."

"Helena?" somebody say in the other room.

"Yes, Alnest?" the old lady say.

"Are you going out there again?"

"I must show the boy where the garbage is," the old lady say.

"Keep that shawl over your head," the old man say.

"You don't have to remind me. Come, boy," the old lady say.

Us go out in the yard. Little old back yard ain't no bigger 'an the store or the kitchen. But it can sleet here jest like it can sleet in any big back yard. And 'fore you know it I'm trembling.

"There," the old lady say, pointing to the cans. I pick up one of the cans. The can so light I put it back down to look inside o' it.

"Here," the old lady say. "Leave that cap alone."

I look at her in the door. She got that black rag wrapped 'round her shoulders, and she pointing one of her fingers at me.

"Pick it up and carry it to the front," she say. I go by her with the can. I'm sure the thing's empty. She could 'a' carried the thing by herself, I'm sure. "Set it on the sidewalk by the door and come back for the other one," she say.

I go and come back. Mama look at me when I pass her. I get

the other can and take it to the front. It don't feel no heavier 'an the other one. I tell myself to look inside and see just what I been hauling. First, I look up and down the street. Nobody coming. Then I look over my shoulder. Little old lady done slipped there jest 's quiet 's mouse, watching me. Look like she knowed I was go'n try that.

"Ehh, Lord," she say. "Children, children. Come in here, boy, and go wash your hands."

I follow her into the kitchen, and she point, and I go to the bathroom. When I came out, the old lady done dished up the food. Rice, gravy, meat, and she even got some lettuce and tomato in a saucer. She even got a glass o' milk and a piece o' cake there, too. It look so good, I almost start eating 'fore I say my blessing.

"Helena?" the old man say.

"Yes, Alnest?" she say.

"Are they eating?"

"Yes," she say.

"Good," he say. "Now you'll stay inside."

The old lady go in there where he is and I can hear 'em talking. I look at Mama. She eating slow like she thinking. I wonder what's the matter now. I reckond she think 'bout home.

The old lady come back in the kitchen.

"I talked to Dr. Bassett's nurse," she says. "Dr. Bassett will take you as soon as you get there."

"Thank you, ma'am," Mama say.

"Perfectly all right," the old lady say. "Which one is it?"

Mama nod towards me. The old lady look at me real sad. I look sad, too.

"You're not afraid, are you?" she say.

"No'm," I say.

"That's a good boy," the old lady say. "Nothing to be afraid of."

When me and Mama get through eating, us thank the old lady again.

"Helena, are they leaving?" the old man say.

"Yes, Alnest."

"Tell them I say goodbye."

"They can hear you, Alnest."

"Goodbye both mother and son," the old man say. "And may God be with you."

Me and Mama tell the old man goodbye, and us follow the old lady in the front. Mama open the door to go out, but she stop and come back in the store.

"You sell salt meat?" she say.

"Yes."

"Give me two bits worse."

"That isn't very much salt meat," the old lady say.

"That's all I have," Mama say.

The old lady go back o' the counter and cut a big piece off the chunk. Then she wrap it and put it in a paper bag.

"Two bits," she say.

"That look like awful lot of meat for a quarter," Mama say.

"Two bits," the old lady say. "I've been selling salt meat behind this counter twenty-five years. I think I know what I'm doing."

"You got a scale there," Mama say.

"What?" the old lady say.

"Weigh it," Mama say.

"What?" the old lady say. "Are you telling me how to run my business?"

"Thanks very much for the food," Mama say.

"Just a minute," the old lady say.

"James," Mama say to me. I move toward the door.

Me and Mama stop again and look at her. The old lady take the meat out the bag and unwrap it and cut 'bout half of it off. Then she wrap it up again and jugg it back in the bag and give it to Mama. Mama lay the quarter on the counter.

"Your kindness will never be forgotten," she say. "James," she say to me.

Us go out and the old lady come to the door to look at us. After us go a little piece I look back, and she still there watching us.

The sleet's coming down heavy, heavy now, and I turn up my collar to keep my neck warm. My mama tell me turn it right back down.

"You not a bum," she say. "You a man."

A Girl's Story

❧ TONI CADE BAMBARA

She was afraid to look at herself just yet. By the time I count to twenty, she decided, if the bleeding hasn't stopped ... she went blank. She hoisted her hips higher toward the wall. Already her footprints were visible. Sweat prints on the wall, though she was shivering. She swung her feet away from the map she'd made with Dada Bibi, the map of Africa done in clay and acrylics. The bright colors of Mozambique distracted her for a moment. She pictured herself in one of the wraps Dada Bibi had made for them to dance in. Pictured herself in Africa talking another language in that warm, rich way Dada Bibi and the brother who tutored the little kids did. Peaceful, friendly, sharing.

Rae Ann swept through her head again for other possible remedies to her situation. For a nosebleed, you put your head way back and stuffed tissue up your nostrils. Once she'd seen her brother Horace plaster his whole set of keys on the back of the neck. The time he had the fight with Joe Lee and his nose bled. Well, she'd tried ice cubes on the neck, on the stomach, on the thighs. Had stuffed herself with tissue. Had put her hips atop a pile of sofa cushions. And still she was bleeding. And what was she going to do about M'Dear's towels? No one would miss the panties and skirt she'd bundled up in the bottom of the garbage. But she couldn't just disappear a towel, certainly not two. M'Dear always counted up the stacks of laundry before the Saturday put-away.

Rae Ann thought about Dada Bibi over at the Center. If the shiny-faced woman were here now with her, it wouldn't be so bad. She'd know exactly what to do. She would sit in the chair and examine Rae Ann's schoolbooks. Would talk calmly. Would help her. Would tell her there was nothing to worry about, that she was a good girl and was not being punished. Would give an explanation and make things right. But between the house and the Center she could bleed to death.

Between her bed and the toilet she'd already left many a trail.

Had already ragged the green sponge a piece, scrubbing up after herself. If Horace came home, she could maybe ask him to run over to the Center. Cept he'd want to know what for. Besides, he didn't go round the Center any more since they jumped on his case so bad about joining the army. He didn't want to hear no more shit about the Vietnamese were his brothers and sisters, were fighting the same enemy as Black folks and was he crazy, stupid or what. And he surely wouldn't want to have to walk all the long way back alone with Dada Bibi in her long skirt and turban, trying to make conversation and getting all tongue-tied sliding around the cussin he always did, and everybody checking them out walking as they were toward his house and all. But maybe if she told him it was an emergency and cried hard, he wouldn't ask her nothing, would just go.

Yesterday Dada Bibi had hugged her hello and didn't even fuss where you been little sister and why ain't you been coming round, don't you want to know about your heritage, ain't you got no pride? Dada Bibi never said none of them things ever. She just hugged you and helped you do whatever it was you thought you came to do at the Center. Rae Ann had come to cut a dress for graduation. She'd be going to intermediate in the fall, and that was a big thing. And maybe she had come to hear about the African queens. Yesterday as they sewed, Dada Bibi told them about some African queen in the old days who kept putting off marriage cause she had to be a soldier and get the Europeans out the land and stop the slaving.

She liked the part where Dada Bibi would have the dude come over to propose umpteen times. Rae Ann could just see him knocking real polite on the screen door and everything. Not like Horace do, or like Pee Wee neither, the boy she was halfway liking but really couldn't say she respected any. They just stood on the corner and hollered for their women, who had better show up quick or later for their ass.

Dada Bibi would have the dude say, "Well, darling, another harvest has past and I now have twenty acres to work and have started building on the new house and the cattle have multiplied. When can we marry?" And then Dada Bibi would have the sister say, "My husband-to-be, there are enemies in the land, crushing our people, our traditions underfoot. We must raise an army and throw them out." And then the dude would go sell a cow or something and help organize the folks on the block to get guns and all. And the sister would get the blacksmith to make her this bad armor stuff. Course Gretchen got to interrupt the story to say the sister chumping the dude, taking his money to have her some boss jewelry made and what a fool he was. But the girls tell her to hush so they can hear the rest. Dada Bibi maintaining it's important to deal with how Gretchen seeing things go down. But no one really wants to give Gretchen's view a play.

Anyway, after many knocks on the screen door and raising of armies and battles, the two of them are old-timers. Then the sister finally says, "My husband-to-be, there is peace in the land now. The children are learning, the folks are working, the elders are happy, our people prosper. Let us get married on the new moon." Gretchen got to spoil it all saying what old folks like that need to get married for, too old to get down anyway. And Dada Bibi try to get the girls to talk that over. But they just tell Gretchen to shut her big mouth and stop hogging all the straight pins. Rae Ann liked to retell the stories to the kids on the block. She always included Gretchen's remarks and everybody's response, since they seemed, in her mind, so much a part of the story.

Rae Ann's legs were tiring. Her left foot was stinging, going to sleep. Her back hurt. And her throat was sore with tension. She looked up at the map and wondered if Dada Bibi had seen the whole trouble coming. When Rae Ann had stayed behind to clean up the sewing scraps, the woman had asked her if there was anything she wanted to talk about now she was getting to be such a young woman. And Rae Ann had hugged her arms across her chest and said, "No, ma'am," cause she figured she might have to hear one of them one-way talks like M'Dear do about not letting boys feel on your tits. But when she got ready to leave, Dada Bibi hugged her like she always did, even to the girls who squirmed out of her reach and would rather not even wave hello and goodbye, just come in and split at their leisure.

"My sister," she had said into her ear, gently releasing her with none of the embarrassed shove her relatives seemed to always punctuate their embraces with. "You're becoming a woman and that's no private thing. It concerns us all who love you. Let's talk sometimes?"

Rae Ann liked the way she always made it a question. Not like the teachers, who just flat-out told you you were going to talk, or rather they were going to talk at you. And not like M'Dear or Aunt Candy, who always just jumped right in talking without even a let's this or could we that.

Maybe Dada Bibi had seen something in her face, in her eyes. Or maybe there had been a telltale spot on the back of her jeans as early as yesterday. Rae Ann twisted her head around toward the pile of clothes on the back of her chair. Upside down her jeans were spotless. Well, then, she reasoned methodically, how did Dada Bibi know? But then who said she had known anything? "That ole plain-face bitch don't know nuthin" was Horace's word to the wise. But just the same, he hung around the bus stop on Tuesday nights, acting blasé like he didn't know Dada Bibi had Tuesday night classes at the college. Not that anybody would speak on this. Joe Lee had cracked and had his ass whipped for his trouble.

Rae Ann was smelling herself and not liking it. She'd already counted three sets of twenties, which meant it was time to move. She rejected the notion of a bath. The last bath had only made it worse. Fore she could even get one foot good out the water, red spots were sliding off the side of the tub onto the tile. She exhaled deeply and tried to make a list in her head. New tissue, tight pants to hold it all in place, the last of the ice tray still in the sink on her twat. She closed her eyes and moaned. Her list was all out of order. She tried again. Check floors and tub. Put towels in bottom of garbage. Put garbage out. Scrape carrots and make salad. Secrete a roll of tissue in her closet for later. Get to the Center. She opened her eyes. What would she say?

Rae Ann pulled her legs down and swung off the bed. She checked to see that the newspaper was still in place before drawing the covers up. She stood and parted the flaps of her bathrobe. Last time she had moved too quickly and the oozing had started, a blob of syrupy brown slipping down the inside of her leg and she afraid to touch it, to stop it, just stood there like a simpleton till it reached her ankle, and then she fled into the bathroom too late. She was looking into the toilet as the water swirled away the first wad of tissue. What if the toilet stuffed up, backed up on the next flush? She could imagine M'Dear bellowing the roof down as the river of red overran the rim and spilled over onto the tiles, flooding the bathroom, splashing past the threshold and onto the hall linoleum.

"Get out the bathroom, willya damn it!"

She jumped and banged an elbow on the sink. She hadn't

heard Horace come into the house. He usually announced his arri-
vals by singing, stamping, and doing a bump-de-bump against the
furniture. Had thought she was all alone with her terror. Hadn't
even locked the door and here she was with her pants down and
the last clump of tissue shredding, sticky red.

"Come on now. I gotta shower fore M'Dear get home."

She was trapped. If she unhooked the roll of toilet paper to
take into her room, he'd see that. And M'Dear would be in any
minute and would come into her room to set her bags down and
get her slippers. If she hid in the closet and squatted down behind
the bundles of mothballed blankets . . .

"Hey," Horace was bamming on the door. "You okay?"

Something in her brother's voice startled her. Before she could
stop herself she was brimming over and shivering hard.

"Rae Ann?" he called through the door. "Rachel?"

"Don't come in!" she screamed. "Don't come in."

The doorknob was being held in position, she could see that.
It had stopped turning. And it seemed to her that he was holding
his breath on his side of the door just like she was holding hers on
hers.

"Hey," he whispered "you okay?" When she didn't answer, he
let go of the knob. She watched it move back into place and then
heard him walk away. She sat there hugging herself, trying to ease
the chattering of her teeth. She leaned over to yank her washcloth
off the hook. And then the smell gripped her. That smell was in
everything. In her bed, her clothes, her breath. The smell of death.
A dry, rank graveyard smell. The smell of her mother's sickroom
years ago, so long ago all the memory that had survived was the
smell and the off-yellow color from the lamp, a color she'd never
ever seen again anywhere. A brown stain was smack in the middle
of the washcloth. She flung it into the basin and ran the water.

"She in there crying."

Rae Ann's heart stopped. M'Dear was in the kitchen. Just behind the medicine cabinet, just behind the wall, they were talking
about her. She jumped up and ran to the door.

"Don't be locking that door," the voice boomed through the
wall. "We hear you in there."

"And we know what you been doin too," her brother's voice
rang out. She wondered what happened to that something that was
in his voice just minutes ago. Where had that brother gone to so

quick? Maybe cause he was scared he sounded so nice. That time when Furman and his gang were after Pee Wee he had sounded like that. Up on the roof, scrunched between the pigeon coop and the chimney, Pee Wee revealed a voice Rae Ann had never known he had. Told her she was a nice girl and shouldn't mess around with guys like him, would have to be careful. Not at all the voice bragging on the handball court, Pee Wee mounting his motorbike, Pee Wee in the schoolyard smoking. Why did it take scarifying to bring out the voice?

"Horace just scared I may die in here and he won't be able to take his damn shower," she mumbled into the washcloth, gagging on the smell. She was too afraid to think anything else.

"You best get in here, Madame." The voice came at her through the mirror. Madame. She was freezing again. Madame never meant anything good. Madame, you best cut a switch. Madame, there's a letter here from school. Madame, where's the receipt from the telephone bill. Madame, do you think you too grown to mind.

Rae Ann swished around some mouthwash and rewrapped her bathrobe tight. She knew she was waddling, the minute she saw the way they looked at her, but she couldn't get herself together. Horace turned back to a plate in the icebox he was eating from. M'Dear was leaning up against the sink, her hat still on her head, the shopping bags leaning against her legs, her shoes not even unlaced.

"You had somebody in here?"

"No, ma'am."

"Ask her how come she in her bathrobe."

"You hush," the old woman warned, and Horace disappeared behind the icebox door.

"What you been doin?"

"Nothin."

"Don't tell me nothin when I'm trying to find out somethin. Miz Gladys run all the way up to the bus stop to tell me she seen you comin home from school way before three o'clock."

Rae Ann heard the pause, felt the pause on top of her head, weighing down into her shoulders. She shrugged. She didn't know how to fill it and lift it.

"You play hookey from school today? Went somewhere with somebody?"

"No, ma'am."

M'Dear breathing in and out, the huffin-puffin getting wheezy. It was clear Rae Ann had better say something, cause there wouldn't be too many more questions, just a heavier pausing swelling, swelling to crush her.

"You cold or somethin?" A question that came out finally and lifted her from her knees. She didn't know why she was so grateful to hear it. She hadn't expected it. Was nodding yes while her mouth said no and smiling and fixing to cry all at the same time.

"Tears don't tell me a damn thing, Rachel Ann."

"Tears say a whole lot to me," Horace was telling the toaster, singing it lest the woman get on him again for butting in.

"I sure wish you'd go somewhere," Rae Ann said over her shoulder. It might be easier to talk with just her grandmother. Though she was still a blank as to what she could possibly say to take the hardness out of her grandmother's face. M'Dear's eyes shot from the boy to the girl to the boy then back again, her head swiveling, her eyes flashing, like she was on the trail of something and there was danger sure for somebody.

"M'Dear, I'm bleeding," she heard herself say, huddling smaller into her bathrobe, feeling an oozing on the inside of her leg.

The old woman's face looked red-hot and strangled, and for a minute the girl thought she was going to be slapped.

"Whatcha been doin?" she hissed through clenched teeth. Rae Ann backed up as a whole bunch of questions and accusations tumbled out of the woman's mouth ramming into her. "You been to the barbershop, haven't you? Let that filthy man go up inside you with a clothes hanger. You going to be your mama all over again. Why didn't you come to me? Who's the boy? Tell me his name quick. And you better not lie."

M'Dear had snatched up her pocketbook, not waiting on an answer in the meantime, and was heading out the door, waving Horace to come on. He burned his fingers pulling out the toast, eager for the adventure.

"I didn't do anything," Rae Ann screamed, racing to the door before it closed against the back of her brother. "I didn't do anything, I swear to God," her throat raspy, failing her, the words barely pushed out and audible.

"Ooooooh," she heard echoing in the tiled hallway, the word hollow and cool, bouncing off the walls as the old woman shoved

71

past the boy back into the kitchen. "Oh, my goodness," she said through her hands. And then Rae Ann felt the hands on her shoulders moist from the mouth coming right through the terry cloth. The hands giving slight pull, pat, tug but not a clear embrace. "Oh, Rachel Ann," the woman whispered, steering her gently down the hall. "Girl, why didn't you say so?" she said, helping her into bed.

Rae Ann bent her knees and eased herself down onto the newspapers. She watched the woman back out of the room, her hands smoothing her waistband, as though she were leaving the dishes to make a call or leaning up from the dough on the breadboard to shout across the air shaft to Miz Gladys. Smoothing the bulk that bunched up over the waistband, nervous.

"Be right back, sugar," still backing out the room. And Rae Ann glad she'd moved her sneakers out the doorway. That'd be all she needed, M'Dear falling over some sneakers.

"Hush your ugly mouth, cause you don't know what you talkin about," she heard in the kitchen just before the front door slammed. Was she going to get a doctor? Maybe she'd gone for Dada Bibi? That wasn't likely. I ain't studyin them folks over there, M'Dear and Miz Gladys like to say, sucking their teeth at the letters, flyers, posters, numerous papers that came into the block, the building, the house, explaining what the Center was about.

"I ain't nobody's African," Miz Gladys had said. "One hundred percent American and proud of it." And M'Dear had jerked her head in agreement, trashing the latest flyer Rae Ann had slipped onto the table.

Rae Ann had tried to push all they said up against other things in her head. Being American and being proud and they weren't the same in her head. When Dada Bibi talked about Harriet Tubman and them, she felt proud. She felt it in her neck and in her spine. When the brother who ran the program for the little kids talked about powerful white Americans robbing Africa and bombing Vietnam and doing ugly all over the world, causing hard times for Black folks and other colored people, she was glad not to be American. And when she watched the films about Africans fighting white folks so that hospitals and schools could be built for the kids, and the books about Fanny Lew somebody and Malcolm fighting for freedom, and the posters about the kids, kids littler than her even, studying and growing vegetables and all and the print saying how even kids were freedom fighters—she was proud not to be American. What she heard in school she pushed up against what was in her head. Then she started looking, just looking in the teacher's bloodshot eyes, looking at M'Dear's fat, looking at Dada Bibi's shiny skin, to decide just how she was going to arrange things in her head. It was simpler to watch than to listen.

"Ma Dear gone for the ambulance?" Horace in the doorway grinning, biting at the toast. "Old Freeny botch up the job? Next time I can take you to this nurse who—"

"Go to hell, nigger."

"Okay, okay," he said, closing his eyes and raising his hands like he wouldn't dream of pressing the magic number on nobody, would gladly take his pot of gold elsewhere. "But when that dead baby drops down and rips you open, don't yell for me to save ya. You'll bleed to death first."

Her sneaker missed his head by a fraction of an inch. And she sang real loud the Guinea-Bissau marching song the brother at the Center had taught her, to drown out his laughing. Her song ended as the door slammed. She eased into the mattress, not realizing she'd been tensed up and inches off the newspaper. Her body was sore with the clutching. She wanted to sleep, her eyes dry and stinging. She'd been afraid that if she blinked too long, she'd never open them again in life.

"To die for the people." Somebody in one of the films had said that. It had seemed okay to her at first. She tried to picture Pee Wee willing to die for the people. But all the pictures that came into her head about Pee Wee dying were mostly about Pee Wee and not the people. She tried to picture Horace standing up against the cops in the name of the kids, protecting Pee Wee maybe, or the other boys the pigs liked to beat up on. But it didn't exactly fit. She dreamed up another dude altogether. He looked a little like the brother in the film, only he was different cause he was hers. And he was blowing up police stations and running through the alleyways back of the projects, and she hiding him in her closet, sneaking him food from the kitchen. Was helping him load his guns to shoot the big businessmen with. And she was seeing him dragging through the streets, one leg shot off. And the President's special cops bending in the street to squeeze off the final bullet in his back. And she'd be holding his head in her lap, the blood trickling out of the side of his mouth, just like in the movies. But the pictures were no fun after a while.

So when Dada Bibi was rewinding, just looking at them, one at a time, but not pressing any discussion, Rae Ann'd said, "I want to live for the people." And Gretchen had said, "Right on." Wasn't nothin hip about dying. Then they started talking about what they could do with their lives to help Black people, to free Black people. And Gretchen said she didn't know if she'd feel like going to school long enough to teach, and she knew for sure she didn't feel like going back to the country so she couldn't see herself feeding nobody directly.

"Shit. I'm just here and ain't nobody gonna run no lame shit on me. Specially them teachers up at the school. Shit. That's the best I can do for the people, give them teachers hell. Shit," she added again, just to make clear no one had better ask her anything else about what she was prepared to do for her people.

"That's cool," said Dada Bibi, surprising them all. "Giving the teachers some static means you gotta hit them books, eat well, get plenty rest to keep the mind alert. Can't hit them with no lame shit, right?" She nodding to Gretchen.

"That's right," Gretchen said, her ass off her shoulders and her whole self trapped.

Rae Ann sniffled back a tear. She wasn't convinced she was really dying, but there was something righteous in the pain that came with thinking it. Something was wrong. She was being punished, that she knew. But she probably wasn't going to really die. She looked hard at the posters by the window, the wood carving she'd made for Kwanza on her desk, the map on the wall, the picture of Jesus on the closet she shared with her grandmother. She wasn't sure just who to make the promise to. So she simply addressed it to them all. If I can get through this time, she promised, I'm going to do something good. It left her dissatisfied, cold. To die for the people left her scared, mad, it wasn't fair. To live for the people left her confused, faintly inadequate. Was she up to it? And what?

"Here you go," M'Dear was saying, pitching the bag onto her bed. "Dinner be on in a minute."

What's wrong with me, she thought, M'Dear fraid to come in the room and get her slippers, fraid to come near me. What have I done? She up-ended the bag and set everything out neatly. A plan.

She had to think methodically and stop all this crying and confusion. I will read everything two times. Then I'll know what to do. She allowed herself a moist blink. She would find out what she had done and take her whipping. Then everything would be like before. M'Dear would come into the room again and set awhile talking while she changed her shoes. Dada Bibi would hug her again. But then Dada Bibi would hug her no matter what. She even hugged the dirty kids from Mason Street. And drank behind them too without even rinsing the cup. Either Dada Bibi had a powerful health to combat germs, she thought, ripping open the packages, or the woman was crazy.

Strong Horse Tea
❧ ALICE WALKER

R annie Toomer's little baby boy Snooks was dying from double pneumonia and whooping cough. She sat away from him, gazing into the low fire, her long crusty bottom lip hanging. She was not married. Was not pretty. Was not anybody much. And he was all she had.

"Lawd, why don't that doctor come on here?" she moaned, tears sliding from her sticky eyes. She had not washed since Snooks took sick five days ago and a long row of whitish snail tracks laced her ashen face.

"What you ought to try is some of the old home remedies," Sarah urged. She was an old neighboring lady who wore magic leaves round her neck sewed up in possumskin next to a dried lizard's foot. She knew how magic came about, and could do magic herself, people said.

"We going to have us a doctor," Rannie Toomer said fiercely, walking over to shoo a fat winter fly from her child's forehead. "I don't believe in none of that swamp magic. All the old home remedies I took when I was a child come just short of killing me."

Snooks, under a pile of faded quilts, made a small gravelike mound in the bed. His head was like a ball of black putty wedged between the thin covers and the dingy yellow pillow. His little eyes were partly open, as if he were peeping out of his hard wasted skull at the chilly room, and the forceful pulse of his breathing caused a faint rustling in the sheets near his mouth like the wind pushing damp papers in a shallow ditch.

"What time you reckon that doctor'll git here?" asked Sarah, not expecting Rannie Toomer to answer her. She sat with her knees wide apart under many aprons and long dark skirts heavy with stains. From time to time she reached long cracked fingers down to sweep her damp skirts away from the live coals. It was almost spring, but the winter cold still clung to her bones and she had to almost sit in the fireplace to be warm. Her deep sharp eyes set in

76

the rough leather of her face had aged a moist hesitant blue that gave her a quick dull stare like a hawk's. Now she gazed coolly at Rannie Toomer and rapped the hearthstones with her stick.

"White mailman, white doctor," she chanted skeptically, under her breath, as if to banish spirits.

"They gotta come see 'bout this baby," Rannie Toomer said wistfully. "Who'd go and ignore a little sick baby like my Snooks?"

"Some folks we don't know so well as we thinks we do might," the old lady replied. "What you want to give that boy of yours is one or two of the old home remedies; arrowsroot or sassyfras and cloves, or a sugar tit soaked in cat's blood."

Rannie Toomer's face went tight.

"We don't need none of your witch's remedies," she cried, grasping her baby by his shrouded toes, trying to knead life into him as she kneaded limberness into flour dough.

"We going to git some of them shots that makes peoples well, cures 'em of all they ails, cleans 'em out and makes 'em strong all at the same time."

She spoke upward from her son's feet as if he were an altar. "Doctor'll be here soon, baby," she whispered to him, then rose to look out the grimy window. "I done sent the mailman." She rubbed her face against the glass, her flat nose more flattened as she peered out into the rain.

"Howdy, Rannie Mae," the red-faced mailman had said pleasantly as he always did when she stood by the car waiting to ask him something. Usually she wanted to ask what certain circulars meant that showed pretty pictures of things she needed. Did the circulars mean that somebody was coming around later and would give her hats and suitcases and shoes and sweaters and rubbing alcohol and a heater for the house and a fur bonnet for her baby? Or, why did he always give her the pictures if she couldn't have what was in them? Or, what did the words say . . . especially the big word written in red: "S-A-L-E!"?

He would explain shortly to her that the only way she could get the goods pictured on the circulars was to buy them in town and that town stores did their advertising by sending out pictures of their goods. She would listen with her mouth hanging open until he finished. Then she would exclaim in a dull amazed way that *she* never *had* any money and he could ask anybody. *She* couldn't ever buy any of the things in the pictures—so why did the stores keep sending them to her?

He tried to explain to her that *everybody* got the circulars, whether they had any money to buy with or not. That this was one of the laws of advertising and he could do nothing about it. He was sure she never understood what he tried to teach her about advertising, for one day she asked him for any extra circulars he had and when he asked what she wanted them for—since she couldn't afford to buy any of the items advertised—she said she needed them to paper the inside of her house to keep out the wind.

Today he thought she looked more ignorant than usual as she stuck her dripping head inside his car. He recoiled from her breath and gave little attention to what she was saying about her sick baby as he mopped up the water she dripped on the plastic door handle of the car.

"Well, never *can* keep 'em dry, I mean *warm* enough, in rainy weather like this here," he mumbled absently, stuffing a wad of circulars advertising hair driers and cold creams into her hands. He wished she would stand back from his car so he could get going. But she clung to the side gabbing away about "Snooks" and "NEW-monia" and "shots" and how she wanted a "REAL doctor."

"That right?" he injected sympathetically from time to time, and from time to time he sneezed, for she was letting in wetness and damp, and he felt he was coming down with a cold. Black people as black as Rannie Mae always made him uneasy, especially when they didn't smell good, and when you could tell they didn't right away. Rannie Mae, leaning in over him out of the rain, smelt like a wet goat. Her dark dirty eyes clinging to his face with such hungry desperation made him nervous.

Why did colored folks always want you to do something for them?

Now he cleared his throat and made a motion forward as if to roll up his window. "Well, ah, *mighty* sorry to hear 'bout that little fella," he said, groping for the window crank. "We'll see what we can do!" He gave her what he hoped was a big friendly smile. God! He didn't want to hurt her feelings! She looked so pitiful hanging there in the rain. Suddenly he had an idea.

"Whyn't you try some of old Aunt Sarah's home remedies?" he suggested brightly, still smiling. He half believed with everybody else in the county that the old blue-eyed black woman possessed magic. Magic that if it didn't work on whites probably would on blacks. But Rannie Mae almost turned the car over shaking her head and body with an emphatic "NO!" She reached in a wet crusted hand to grasp his shoulder.

"We wants a doctor, a real doctor!" she screamed. She had begun to cry and drop her tears on him. "You git us a doctor from town," she bellowed, shaking the solid shoulder that bulged under his new tweed coat.

"Like I say," he drawled lamely although beginning to be furious with her, "we'll do what we can!" And he hurriedly rolled up the window and sped down the road, cringing from the thought that she had put her hands on him.

"Old home remedies! Old home remedies!" Rannie Toomer cursed the words while she licked at the hot tears that ran down her face, the only warmth about her. She turned back to the trail that led to her house, trampling the wet circulars under her feet. Under the fence she went and was in a pasture, surrounded by dozens of fat white folks' cows and an old gray horse and a mule or two. Animals lived there in the pasture all around her house, and she and Snooks lived in it.

It was less than an hour after she had talked to the mailman that she looked up expecting the doctor and saw old Sarah tramping through the grass on her walking stick. She couldn't pretend she wasn't home with the smoke climbing out the chimney, so she let her in, making her leave her bag of tricks on the front porch.

Old woman old as that ought to forgit trying to cure other people with her nigger magic . . . ought to use some of it on herself, she thought. She would not let her lay a finger on Snooks and warned her if she tried she would knock her over the head with her own cane.

"He coming all right," Rannie Toomer said firmly, looking, straining her eyes to see through the rain.

"Let me tell you, child," the old woman said almost gently, "he ain't." She was sipping something hot from a dish. When would this one know, she wondered, that she could only depend on those who would come.

"But I *told* you," Rannie Toomer said in exasperation, as if

79

explaining something to a backward child. "I asked the mailman to bring a doctor for my Snooks!"

Cold wind was shooting all around her from the cracks in the window framing, faded circulars blew inward from the walls. The old woman's gloomy prediction made her tremble.

"He done fetched the doctor," Sarah said, rubbing her dish with her hand. "What you reckon brung me over here in this here flood? Wasn't no desire to see no rainbows, I can tell you."

Rannie Toomer paled.

"I's the doctor, child." Sarah turned to Rannie with dull wise eyes. "That there mailman didn't git no further with that message than the road in front of my house. Lucky he got good lungs—deef as I is I had myself a time trying to make out what he was yellin'."

Rannie began to cry, moaning.

Suddenly the breathing of Snooks from the bed seemed to drown out the noise of the downpour outside. Rannie Toomer could feel his pulse making the whole house tremble.

"Here," she cried, snatching up the baby and handing him to Sarah. "Make him well. *O my lawd,* make him well!"

Sarah rose from her seat by the fire and took the tiny baby, already turning a purplish blue around the eyes and mouth.

"Let's not upset this little fella unnessarylike," she said, placing the baby back on the bed. Gently she began to examine him, all the while moaning and humming some thin pagan tune that pushed against the sound of the wind and rain with its own melancholy power. She stripped him of all his clothes, poked at his fibreless baby ribs, blew against his chest. Along his tiny flat back she ran her soft old fingers. The child hung on in deep rasping sleep, and his small glazed eyes neither opened fully nor fully closed.

Rannie Toomer swayed over the bed watching the old woman touching the baby. She thought of the time she had wasted waiting for the real doctor. Her feeling of guilt was a stone.

"I'll do anything you say do, Aunt Sarah," she cried, mopping at her nose with her dress. "Anything. Just, please God, make him git better!"

Old Sarah dressed the baby again and sat down in front of the fire. She stayed deep in thought for several moments. Rannie Toomer gazed first into her silent face and then at the baby, whose breathing seemed to have eased since Sarah picked him up.

Do something quick, she urged Sarah in her mind, wanting to

believe in her powers completely. Do something that'll make him rise up and call his mama!

"The child's dying," said Sarah bluntly, staking out beforehand some limitation to her skill. "But there still might be something we can do. . . ."

"What, Aunt Sarah, what?" Rannie Toomer was on her knees before the old woman's chair, wringing her hands and crying. She fastened hungry eyes on Sarah's lips.

"What can I *do*?" she urged fiercely, hearing the faint labored breathing from the bed.

"It's going to take a strong stomach," said Sarah slowly. "A *mighty* strong stomach. And most you young peoples these days don't have 'em."

"Snooks got a strong stomach," said Rannie Toomer, looking anxiously into the old serious face.

"It ain't him that's got to have the strong stomach," Sarah said, glancing down at Rannie Toomer. *"You* the one got to have a strong stomach . . . he won't know *what* it is he's drinking."

Rannie Toomer began to tremble way down deep in her stomach. It sure was weak, she thought. Trembling like that. But what could she mean her Snooks to drink? Not cat's blood—! And not some of the messes with bat's wings she'd heard Sarah mixed for people sick in the head? . . .

"What is it?" she whispered, bringing her head close to Sarah's knee. Sarah leaned down and put her toothless mouth to her ear.

"The only thing that can save this child now is some good strong horse tea," she said, keeping her eyes on the girl's face. "The *only* thing. And if you wants him out of that bed you better make tracks to git some."

Rannie Toomer took up her wet coat and stepped across the porch into the pasture. The rain fell against her face with the force of small hailstones. She started walking in the direction of the trees where she could see the bulky lightish shapes of cows. Her thin plastic shoes were sucked at by the mud, but she pushed herself forward in search of the lone gray mare.

All the animals shifted ground and rolled big dark eyes at Rannie Toomer. She made as little noise as she could and leaned against a tree to wait.

Thunder rose from the side of the sky like tires of a big truck rumbling over rough dirt road. Then it stood a split second in the middle of the sky before it exploded like a giant firecracker, then rolled away again like an empty keg. Lightning streaked across the sky, setting the air white and charged.

Rannie Toomer stood dripping under her tree, hoping not to be struck. She kept her eyes carefully on the behind of the gray mare, who, after nearly an hour, began nonchalantly to spread her muddy knees.

At that moment Rannie Toomer realized that she had brought nothing to catch the precious tea in. Lightning struck something not far off and caused a crackling and groaning in the woods that frightened the animals away from their shelter. Rannie Toomer slipped down in the mud trying to take off one of her plastic shoes to catch the tea. And the gray mare, trickling some, broke for a clump of cedars yards away.

Rannie Toomer was close enough to catch the tea if she could keep up with the mare while she ran. So alternately holding her breath and gasping for air she started after her. Mud from her fall clung to her elbows and streaked her frizzy hair. Slipping and sliding in the mud she raced after the mare, holding out, as if for alms, her plastic shoe.

In the house Sarah sat, her shawls and sweaters tight around her, rubbing her knees and muttering under her breath. She heard the thunder, saw the lightning that lit up the dingy room and turned her waiting face to the bed. Hobbling over on stiff legs she could hear no sound; the frail breathing had stopped with the thunder, not to come again.

Across the mud-washed pasture Rannie Toomer stumbled, holding out her plastic shoe for the gray mare to fill. In spurts and splashes mixed with rainwater she gathered her tea. In parting, the old mare snorted and threw up one big leg, knocking her back into the mud. She rose, trembling and crying, holding the shoe, spilling none over the top but realizing a leak, a tiny crack at her shoe's front. Quickly she stuck her mouth there, over the crack, and ankle deep in the slippery mud of the pasture and freezing in her shabby wet coat, she ran home to give the still warm horse tea to her baby Snooks.

From **The Cancer Journals**
૨⋇ AUDRE LORDE

These excerpts are included here in the order in which they were placed in the published journal—where they did not appear chrono-logically. The reader is encouraged to read the entire journal.

1/26/79

I'm not feeling very hopeful these days, about selfhood or anything else. I handle the outward motions of each day while pain fills me like a puspocket and every touch threatens to breech the taut membrane that keeps it from flowing through and poisoning my whole existence. Sometimes despair sweeps across my consciousness like luna winds across a barren moonscape. Ironshod horses rage back and forth over every nerve. Oh Seboulisa ma, help me remember what I have paid much to learn. I could die of difference, or live— myriad selves.

2/5/79

The terrible thing is that nothing goes past me these days, nothing. Each horror remains like a steel vise in my flesh, another magnet to the flame. Buster has joined the rolecall of useless wasteful deaths of young Black people; in the gallery today everywhere ugly images of women offering up distorted bodies for whatever fantasy passes in the name of male art. Gargoyles of pleasure. Beautiful laughing Buster, shot down in a hallway for ninety cents. Shall I unlearn that tongue in which my curse is written?

3/1/79

It is such an effort to find decent food in this place, not to just give up and eat the old poison. But I must tend my body with at least as much care as I tend the compost, particularly now when it seems

83

so beside the point. Is this pain and despair that surround me a result of cancer, or has it just been released by cancer? I feel so unequal to what I always handled before, the abominations outside that echo the pain within. And yes I am completely self-referenced right now because it is the only translation I can trust, and I do believe not until every woman traces her weave back strand by bloody self-referenced strand, will we begin to alter the whole pattern.

4/16/79

The enormity of our task, to turn the world around. It feels like turning my life around, inside out. If I can look directly at my life and my death without flinching I know there is nothing they can ever do to me again. I must be content to see how really little I can do and still do it with an open heart. I can never accept this, like I can't accept that turning my life around is so hard, eating differently, sleeping differently, moving differently, being differently. Like Martha said, I want the old me, bad as before.

4/22/79

I must let this pain flow through me and pass on. If I resist or try to stop it, it will detonate inside me, shatter me, splatter my pieces against every wall and person that I touch.

5/1/79

Spring comes, and still I feel despair like a pale cloud waiting to consume me, engulf me like another cancer, swallow me into immobility, metabolize me into cells of itself; my body, a barometer. I need to remind myself of the joy, the lightness, the laughter so vital to my living and my health. Otherwise, the other will always be waiting to eat me up into despair again. And that means destruction. I don't know how, but it does.

9/79

There is no room around me in which to be still, to examine and explore what pain is mine alone—no device to separate my struggle within from my fury at the outside world's viciousness, the stupid brutal lack of consciousness or concern that passes for the way things are. The arrogant blindness of comfortable white women. What is this work all for? What does it matter whether I ever speak again or not? I try. The blood of black women sloshes from coast to coast and Daly says race is of no concern to women. So that means we are either immortal or born to die and no note taken, un-women.

10/3/79

I don't feel like being strong, but do I have a choice? It hurts when even my sisters look at me in the street with cold and silent eyes. I am defined as other in every group I'm a part of. The outsider, both strength and weakness. Yet without community there is certainly no liberation, no future, only the most vulnerable and temporary armistice between me and my oppression.

11/19/79

I want to write rage but all that comes is sadness. We have been sad long enough to make this earth either weep or grow fertile. I am an anachronism, a sport, like the bee that was never meant to fly. Science said so. I am not supposed to exist. I carry death around in my body like a condemnation. But I do live. The bee flies. There must be some way to integrate death into living, neither ignoring it nor giving in to it.

1/1/80

Faith is the last day of Kwanza, and the name of the war against despair, the battle I fight daily. I become better at it. I want to write about that battle, the skirmishes, the losses, the small yet so important victories that make the sweetness of my life.

1/20/80

The novel is finished at last. It has been a lifeline. I do not have to win in order to know my dreams are valid, I only have to believe in a process of which I am a part. My work kept me alive this past year, my work and the love of women. They are inseparable from each other. In the recognition of the existence of love lies the answer to despair. Work is that recognition given voice and name.

2/18/80

I am 46 years living today and very pleased to be alive, very glad and very happy. Fear and pain and despair do not disappear. They only become slowly less and less important. Although sometimes I still long for a simple orderly life with a hunger sharp as that sudden vegetarian hunger for meat.

4/6/80

Somedays, if bitterness were a whetstone, I could be sharp as grief.

5/30/80

Last spring was another piece of the fall and winter before, a progression from all the pain and sadness of that time, ruminated over. But somehow this summer which is almost upon me feels like a part of my future. Like a brand new time, and I'm pleased to know it, wherever it leads. I feel like another woman, de-chrysalised and become a broader, stretched-out me, strong and excited, a muscle flexed and honed for action.

6/20/80

I do not forget cancer for very long, ever. That keeps me armed and on my toes, but also with a slight background noise of fear. Carl Simonton's book, *Getting Well Again,* has been really helpful to me, even though his smugness infuriates me sometimes. The visualizations and deep relaxing techniques that I learned from it help make me a less anxious person, which seems strange, because in other ways, I live with the constant fear of recurrence of another cancer. But fear and anxiety are not the same at all. One is an appropriate response to a real situation which I can accept and learn to work through just as I work through semi-blindness. But the other, anxiety, is an immobilizing yield to things that go bump in the night, a surrender to namelessness, formlessness, voicelessness, and silence.

7/10/80

I dreamt I had begun training to change my life, with a teacher who is very shadowy. I was not attending classes, but I was going to learn how to change my whole life, live differently, do everything in a new and different way. I didn't really understand, but I trusted this shadowy teacher. Another young woman who was there told me she was taking a course in "language crazure," the opposite of discrazure (the cracking and wearing away of rock). I thought it would be very exciting to study the formation and crack and composure of words, so I told my teacher I wanted to take that course. My teacher said okay, but it wasn't going to help me any because I had to learn something else, and I wouldn't get anything new from that class. I replied maybe not, but even though I knew all about rocks, for instance, I still liked studying their composition, and giving a name to the different ingredients of which they were made. It's very exciting to think of me being all the people in this dream.

* * *

Breast Cancer:
A Black Lesbian Feminist Experience

March 25, 1978

The idea of knowing, rather than believing, trusting, or even understanding, has always been considered heretical. But I would willingly pay whatever price in pain was needed, to savor the weight of completion; to be utterly filled, not with conviction nor with faith, but with experience—knowledge, direct and different from all other certainties.

October 10, 1978

I want to write about the pain. The pain of waking up in the recovery room which is worsened by that immediate sense of loss. Of going in and out of pain and shots. Of the correct position for my

87

arm to drain. The euphoria of the 2nd day, and how it's been downhill from there.

I want to write of the pain I am feeling right now, of the lukewarm tears that will not stop coming into my *eyes*—for what? For my lost breast? For the lost me? And which me was that again anyway? For the death I don't know how to postpone? Or how to meet elegantly?

I'm so tired of all this. I want to be the person I used to be, the real me. I feel sometimes that it's all a dream and surely I'm about to wake up now.

November 2, 1978

How do you spend your time, she said. Reading, mostly, I said. I couldn't tell her that mostly I sat staring at blank walls, or getting stoned into my heart, and then, one day when I found I could finally masturbate again, making love to myself for hours at a time. The flame was dim and flickering, but it was a welcome relief to the long coldness.

December 29, 1978

What is there possibly left for us to be afraid of, after we have dealt face to face with death and not embraced it? Once I accept the existence of dying, as a life process, who can ever have power over me again?

* * *

Editor's note: The entries which follow constitute a kind of flashback within a flashback, which the author structures into the presentation of her journal in order to stress certain of her thoughts and experiences.

September 21, 1978

The anger that I felt for my right breast last year has faded, and I'm glad because I have had this extra year. My breasts have always been so very precious to me, since I accepted having them, it would have been a shame not to have enjoyed the last year of one of them. And I think I am prepared to lose it now in a way I was not quite ready to last November, because now I really see it as a choice between my breast and my life, and in that view there cannot be any question.

Somehow I always knew this would be the final outcome, for it never did seem like a finished business for me. This year between was like a hiatus, an interregnum in a battle within which I could so easily be a casualty, since I certainly was a warrior. And in that brief time the sun shone and the birds sang and I wrote important words and have loved richly and been loved in return. And if a lifetime of furies is the cause of this death in my right breast, there is still nothing I've never been able to accept before that I would accept now in order to keep my breast. It was a 12 month reprieve in which I could come to accept the emotional fact/truths I came to see first in those horrendous weeks last year before the biopsy. If I do what I need to do because I want to do it, it will matter less when death comes, because it will have been an ally that spurred me on.

I was relieved when the first tumor was benign, but I said to Frances at the time that the true horror would be if they said it was benign and it wasn't. I think my body knew there was a malignancy there somewhere, and that it would have to be dealt with eventually. Well, I'm dealing with it as best I can. I wish I didn't have to, and I don't even know if I'm doing it right, but I sure am glad that I had this extra year to learn to love me in a different way.

I'm going to have the mastectomy, knowing there are alternatives, some of which sound very possible in the sense of right thinking, but none of which satisfy me enough.... Since it is my life that I am gambling with, and my life is worth even more than the sensual delights of my breast, I certainly can't take that chance.

7:30 p.m. And yet if I cried for a hundred years I couldn't possibly express the sorrow I feel right now, the sadness and the loss. How did the Amazons of Dahomey feel? They were only little girls. But they did this willingly, for something they believed in. I suppose I am too but I can't feel that now.

89

* * *

September 22, 1978

Today is the day in the grim rainy morning and all I can do now is weep. Eudora, what did I give you in those Mexican days so long ago? Did you know how I loved you? You never talked of your dying, only of your work.

* * *

October 5, 1978

I feel like I'm counting my days in milliseconds, never mind hours. And it's a good thing, that particular consciousness of the way in which each hour passes, even if it is a boring hour. I want it to become permanent. There is so much I have not said in the past few days, that can only be lived now—the act of writing seems impossible to me sometimes, the space of time for the words to form or be written is long enough for the situation to totally alter, leaving you liar or at search once again for the truth. What seems impossible is made real/tangible by the physical form of my brown arm moving across the page; not that my arm cannot do it, but that something holds it away.

In some way I must aerate this grief, bring heat and light around the pain to lend it some proportion, and god knows the news is nothing to write home about—the new pope is dead, the yankees won the game . . .

Later

If I said this all didn't matter I would be lying. I see this as a serious break in my work/living, but also as a serious chance to learn something that I can share for use. And I mourn the women who limit their loss to the physical loss alone, who do not move into the whole terrible meaning of mortality as both weapon and power. After all, what could we possibly be afraid of after having admitted to ourselves that we had dealt face to face with death and not embraced it? For once we accept the actual existence of our dying, who can ever have power over us again?

90

Now I am anxious for more living—to sample and partake of the sweetness of each moment and each wonder who walks with me through my days. And now I feel again the large sweetness of the women who stayed open to me when I needed that openness like rain, who made themselves available.

* * *

In a perspective of urgency, I want to say now that I'd give anything to have done it differently—it being the birth of a unique and survival-worthy, or survival-effective, perspective. Or I'd give anything not to have cancer and my beautiful breast gone, fled with my love of it. But then immediately after I guess I have to qualify that—there really are some things I wouldn't give. I wouldn't give my life, first of all, or else I wouldn't have chosen to have the operation in the first place, and I did. I wouldn't give Frances, or the children, or even any one of the women I love. I wouldn't give up my poetry, and I guess when I come right down to it I wouldn't give my eyes, nor my arms. So I guess I do have to be careful that my urgencies reflect my priorities.

Sometimes I feel like I'm the spoils in a battle between good and evil, right now, or that I'm both sides doing the fighting, and I'm not even sure of the outcome nor the terms. But sometimes it comes into my head, like right now, what would you really give? And it feels like, even just musing, I could make a terrible and tragic error of judgment if I don't always keep my head and my priorities clear. It's as if the devil is really trying to buy my soul, and pretending that it doesn't matter if I say yes because everybody knows he's not for real anyway. But I don't know that. And I don't think this is all a dream at all, and no, I would not give up love.

Maybe this is the chance to live and speak those things I really do believe, that power comes from moving into whatever I fear most that cannot be avoided. But will I ever be strong enough again to open my mouth and not have a cry of raw pain leap out?

* * *

I think I was fighting the devil of despair within myself for my own soul.

When I started to write this, I went back to the books I had read in the hospital as I made my decision to have a mastectomy. I came across pictures of women with one breast and mastectomy scars, and I remembered shrinking from these pictures before my surgery. Now they seemed not at all strange or frightening to me. At times, I miss my right breast, the actuality of it, its presence, with a great and poignant sense of loss. But in the same way, and just as infrequently, as I sometimes miss being 32, at the same time knowing that I have gained from the very loss I mourn.

Right after surgery I had a sense that I would never be able to bear missing that great well of sexual pleasure that I connected with my right breast. That sense has completely passed away, as I have come to realize that that well of feeling was within me. I alone own my feelings. I can never lose that feeling because I own it, because it comes out of myself. I can attach it anywhere I want to, because my feelings are a part of me, my sorrow and my joy.

I would never have chosen this path, but I am very glad to be who I am, here.   30 March 1979

Dreaming, I Can Dance

❧ GEORGIA L. McMURRAY

In my dreams, I dance,
whirling to the rhythm of drums beating
sounds only I can hear.
How I fly, leap through the air,
multitudes of colors spinning 'round
weaving a web of ecstasy.
I am dressed in white,
red flowers in my hair.
Floating through waves of sound,
I come into arms awaiting me,
willing me through steps unknown.
Toe in, toe out, he leads me,
our feet barely touching the ground.
He speaks of love while we dance,
tilting his head toward mine.
Soft hands gloved in grey,
stroking my face with rhythmic grace,
caressing me to three-quarter time.
Bodies fusing body heat
lighting a darkening sky.
Slowly the music draws to a close,
melancholy echoes lingering on,
kindling desire for a loss so profound.
I cannot move.
My body that wants to fly,
that needs to love,
lies still.
Dreaming, I can dance.
So let me sleep, never to wake again.
I want to dance once more.

Note: Georgia McMurray is paralyzed due to a rare form of muscular dystrophy.

93

The Abortion
❧ ALICE WALKER

They had discussed it, but not deeply, whether they wanted the baby she was now carrying. "I don't *know* if I want it," she said, eyes filling with tears. She cried at anything now, and was often nauseous. That pregnant women cried easily and were nauseous seemed banal to her, and she resented banality.

"Well, think about it," he said, with his smooth reassuring voice (but with an edge of impatience she now felt) that used to soothe her.

It was all she *did* think about, all she apparently *could;* that he could dream otherwise enraged her. But she always lost, when they argued. Her temper would flare up, he would become instantly reasonable, mature, responsible, if not responsive precisely, to her mood, and she would swallow down her tears and hate herself. It was because she believed him "good." The best human being she had ever met.

"It isn't as if we don't already have a child," she said in a calmer tone, carelessly wiping at the tear that slid from one eye.

"We have a perfect child," he said with relish, "thank the Good Lord!"

Had she ever dreamed she'd marry someone humble enough to go around thanking the Good Lord? She had not.

Now they left the bedroom, where she had been lying down on their massive king-size bed with the forbidding ridge in the middle, and went down the hall—hung with bright prints—to the cheerful, spotlessly clean kitchen. He put water on for tea in a bright yellow pot.

She wanted him to want the baby so much he would try to save its life. On the other hand, she did not permit such presumptuousness. As he praised the child they already had, a daughter of sunny disposition and winning smile, Imani sensed subterfuge, and hardened her heart.

"What am I talking about," she said, as if she'd been talking about it. "Another child would kill me. I can't imagine life with two children. Having a child is a good experience *to have had,* like graduate school. But if you've had one, you've had the experience and that's enough."

He placed the tea before her and rested a heavy hand on her hair. She felt the heat and pressure of his hand as she touched the cup and felt the odor and steam rise up from it. Her throat contracted.

"I can't drink that," she said through gritted teeth. "Take it away."

There were days of this.

Clarice, their daughter, was barely two years old. A miscarriage brought on by grief (Imani had lost her fervidly environmentalist mother to lung cancer shortly after Clarice's birth; the asbestos ceiling in the classroom where she taught first graders had leaked for twenty years) separated Clarice's birth from the new pregnancy. Imani felt her body had been assaulted by these events and was, in fact, considerably weakened, and was also, in any case, chronically anaemic and run down. Still, if she had wanted the baby more than she did not want it, she would not have planned to abort it.

They lived in a small town in the South. Her husband, Clarence, was, among other things, legal adviser and defender of the new black mayor of the town. The mayor was much in their lives because of the difficulties being the first black mayor of a small town assured, and because, next to the major leaders of black struggles in the South, Clarence respected and admired him most.

Imani reserved absolute judgment, but she did point out that Mayor Carswell would never look at her directly when she made a comment or posed a question, even sitting at her own dinner table, and would instead talk to Clarence as if she were not there. He assumed that as a woman she would not be interested in, or even understand, politics. (He would comment occasionally on her cooking or her clothes. He noticed when she cut her hair.) But Imani understood every shade and variation of politics: she understood, for example, why she fed the mouth that did not speak to her; because for the present she must believe in Mayor Carswell, even as he could not believe in her. Even understanding this, however, she found dinners with Carswell hard to swallow.

But Clarence was dedicated to the mayor, and believed his success would ultimately mean security and advancement for them all.

On the morning she left to have the abortion, the mayor and Clarence were to have a working lunch, and they drove her to the airport deep in conversation about municipal funds, racist cops, and the facilities for teaching at the chaotic, newly integrated schools. Clarence had time for the briefest kiss and hug at the airport ramp.

"Take care of yourself," he whispered lovingly as she walked away. He was needed, while she was gone, to draft the city's new charter. She had agreed this was important; the mayor was already being called incompetent by local businessmen and the chamber of commerce, and one inferred from television that no black person alive even knew what a city charter was.

"Take care of myself." Yes, she thought. I see that is what I have to do. But she thought this self-pityingly, which invalidated it. She had expected *him* to take care of her, and she blamed him for not doing so now.

Well, she was a fraud, anyway. She had known after a year of marriage that it bored her. "The Experience of Having a Child" was to distract her from this fact. Still, she expected him to "take care of her." She was lucky he didn't pack up and leave. But he seemed to know, as she did, that if anyone packed and left, it would be her. Precisely *because* she was a fraud and because in the end he would settle for fraud and she could not.

On the plane to New York her teeth ached and she vomited bile—bitter, yellowish stuff she hadn't even been aware her body produced. She resented and appreciated the crisp help of the stewardess, who asked if she needed anything, then stood chatting with the cigarette-smoking white man next to her, whose fat hairy wrist, like a large worm, was all Imani could bear to see out of the corner of her eye.

Her first abortion, when she was still in college, she frequently remembered as wonderful, bearing as it had all the marks of a supreme coming of age and a seizing of the direction of her own life, as well as a comprehension of existence that never left her: that life—what one saw about one and called Life—was not a facade. There was nothing behind it which used "Life" as its manifestation. Life was itself. Period. At the time, and afterwards, and even now, this seemed a marvelous thing to know.

The abortionist had been a delightful Italian doctor on the Upper East Side in New York, and before he put her under he told her about his own daughter who was just her age, and a junior at Vassar. He babbled on and on until she was out, but not before Imani had thought how her thousand dollars, for which she would be in debt for years, would go to keep her there.

When she woke up it was all over. She lay on a brown Naugahyde sofa in the doctor's outer office. And she heard, over her somewhere in the air, the sound of a woman's voice. It was a Saturday, no nurses in attendance, and she presumed it was the doctor's wife. She was pulled gently to her feet by this voice and encouraged to walk.

"And when you leave, be sure to walk as if nothing is wrong," the voice said.

Imani did not feel any pain. This surprised her. Perhaps he didn't do anything, she thought. Perhaps he took my thousand dollars and put me to sleep with two dollars' worth of ether. Perhaps this is a racket.

But he was so kind, and he was smiling benignly, almost fatherly, at her (and Imani realized how desperately she needed this "fatherly" look, this "fatherly" smile). "Thank you," she murmured sincerely: she was thanking him for her life.

Some of Italy was still in his voice. "It's nothing, nothing," he said. "A nice, pretty girl like you; in school like my own daughter, you didn't need this trouble."

"He's nice," she said to herself, walking to the subway on her way back to school. She lay down gingerly across a vacant seat, and passed out.

She hemorrhaged steadily for six weeks, and was not well again for a year.

* * *

But this was seven years later. An abortion law now made it possible to make an appointment at a clinic, and for seventy-five dollars a safe, quick, painless abortion was yours.

Imani had once lived in New York, in the Village, not five blocks from where the abortion clinic was. It was also near the Margaret Sanger clinic, where she had received her very first diaphragm, with utter gratitude and amazement that someone apparently understood and actually cared about young women as alone and ignorant as she. In fact, as she walked up the block, with its modern office buildings side by side with older, more elegant brownstones, she felt how close she was still to that earlier self. Still not in control of her sensuality, and only through violence and with money (for the flight, for the operation itself) in control of her body.

She found that abortion had entered the age of the assembly line. Grateful for the lack of distinction between herself and the other women—all colors, ages, states of misery or nervousness—she was less happy to notice, once the doctor started to insert the catheter, that the anesthesia she had been given was insufficient. But assembly lines don't stop because the product on them has a complaint. Her doctor whistled, and assured her she was all right, and carried the procedure through to the horrific end. Imani fainted some seconds before that.

They laid her out in a peaceful room full of cheerful colors. Primary colors: yellow, red, blue. When she revived she had the feeling of being in a nursery. She had a pressing need to urinate.

A nurse, kindly, white-haired and with firm hands, helped her to the toilet. Imani saw herself in the mirror over the sink and was alarmed. She was literally gray, as if all her blood had leaked out.

"Don't worry about how you look," said the nurse. "Rest a bit here and take it easy when you get back home. You'll be fine in a week or so."

She could not imagine being fine again. Somewhere her child—she never dodged into the language of "fetuses" and "amorphous growths"—was being flushed down a sewer. Gone all her or his chances to see the sunlight, savor a fig.

"Well," she said to this child, "It was you or me, Kiddo, and I chose me."

There were people who thought she had no right to choose herself, but Imani knew better than to think of those people now.

It was a bright, hot Saturday when she returned.

Clarence and Clarice picked her up at the airport. They had brought flowers from Imani's garden, and Clarice presented them with a stout-hearted hug. Once in her mother's lap she rested content all the way home, sucking her thumb, stroking her nose with the forefinger of the same hand, and kneading a corner of her blanket with the three fingers that were left.

"How did it go?" asked Clarence.

"It went," said Imani.

There was no easy way to explain abortion to a man. She thought castration might be an apt analogy, but most men, perhaps all, would insist this could not possibly be true.

"The anesthesia failed," she said. "I thought I'd never faint in time to keep from screaming and leaping off the table."

Clarence paled. He hated the thought of pain, any kind of violence. He could not endure it; it made him physically ill. This was one of the reasons he was a pacifist, another reason she admired him.

She knew he wanted her to stop talking. But she continued in a flat, deliberate voice.

"All the blood seemed to run out of me. The tendons in my legs felt cut. I was gray."

He reached for her hand. Held it. Squeezed.

"But," she said, "at least I know what I don't want. And I intend never to go through any of this again."

They were in the living room of their peaceful, quiet and colorful house. Imani was in her rocker, Clarice dozing on her lap. Clarence sank to the floor and rested his head against her knees. She felt he was asking for nurture when she needed it herself. She felt the two of them, Clarence and Clarice, clinging to her, using her. And that the only way she could claim herself, feel herself distinct from them, was by doing something painful, self-defining but self-destructive.

She suffered the pressure of his head as long as she could.

"Have a vasectomy," she said, "or stay in the guest room. Nothing is going to touch me anymore that isn't harmless."

He smoothed her thick hair with his hand. "We'll talk about it," he said, as if that was not what they were doing. "We'll see. Don't worry. We'll take care of things."

She had forgotten that the third Sunday in June, the following day, was the fifth memorial observance for Holly Monroe, who had been shot down on her way home from her high-school graduation ceremony five years before. Imani *always* went to these memorials. She liked the reassurance that her people had long memories, and that those people who fell in struggle or innocence were not forgotten. She was, of course, too weak to go. She was dizzy and still losing blood. The white lawgivers attempted to get around assassi-nation—which Imani considered extreme abortion—by saying the victim provoked it (there had been some difficulty saying this about Holly Monroe, but they had tried) but were antiabortionist to a man. Imani thought of this as she resolutely showered and washed her hair.

Clarence had installed central air conditioning their second year in the house. Imani had at first objected. "I want to smell the trees, the flowers, the natural air!" she cried. But the first summer of 110-degree heat had cured her of giving a damn about any of that. Now she wanted to be cool. As much as she loved trees, on a hot day she would have sawed through a forest to get to an air conditioner.

In fairness to him, she had to admit he asked her if she thought she was well enough to go. But even to be asked annoyed her. She was not one to let her own troubles prevent her from showing proper respect and remembrance toward the dead, although she understood perfectly well that once dead, the dead do not exist. So respect, remembrance was for herself, and today herself needed rest. There was something mad about her refusal to rest, and she felt it as she tottered about getting Clarice dressed. But she did not stop. She ran a bath, plopped the child in it, scrubbed her plump body on her knees, arms straining over the tub awkwardly in a way that made her stomach hurt—but not yet her uterus—dried her hair, lifted her out and dried the rest of her on the kitchen table.

"You are going to remember as long as you live what kind of people they are," she said to the child, who, gurgling and cooing, looked into her mother's stern face with light-hearted fixation.

"You are going to hear the music," Imani said. "The music they've tried to kill. The music they try to steal." She felt feverish and was aware she was muttering. She didn't care.

"They think they can kill a continent—people, trees, buffalo—and then fly off to the moon and just forget about it. But you and me we're going to remember the people, the trees and the fucking buffalo. Goddammit."

"Buffwoe," said the child, hitting at her mother's face with a spoon.

She placed the baby on a blanket in the living room and turned to see her husband's eyes, full of pity, on her. She wore pert green velvet slippers and a lovely sea green robe. Her body was bent within it. A reluctant tear formed beneath his gaze.

"Sometimes I look at you and I wonder 'What is this man doing in my house?' "

This had started as a joke between them. Her aim had been never to marry, but to take in lovers who could be sent home at dawn, freeing her to work and ramble.

"I'm here because you love me," was the traditional answer. But Clarence faltered, meeting her eyes, and Imani turned away.

It was a hundred degrees by ten o'clock. By eleven, when the memorial service began, it would be ten degrees hotter. Imani staggered from the heat. When she sat in the car she had to clench her teeth against the dizziness until the motor prodded the air conditioning to envelop them in coolness. A dull ache started in her uterus.

The church was not of course air conditioned. It was authentic Primitive Baptist in every sense.

Like the four previous memorials this one was designed by Holly Monroe's classmates. All twenty-five of whom—fat and thin—managed to look like the dead girl. Imani had never seen Holly Monroe, though there were always photographs of her dominating the pulpit of this church where she had been baptized and where she had sung in the choir—and to her, every black girl of a certain vulnerable age *was* Holly Monroe. And an even deeper truth was that Holly Monroe was herself. Herself shot down, aborted on the eve of becoming herself.

She was prepared to cry and to do so with abandon. But she did not. She clenched her teeth against the steadily increasing pain and her tears were instantly blotted by the heat.

Mayor Carswell had been waiting for Clarence in the vestibule of the church, mopping his plumply jowled face with a voluminous handkerchief and holding court among half a dozen young men and women who listened to him with awe. Imani exchanged greetings with the mayor, he ritualistically kissed her on the cheek, and kissed Clarice on the cheek, but his rather heat-glazed eye was already fastened on her husband. The two men huddled in a corner away from the awed young group. Away from Imani and Clarice, who passed hesitantly, waiting to be joined or to be called back, into the church.

There was a quarter hour's worth of music.

"Holly Monroe was five feet, three inches tall, and weighed one hundred and eleven pounds," her best friend said, not reading from notes, but talking to each person in the audience. "She was a stubborn, loyal Aries, the best kind of friend to have. She had black kinky hair that she experimented with a lot. She was exactly the color of this oak church pew in the summer; in the winter she was the color [pointing up] of this heart pine ceiling. She loved green. She did not like lavender because she said she also didn't like pink. She had brown eyes and wore glasses, except when she was meeting someone for the first time. She had a sort of rounded nose. She had beautiful large teeth, but her lips were always chapped so she didn't smile as much as she might have if she'd ever gotten used to carrying Chap Stick. She had elegant feet.

"Her favorite church song was 'Leaning on the Everlasting Arms.' Her favorite other kind of song was 'I Can't Help Myself—I Love You and Nobody Else.' She was often late for choir rehearsal though she loved to sing. She made the dress she wore to her graduation in Home Ec. She *hated* Home Ec. . . . "

Imani was aware that the sound of low, murmurous voices had been the background for this statement all along. Everything was quiet around her, even Clarice sat up straight, absorbed by the simple friendliness of the young woman's voice. All of Holly Monroe's classmates and friends in the choir wore vivid green. Imani imagined Clarice entranced by the brilliant, swaying color as by a field of swaying corn.

Lifting the child, her uterus burning, and perspiration already a stream down her back, Imani tiptoed to the door. Clarence and the mayor were still deep in conversation. She heard "board meeting . . . aldermen . . . city council." She beckoned to Clarence.

"Your voices are carrying!" she hissed.

She meant: How dare you not come inside.

They did not. Clarence raised his head, looked at her, and shrugged his shoulders helplessly. Then, turning, with the abstracted air of priests, the two men moved slowly toward the outer door, and into the churchyard, coming to stand some distance from the church beneath a large oak tree. There they remained throughout the service.

Two years later, Clarence was furious with her: What is the matter with you? he asked. You never want me to touch you. You told me to sleep in the guest room and I did. You told me to have a vasectomy I didn't want and *I did*. (Here, there was a sob of hatred for her somewhere in the anger, the humiliation; he thought of himself as a eunuch, and blamed her.)

She was not merely frigid, she was remote.

She had been amazed after they left the church that the anger she'd felt watching Clarence and the mayor turn away from the Holly Monroe memorial did not prevent her accepting a ride home with him. A month later it did not prevent her smiling on him fondly. Did not prevent a trip to Bermuda, a few blissful days of very good sex on a deserted beach screened by trees. Did not prevent her listening to his mother's stories of Clarence's youth as though she would treasure them forever.

And yet. From that moment in the heat of the church door, she had uncoupled herself from him, in a separation that made him, except occasionally, little more than a stranger.

And he had not felt it, had not known.

"What have I done?" he asked, all the tenderness in his voice breaking over her. She smiled a nervous smile at him, which he interpreted as derision—so far apart had they drifted.

They had discussed the episode at the church many times. Mayor Carswell—whom they never saw anymore—was now a model mayor, with wide biracial support in his campaign for the legislature. Neither could easily recall him, though television frequently brought him into the house.

"It was so important that I help the mayor!" said Clarence. "He was our *first!*"

Imani understood this perfectly well, but it sounded humorous to her. When she smiled, he was offended.

She had known the moment she left the marriage, the exact second. But apparently that moment had left no perceptible mark.

They argued, she smiled, they scowled, blamed and cried—as she packed.

Each of them almost recalled out loud that about this time of the year their aborted child would have been a troublesome, "terrible" two-year-old, a great burden on its mother, whose health was by now in excellent shape, each wanted to think aloud that the marriage would have deteriorated anyway, because of that.

The Mother

❧ GWENDOLYN BROOKS

Abortions will not let you forget.
You remember the children you got that you did not get,
The damp small pulps with a little or with no hair,
The singers and workers that never handled the air.
You will never neglect or beat
Them, or silence or buy with a sweet.
You will never wind up the sucking-thumb
Or scuttle off ghosts that come.
You will never leave them, controlling your luscious sigh,
Return for a snack of them, with gobbling mother-eye.

I have heard in the voices of the wind the voices of my
    dim killed children.
I have contracted. I have eased
My dim dears at the breasts they could never suck.
I have said, Sweets, if I sinned, if I seized
Your luck
And your lives from your unfinished reach,
If I stole your births and your names,
Your straight baby tears and your games,
Your stilted or lovely loves, your tumults, your
    marriages, aches, and your deaths,
If I poisoned the beginnings of your breaths,
Believe that even in my deliberateness I was not
    deliberate.
Though why should I whine,
Whine that the crime was other than mine?—
Since anyhow you are dead.
Or rather, or instead,
You were never made.
But that too, I am afraid,
Is faulty: oh, what shall I say, how is the truth to be
    said?
You were born, you had body, you died.
It is just that you never giggled or planned or cried.

104

Believe me, I loved you all.
Believe me, I knew you, though faintly, and I loved, I
    loved you
All.

Illness and
Health-Seeking Behavior
Discussion Questions

1. Which of the characters in these stories and poems have you met before and under what circumstances?

2. How did you feel after reading "The Sky Is Gray"?

3. Do you know a nonblack counterpart for Dr. Sidesaddle? Can you understand the author's motivation for writing such a letter?

4. Zora Neale Hurston describes an experience that was humiliating. Have you witnessed or experienced a similar kind of occurrence? If so, describe your reactions and feelings.

5. In the story "If We Must Die," a black physician is threatened with physical harm for the care he is trying to provide to a seriously injured white girl. Does the event reflect behavior only of a former time or is that kind of prejudice still manifest today?

6. What is happening in Toni Cade Bambara's story and how does it tie into some of the problems facing us today?

7. What is gained from the child's perspective in "The Sky Is Gray" and how does this mother compare to the mother in "Strong Horse Tea"?

8. There are some who believe that low-income families ought to limit family size through tubal ligation, birth control, or abortion. In terms of abortion as an alternative, what have you discovered from these selections?

9. In the story and poem which deal with the abortion issue, what sympathies are aroused in you, and are your own attitudes about abortion changed in any way?

10. What have you learned from these stories about society, and health-care professionals, about feelings, about some black men and women?

SECTION II

✺

Aging

'Cause tired don't mean lazy and every goodbye ain't gone.
                                                MAYA ANGELOU

To grow old is to pass from passion to compassion.

                                                ALBERT CAMUS

Introduction

In Robert Frost's well-known poem, "Nothing Gold Can Stay," the poetic voice reminds readers that the garden of earthly perfection, the golden paradise of Genesis, is not attainable for real-life human beings. Instead, we, like nature, are subjected to seasons including those of decay and death. Nothing gold can stay.

This section on aging contains creative works inspired by the black aging experience. Most are not commonly found in anthologies and will provide, therefore, an unfamiliar but important perspective about a period of time in the season of decline and disability in individual blacks. The current population of elderly blacks, who serve as subjects in the works presented here, have borne a heavy burden of discriminatory treatment. For them the combined influence of poor education and job inequities has often resulted in sporadic and menial employment and unacceptable living conditions. Health-care providers and decision makers working with elderly blacks need to be aware of the role that education and employment histories play in the well-being of those under their care.

In the complex configuration of differences and similarities among ethnic groups, norms and values of the predominant culture

107

have significant impact. However, while minority status frequently results in more problems and greater obstacles, especially in health care, the cultural symbols, rituals, and meanings shared by minority group members are important positive resources in the aging process. Readers with residual stereotypical impressions of older black men and women will discover characters who will dispel their misconceptions.

The glory, beauty, pain, and ugliness of aging are captured by the authors in our selections. Some praise and revere the wisdom, the enduring strength, and the bravery of the old. Others respond specifically to the decay and sadness associated with loss of physical and social function. Many focus on poverty and its soul-killing effects on disadvantaged African-Americans. Above all, the selections reveal what we intuitively know: all people, whether black or white, are buffeted by the cold winds of the aging process. For many it is a time of disability, vulnerability, and fear; for others, aging is but a period in life's cyclical pattern. Either way, the final season of winter is not too far away.

In "Aunt Sue's Stories," which appears at the beginning of the book, Langston Hughes evokes the power of stories which are part of the black oral history tradition as they affect "the dark-faced child" sitting at the storyteller's knee. Sue's stories came from her head, what she had learned as a child listener, and are passed on from her to storytellers of the future. Like many other elderly black figures, Sue is the keeper of black history, a history of slavery, sorrow, and heroic resilience. Clearly, the speaker, the now grown-up child, continues the tradition, another link in an unending chain of storytellers.

This section begins with two selections by writers remembering elderly women from their childhood experiences. Both stories express the fragile but special bond between an aged figure and a small child which has contributed significantly to the storyteller's character and outlook.

In "Maggie of the Green Bottles," we meet Granny Maggie, a concocter of herbed potions in jeweled green jars, through the eyes of her great-granddaughter, Peaches, now grown up, recalling from the perspective of her childhood the old woman's secret conjurings. In an extended household, where adults considered the eccentric old woman a nuisance and a burden, the relationship between the child and her mesmerizing granny was strengthened by their status as peripheral family members, the one in-coming and the other out-going. When death enters, we learn that the little girl has been the unwitting messenger and that the lovely green bottles, the containers of granny's most powerful wisdoms, have disappeared. Maggie's death marks the end of Peaches' childhood; she loses that sense of wonderment, instilled by the old woman's eccentricities, and becomes "ordinary, mortal," like her "everyday-type" baby brother. Maggie, we sense, is ultimately a metaphor for the condition of childhood that must one day be left. The jeweled green bottles, she retrospectively realizes, contained lethal doses of sleep, then death; they symbolize the transference of life force from one generation to the next.

"To Da-duh, in Memoriam," by Paule Marshall, similarly recalls an encounter by a thoughtful adult with a now-deceased grandmother in which the reader experiences the love between grandmother and granddaughter, as well as the child's pain on the occasion of the old woman's death. Marshall's story is autobiographical, an account of the visit she made to Barbados, her grandmother's home, when she was a saucy nine-year-old from New York City. According to Marshall, Da-duh is "an ancestor figure, symbolic . . . for me of the long lives of black women and men—African and New World—who made my being possible and whose spirit I believe continues to animate my life and work."[1]

The poem "George," by Dudley Randall, moves us into a different mood and impression of aging. As children, we watch old people shuffle from room to room and trace the furrows in their wrinkled faces. They are old, these observed beings; we, in contrast, are permanently young with no thoughts of becoming like them. Randall's poem comments on the shock he feels when he witnesses firsthand the gradual transformation of an older male coworker from a figure of physical strength and power to one of diminishment in a hospital. George's fate, of course, is a vicarious rendering of our own worst fears of illness and incapacity, dependency and institutionalization.

Destruction by time and the accompanying stench of mortality is presented by Lucille Clifton's urban portrait of "Miss Rosie." Omnipresent bag ladies litter our city streets like bulky shadows of shame. Clifton brings us face-to-face with the effects of poverty and

1. From an interview with Paule Marshall, n.d.

societal indifference when she considers Rosie in her "old man's shoes/ with the little toe cut out," "wrapped up like garbage. . . ." This woman used to be the best-looking woman in Georgia, the "Georgia Rose," and the poetic voice decries this tragic fall with a tribute and lament: "I stand up/ through your destruction/ I stand up."

The story of Lizabeth in "Marigolds" by Eugenia Collier is painfully familiar. As children, many of us harassed or taunted enfeebled elders in our neighborhoods. It is not a happy memory. Because the experience is common, Collier's account invites a study of our actions. Why did we behave so despicably? Often, the desultory action is group-inspired, the plot of several children, a small gang. It is mindless and wanton, an action to be remembered with shame by the child grown up.

> When we were tiny children, we thought Miss Lottie was a witch and we made up tales, that we half believed ourselves, about her exploits. We were far too sophisticated now, of course, to believe the witch-nonsense. But old fears have a way of clinging like cobwebs, and so when we sighted the tumble-down shack, we had to stop to reinforce our nerves.

When the old woman occupying the ramshackle house "dared to create beauty in the midst of ugliness and sterility" by planting passionate mounds of marigolds, the children took note. The show of brilliant yellow flowers drew them, ironically, to cruelty. The destruction of the flowers by the prepubescent child, now narrator, symbolized a loss of innocence, a childish fist pounding at the borders of adulthood, which were finally and irrevocably breached when she looked up into the face of the broken old woman, Lottie. It is a difficult recollection.

Relationships between children and adults vary. Alice Walker describes a situation in which children infuse a dying old man with life, not just once, but many times, as they move from childhood into adulthood. "To Hell with Dying" introduces Mr. Sweet, who for two decades is like a dying ember, requiring that life be blown into him ritualistically.

> "To hell with dying, man, these children want Mr. Sweet"—which was my cue to throw myself upon the bed and kiss Mr. Sweet all

around the whiskers and under the eyes and around the collar of his nightshirt where he smelled so strongly of all sorts of things, mostly liniment.

When necessary, the entire family rallies around the old diabetic and alcoholic guitar player, infusing him with an incentive to live. The narrator, as the youngest child, recalls her wonderful moments with him when she and her brothers and sisters "never felt anything of Mr. Sweet's age when we played with him." Despite all efforts, Mr. Sweet, who was "like a piece of rare and delicate china which was always being saved from breaking," finally died at age ninety. This experience was indeed strange and revelatory to the now-grown children, who, until this moment, had not come to grips with the gray ashes of death.

Poems by Maya Angelou and Sterling Brown are portraits of individual speakers whose perspectives vary. The discomfort of being old and incapacitated nudges the old woman in "The Last Decision" toward resignation. She is tired, weary: "The print is too small," "The food is too rich," "I cannot hear one single word."

A second poem by Maya Angelou, "On Aging," speaks to human spirit and pride. The speaker doesn't need chatter; she may want to listen herself. If she stumbles, don't rush forward with a rocking chair. Independence and spirit characterize this exhilarated fighter who knows it ain't over till it's over. She understands the cyclical rhythms of life: " ... tired don't mean lazy/ And every goodbye ain't gone."

A woman's graceful acceptance of aging and abiding faith is presented in "Virginia Portrait" by Sterling Brown. In the seasons preceding the winter of age the speaker reviews the grief and pain that have mingled with happiness to bring a full life. She is strong, steadfast, deep-rooted, a woman whose modest circumstances have not deprived her of her life's greatest riches: laughter, wisdom, and a sense of spiritual dignity. Now she is ready to lay down her burdens; it is time. "The winter of her year has come to her, this wizened woman, spare of frame, but great of heart, erect, and undefeated yet."

Many stories in newspapers describe despairing elderly couples whose lives end abruptly in suicide. Infirmity, reduced resources, and loneliness are frequently factors contributing to the incidence of euthanasia and suicide. Couples look into a deteriorating future with greater dependency on others. For some this eventuality is impossible; they choose, instead, a final act of independence, selecting other terms for death, terms that offer greater dignity and control. In Arna Bontemps's story, "A Summer Tragedy," we meet Jeff and Jenny Patton, who are journeying toward death. With some fumbling, the elegant pair dress in their Sunday best. He struggles with his high, stiff collar; she, now blind, gropes with her hands and cane to find her old shoes and stockings. There is an ironic grace, sweetness, and charm to this couple and the course they have chosen, especially in noting that the story was written in 1928, decades before the word *bioethics* and the phrase "death with dignity" were coined. That the couple is black and in circumstances we can identify for ourselves lends an unforgettable poignancy to the story.

This section on aging concludes with a poem by Gwendolyn Brooks called "The Bean Eaters." "They eat beans mostly, this old yellow pair." An artist could translate easily to canvas what Brooks describes with words. But without that visual portrayal an image will appear anyway: one that will etch in our minds the bittersweet nature of age. It, like autumn, stirs a sense of sadness and loss. Although the edges are frayed and bareness is apparent, a parallel image of fullness and richness lingers "As they lean over the beans in their rented back room that/ is full of beads and receipts and dolls and clothes,/ tobacco crumbs, vases and fringes," "remembering . . . / Remembering, with twinklings and twinges. . . ."

Soon all autumn leaves will be gone.

Maggie of the Green Bottles
❧ TONI CADE BAMBARA

Maggie had not intended to get sucked in on this thing, sleeping straight through the christening, steering clear of the punch bowl, and refusing to dress for company. But when she glanced over my grandfather's shoulder and saw "Aspire, Enspire, Perspire" scrawled across the first page in that hard-core Protestant hand, and a grease stain from the fried chicken too, something snapped in her head. She snatched up the book and retired rapidly to her room, locked my mother out, and explained through the door that my mother was a fool to encourage a lot of misspelled nonsense from Mr. Tyler's kin, and an even bigger fool for having married the monster in the first place.

I imagine that Maggie sat at her great oak desk, rolled the lace cuffs gently back, and dipped her quill into the lavender ink pot with all the ceremony due the Emancipation Proclamation, which was, after all, exactly what she was drafting. Writing to me, she explained, was serious business, for she felt called upon to liberate me from all historical and genealogical connections except the most divine. In short, the family was a disgrace, degrading Maggie's and my capacity for wings, as they say. I can only say that Maggie was truly inspired. And she probably ruined my life from the get-go.

There is a photo of the two of us on the second page. There's Maggie in Minnie Mouse shoes and a long polka-dot affair with her stockings rolled up at the shins, looking like muffins. There's me with nothing much at all on, in her arms, and looking almost like a normal, mortal, everyday-type baby—raw, wrinkled, ugly. Except that it must be clearly understood straightaway that I sprang into the world full wise and invulnerable and gorgeous like a goddess. Behind us is the player piano with the spooky keys. And behind that, the window outlining Maggie's crosshatched face and looking out over the yard, overgrown even then, where later I lay lost in the high grass, never hoping to be found till Maggie picked me up into her hair and told me all about the earth's moons.

Once just a raggedy thing holding telegrams from well-wishers, the book was pleasant reading on those rainy days when I didn't risk rusting my skates, or maybe just wasn't up to trailing up and down the city streets with the kids, preferring to study Maggie's drawings and try to grab hold of the fearsome machinery which turned the planets and coursed the stars and told me in no uncertain terms that as an Aries babe I was obligated to carry on the work of other Aries greats from Alexander right on down to anyone you care to mention. I could go on to relate all the wise-alecky responses I gave to Maggie's document as an older child rummaging in the trunks among the canceled checks and old sheet music, looking for some suspicioned love letters or some small proof that my mother had once had romance in her life, and finding instead the raggedy little book I thought was just a raggedy little book. But it is much too easy to smile at one's ignorant youth just to flatter one's present wisdom, but I digress.

Because, on my birthday, Saturn was sitting on its ass and Mars was taken unawares, getting bumped by Jupiter's flunkies, I would not be into my own till well past twenty. But according to the cards, and my palm line bore it out, the hangman would spare me till well into my hundredth year. So all in all, the tea leaves having had their say and the coffee-ground patterns being what they were, I was destined for greatness. She assured me. And I was certain of my success, as I was certain that my parents were not my parents, that I was descended, anointed and ready to gobble up the world from urgent, noble Olympiads.

I am told by those who knew her, whose memories consist of something more substantial than a frantic gray lady who poured coffee into her saucer, that Margaret Cooper Williams wanted something she could not have. And it was the sorrow of her life that all her children and theirs and theirs were uncooperative—worse, squeamish. Too busy taking in laundry, buckling at the knees, putting their faith in Jesus, mute and sullen in their sorrow, too squeamish to band together and take the world by storm, make history, or even to appreciate the calling of Maggie the Ram, or the Aries that came after. Other things they told me too, things I put aside to learn later though I always knew, perhaps, but never quite wanted to, the way you hold your breath and steady yourself to the knowledge secretly, but never let yourself understand. They called her crazy.

It is to Maggie's guts that I bow forehead to the floor and kiss her hand, because she'd tackle the lot of them right there in the yard, blood kin or by marriage, and neighbors or no. And anybody who'd stand up to my father, gross Neanderthal that he was, simply had to be some kind of weird combination of David, Aries, and lunatic. It began with the cooking usually, especially the pots of things Maggie concocted. Witchcraft, he called it. Home cooking, she'd counter. Then he'd come over to the stove, lift a lid with an incredible face, and comment about cesspools and fertilizers. But she'd remind him of his favorite dish, chitlins, addressing the bread box, though. He'd turn up the radio and make some remark about good church music and her crazy voodoo records. Then she'd tell the curtains that some men, who put magic down with nothing to replace it and nothing much to recommend them in the first place but their magic wand, lived a runabout life, practicing black magic on other men's wives. Then he'd say something about freeloading relatives and dancing to the piper's tune. And she'd whisper to the kettles that there wasn't no sense in begging from a beggar. Depending on how large an audience they drew, this could go on for hours until my father would cock his head to the side, listening, and then try to make his getaway.

"Ain't nobody calling you, Mr. Tyler, cause don't nobody want you." And I'd feel kind of bad about my father like I do about the wolf man and the phantom of the opera. Monsters, you know, more than anybody else, need your pity cause they need beauty and love so bad.

One day, right about the time Maggie would say something painful that made him bring up freeloaders and piper's tunes, he began to sputter so bad it made me want to cry. But Maggie put the big wooden spoon down and whistled for Mister T—at least that's what Maggie and my grandmother, before she died, insisted on calling him. The dog, always hungry, came bounding through the screen door, stopped on a dime by the sink, and slinked over to Maggie's legs the way beat-up dogs can do, their tails all confused as to just what to do, their eyes unblinkingly watchful. Maggie offered him something from the pot. And when Mister T had finished, he licked Maggie's hand. She began to cackle. And then, before I could even put my milk down, up went Maggie's palm, and *bam,* Mister T went skidding across the linoleum and banged all the seltzer bottles down.

"Damn-fool mutt," said Maggie to her wooden spoon, "too

dumb to even know you're supposed to bite the hand that feeds you."

My father threw his hand back and yelled for my mother to drop whatever she was doing, which was standing in the doorway shaking her head, and pack up the old lady's things posthaste. Maggie went right on laughing and talking to the spoon. And Mister T slinked over to the table so Baby Jason could pet him. And then it was name-calling time. And again I must genuflect and kiss her ring, because my father was no slouch when it came to names. He could malign your mother and work your father's lineage over in one short breath, describing in absolute detail all the incredible alliances made between your ancestors and all sorts of weird creatures. But Maggie had him beat there too, old lady in lace talking to spoons or no.

My mother came in weary and worn and gave me a nod. I slid my peanut-butter sandwich off the icebox, grabbed Baby Jason by his harness, and dragged him into our room, where I was supposed to read to him real loud. But I listened, I always listened to my mother's footfalls on the porch to the gravel path and down the hard mud road to the woodshed. Then I could give my attention to the kitchen, for "Goldilocks," keep in mind, never was enough to keep the brain alive. Then, right in the middle of some fierce curse or other, my father did this unbelievable thing. He stomped right into Maggie's room—that sanctuary of heaven charts and incense pots and dream books and magic stuffs. Only Jason, hiding from an August storm, had ever been allowed in there, and that was on his knees crawling. But in he stomped all big and bad like some terrible giant, this man whom Grandma Williams used to say was just the sort of size man put on this earth for the " 'spress purpose of clubbing us all to death." And he came out with these green bottles, one in each hand, snorting and laughing at the same time. And I figured, peeping into the kitchen, that these bottles were enchanted, for they had a strange effect on Maggie, she shut right up. They had a strange effect on me too, gleaming there up in the air, nearly touching the ceiling, glinting off the shots of sunshine, grasped in the giant's fist. I was awed.

Whenever I saw them piled in the garbage out back I was tempted to touch them and make a wish, knowing all the while that the charm was all used up and that that was why they were in the garbage in the first place. But there was no doubt that they were

116

special. And whenever Baby Jason managed to drag one out from under the bed, there was much whispering and shuffling on my mother's part. And when Sweet Basil, the grocer's boy, delivered these green bottles to Maggie, it was all hush-hush and backdoor and in the corner dealings, slipping it in and out of innumerable paper bags, holding it up to the light, then off she'd run to her room and be gone for hours, days sometimes, and when she did appear, looking mysterious and in a trance, her face all full of shadows. And she'd sit at the sideboard with that famous cup from the World's Fair, pouring coffee into the saucer and blowing on it very carefully, nodding and humming and swirling the grinds. She called me over once to look at the grinds.

"What does this look like, Peaches?"

"Looks like a star with a piece out of it."

"Hmm," she mumbled, and swirled again. "And now?"

Me peering into the cup and lost for words. "Looks like a face that lost its eyes."

"Hmm," again, as she thrust the cup right under my nose, and me wishing it was a box of falling glass I could look at where I knew what was what instead of looking into the bottom of a fat yellow cup at what looked like nothing but coffee grinds.

"Looks like a mouth losing its breath, Great Granny."

"Let's not get too outrageous, Peaches. This is serious business."

"Yes ma'am." Peering again and trying to be worthy of Alexander and the Ram and all my other forebears. "What it really seems to be"—stalling for time and praying for inspiration—"is an upside-down bird, dead on its back with his heart chopped out and the hole bleeding."

She flicked my hand away when I tried to point the picture out which by now I was beginning to believe. "Go play somewhere, girl," she said. She was mad. "And quit calling me Granny."

"What happened here today?" my mother kept asking all evening, thumping out the fragrant dough and wringing the dishtowel, which was supposed to help the dough rise, wringing it to pieces. I couldn't remember anything in particular, following her gaze to Maggie's door. "Was Sweet Basil here this afternoon?" Couldn't remember that either, but tried to show I was her daughter by staring hard at the closed door too. "Was Great Granny up and around at all today?" My memory failed me there too. "You ain't

117

got much memory to speak of at all, do you?" said my father. I hung onto my mother's apron and helped her wring the dishtowel to pieces.

They told me she was very sick, so I had to drag Baby Jason out to the high grass to play with him. It was a hot day and the smell of the kerosene soaking the weeds that were stubborn about dying made my eyes tear. I was face down in the grass just listening, waiting for the afternoon siren which last year I thought was Judgment Day because it blew so long to say that the war was over and that we didn't have to eat Spam any more and that there was a circus coming and a parade and Uncle Bubba too, but with only one leg to show for it all. Maggie came into the yard with her basket of vegetables. She sat down at the edge of the gravel path and began stringing the peppers, red and green, red and green. And, like always, she was humming one of those weird songs of hers which always made her seem holier and blacker than she could've been. I tied Baby Jason to a tree so he wouldn't crawl into her lap, which always annoyed her. Maggie didn't like baby boys, or any kind of boys I'm thinking, but especially baby boys born in Cancer and Pisces or anything but in Aries.

"Look here, Peaches," she called, working the twine through the peppers and dropping her voice real low. "I want you to do this thing for your Great Granny."

"What must I do?" I waited a long time till I almost thought she'd fallen asleep, her head rolling around on her chest and her hands fumbling with the slippery peppers, ripping them.

"I want you to go to my room and pull out the big pink box from under the bed." She looked around and woke up a bit. "This is a secret you-and-me thing now, Peaches." I nodded and waited some more. "Open the box and you'll see a green bottle. Wrap this apron around it and tuck it under your arm like so. Then grab up the mushrooms I left on the sideboard like that's what you came for in the first place. But get yourself back here right quick." I repeated the instructions, flopped a necklace of peppers around me, and dashed into the hot and dusty house. When I got back she dumped the mushrooms into her lap, tucked the bottle under her skirt, and smiled at the poor little peppers her nervous hands had strung. They hung wet and ruined off the twine like broken-necked little animals.

I was down in the bottoms playing with the state-farm kids

when Uncle Bubba came sliding down the sand pile on his one good leg. Jason was already in the station wagon hanging onto my old doll. We stayed at Aunt Min's till my father came to get us in the pickup. Everybody was in the kitchen dividing up Maggie's things. The linen chest went to Aunt Thelma. And the souvenirs from Maggie's honeymoons went to the freckle-faced cousins from town. The clothes were packed for the church. And Reverend Elson was directing the piano's carrying from the kitchen window. The scattered sopranos, who never ever seemed to get together on their high notes or on their visits like this, were making my mother drink tea and kept nodding at me, saying she was sitting in the mourner's seat, which was just like all the other chairs in the set; same as the amen corner was no better or any less dusty than the rest of the church and not even a corner. Then Reverend Elson turned to say that no matter how crazy she'd been, no matter how hateful she'd acted toward the church in general and him in particular, no matter how spiteful she'd behaved towards her neighbors and even her blood kin, and even though everyone was better off without her, seeing how she died as proof of her heathen character, and right there in the front yard too, with a bottle under her skirts, the sopranos joined in scattered as ever, despite all that, the Reverend Elson continued, God rest her soul, if He saw fit, that is.

The china darning egg went into Jason's overalls. And the desk went into my room. Bubba said he wanted the books for his children. And they all gave him such a look. My mother just sat in the kitchen chair called the mourner's seat and said nothing at all except that they were selling the house and moving to the city.

"Well, Peaches," my father said. "You were her special, what you want?"

"I'll take the bottles," I said.

"Let us pray," said the Reverend.

That night I sat at the desk and read the baby book for the first time. It sounded like Maggie for the world, holding me in her lap and spreading the charts on the kitchen table. I looked my new bottle collection over. There were purple bottles with glass stoppers and labels. There were squat blue bottles with squeeze tops but nothing in them. There were flat red bottles that could hold only one flower at a time. I had meant the green bottles. I was going to tell them and then I didn't. I was too small for so much enchantment anyway. I went to bed feeling much too small. And it seemed a shame that the hope of the Aries line should have to sleep with a light on still, and blame it on Jason and cry with balled fists in the eyes just like an ordinary, mortal, everyday-type baby.

To Da-duh, In Memoriam
༞ PAULE MARSHALL

> "... Oh Nana! all of you is not involved in this evil business
> Death,
> Nor all of us in life."
>
> —From "At My Grandmother's Grave,"
> by Lebert Bethune

I did not see her at first I remember. For not only was it dark inside the crowded disembarkation shed in spite of the daylight flooding in from outside, but standing there waiting for her with my mother and sister I was still somewhat blinded from the sheen of tropical sunlight on the water of the bay which we had just crossed in the landing boat, leaving behind us the ship that had brought us from New York lying in the offing. Besides, being only nine years of age at the time and knowing nothing of islands I was busy attending to the alien sights and sounds of Barbados, the unfamiliar smells.

I did not see her, but I was alerted to her approach by my mother's hand which suddenly tightened around mine, and looking up I traced her gaze through the gloom in the shed until I finally made out the small, purposeful, painfully erect figure of the old woman headed our way.

Her face was drowned in the shadow of an ugly rolled-brim brown felt hat, but the details of her slight body and of the struggle taking place within it were clear enough—an intense, unrelenting struggle between her back which was beginning to bend ever so slightly under the weight of her eighty-odd years and the rest of her which sought to deny those years and hold that back straight, keep it in line. Moving swiftly toward us (so swiftly it seemed she did not intend stopping when she reached us but would sweep past us out the doorway which opened onto the sea and like Christ walk upon the water!), she was caught between the sunlight at her end of the building and the darkness inside—and for a moment she appeared to contain them both: the light in the long severe old-fashioned white dress she wore which brought the sense of a past that was still alive into our bustling present and in the snatch of white at her eye; the darkness in her black high-top shoes and in her face which was visible now that she was closer.

It was as stark and fleshless as a death mask, that face. The maggots might have already done their work, leaving only the framework of bone beneath the ruined skin and deep wells at the temple and jaw. But her eyes were alive, unnervingly so for one so old, with a sharp light that flicked out of the dim clouded depths like a lizard's tongue to snap up all in her view. Those eyes betrayed a child's curiosity about the world, and I wondered vaguely seeing them, and seeing the way the bodice of her ancient dress had collapsed in on her flat chest (what had happened to her breasts?), whether she might not be some kind of child at the same time that she was a woman, with fourteen children, my mother included, to prove it. Perhaps she was both, both child and woman, darkness and light, past and present, life and death—all the opposites contained and reconciled in her.

"My Da-duh," my mother said formally and stepped forward. The name sounded like thunder fading softly in the distance.

"Child," Da-duh said, and her tone, her quick scrutiny of my mother, the brief embrace in which they appeared to shy from each other rather than touch, wiped out the fifteen years my mother had been away and restored the old relationship. My mother, who was such a formidable figure in my eyes, had suddenly with a word been reduced to my status.

"Yes, God is good," Da-duh said with a nod that was like a tic. "He has spared me to see my child again."

We were led forward then, apologetically because not only did Da-duh prefer boys but she also liked her grandchildren to be "white," that is, fair-skinned; and we had, I was to discover, a number of cousins, the outside children of white estate managers and the like, who qualified. We, though, were as black as she.

My sister being the oldest was presented first. "This one takes after the father," my mother said and waited to be reproved.

Frowning, Da-duh tilted my sister's face toward the light. But her frown soon gave way to a grudging smile, for my sister with her large mild eyes and little broad winged nose, with our father's high-cheeked Barbadian cast to her face, was pretty.

"She's goin' be lucky," Da-duh said and patted her once on the cheek. "Any girl child that takes after the father does be lucky."

She turned then to me. But oddly enough she did not touch me. Instead leaning close, she peered hard at me, and then quickly drew back. I thought I saw her hand start up as though to shield her eyes. It was almost as if she saw not only me, a thin truculent child who it was said took after no one but myself, but something in me which for some reason she found disturbing, even threatening. We looked silently at each other for a long time there in the noisy shed, our gaze locked. She was the first to look away.

"But Adry," she said to my mother and her laugh was cracked, thin, apprehensive. "Where did you get this one here with this fierce look?"

"We don't know where she came out of, my Da-duh," my mother said, laughing also. Even I smiled to myself. After all I had won the encounter. Da-duh had recognized my small strength—and this was all I ever asked of the adults in my life then.

"Come, soul," Da-duh said and took my hand. "You must be one of those New York terrors you hear so much about."

She led us, me at her side and my sister and mother behind, out of the shed into the sunlight that was like a bright driving summer rain and over to a group of people clustered beside a decrepit lorry. They were our relatives, most of them from St. Andrews although Da-duh herself lived in St. Thomas, the women wearing bright print dresses, the colors vivid against their darkness, the men rusty black suits that encased them like straitjackets. Da-duh, holding fast to my hand, became my anchor as they circled round us like a nervous sea, exclaiming, touching us with their calloused hands, embracing us shyly. They laughed in awed bursts: "But look Adry got big-big children!"/"And see the nice things they wearing, wrist watch and all!"/"I tell you, Adry has done all right for sheself in New York. . . ."

Da-duh, ashamed at their wonder, embarrassed for them, admonished them the while. "But oh Christ," she said, "Why you all got to get on like you never saw people from 'Away' before? You would think New York is the only place in the world to hear wunna. That's why I don't like to go anyplace with you St. Andrews people, you know. You all ain't been colonized."

We were in the back of the lorry finally, packed in among the barrels of ham, flour, cornmeal and rice and the trunks of clothes that my mother had brought as gifts. We made our way slowly through Bridgetown's clogged streets, part of a funereal procession of cars and open-sided buses, bicycles and donkey carts. The dim little limestone shops and offices along the way marched with us, at the same mournful pace, toward the same grave ceremony—as did the people, the women balancing huge baskets on top their heads as if they were no more than hats they wore to shade them from the sun. Looking over the edge of the lorry I watched as their feet slurred the dust. I listened, and their voices, raw and loud and dissonant in the heat, seemed to be grappling with each other high overhead.

Da-duh sat on a trunk in our midst, a monarch amid her court. She still held my hand, but it was different now. I had suddenly become her anchor, for I felt her fear of the lorry with its asthmatic motor (a fear and distrust, I later learned, she held of all machines) beating like a pulse in her rough palm.

As soon as we left Bridgetown behind though, she relaxed, and while the others around us talked she gazed at the canes standing tall on either side of the winding marl road. "C'dear," she said softly to herself after a time. "The canes this side are pretty enough."

They were too much for me. I thought of them as giant weeds that had overrun the island, leaving scarcely any room for the small tottering houses of sunbleached pine we passed or the people, dark streaks as our lorry hurtled by. I suddenly feared that we were journeying, unaware that we were, toward some dangerous place where the canes, grown as high and thick as a forest, would close in on us and run us through with their stiletto blades. I longed then for the familiar: for the street in Brooklyn where I lived, for my father who had refused to accompany us ("Blowing out good money on foolishness," he had said of the trip), for a game of tag with my friends under the chestnut tree outside our aging brownstone house.

"Yes, but wait till you see St. Thomas canes," Da-duh was saying to me. "They's canes father, bo," she gave a proud arrogant nod. "Tomorrow, God willing, I goin' take you out in the ground and show them to you."

True to her word Da-duh took me with her the following day out into the ground. It was a fairly large plot adjoining her weathered board and shingle house and consisting of a small orchard, a good-sized canepiece and behind the canes, where the land sloped abruptly down, a gully. She had purchased it with Panama money sent her by her eldest son, my uncle Joseph, who had died working on the canal. We entered the ground along a trail no wider than her body and as devious and complex as her reasons for showing me her land. Da-duh strode briskly ahead, her slight form filled out this morning by the layers of sacking petticoats she wore under her working dress to protect her against the damp. A fresh white cloth, elaborately arranged around her head, added to her height, and lent her a vain, almost roguish air.

Her pace slowed once we reached the orchard, and glancing back at me occasionally over her shoulder, she pointed out the various trees.

"This here is a breadfruit," she said. "That one yonder is a papaw. Here's a guava. This is a mango. I know you don't have anything like these in New York. Here's a sugar apple." (The fruit looked more like artichokes than apples to me.) "This one bears limes. . . ." She went on for some time, intoning the names of the trees as though they were those of her gods. Finally, turning to me, she said, "I know you don't have anything this nice where you come from." Then, as I hesitated: "I said I know you don't have anything this nice where you come from. . . ."

"No," I said and my world did seem suddenly lacking.

Da-duh nodded and passed on. The orchard ended and we were on the narrow cart road that led through the canepiece, the canes clashing like swords above my cowering head. Again she turned and her thin muscular arms spread wide, her dim gaze embracing the small field of canes, she said—and her voice almost broke under the weight of her pride, "Tell me, have you got anything like these in that place where you were born?"

"No."

"I din' think so. I bet you don't even know that these canes here and the sugar you eat is one and the same thing. That they does throw the canes into some damn machine at the factory and squeeze out all the little life in them to make sugar for you all so in New York to eat. I bet you don't know that."

"I've got two cavities and I'm not allowed to eat a lot of sugar."

But Da-duh didn't hear me. She had turned with an inexplicably angry motion and was making her way rapidly out of the canes and down the slope at the edge of the field which led to the gully below. Following her apprehensively down the incline amid a stand of banana plants whose leaves flapped like elephants ears in the wind, I found myself in the middle of a small tropical wood—a place dense and damp and gloomy and tremulous with the fitful play of light and shadow as the leaves high above moved against the sun that was almost hidden from view. It was a violent place, the tangled foliage fighting each other for a chance at the sunlight, the branches of the trees locked in what seemed an immemorial struggle, one both necessary and inevitable. But despite the violence, it was pleasant, almost peaceful in the gully, and beneath the thick undergrowth the earth smelled like spring.

This time Da-duh didn't even bother to ask her usual question, but simply turned and waited for me to speak.

"No," I said, my head bowed. "We don't have anything like this in New York."

"Ah," she cried, her triumph complete. "I din' think so. Why, I've heard that's a place where you can walk till you near drop and never see a tree."

"We've got a chestnut tree in front of our house," I said.

"Does it bear?" She waited. "I ask you, does it bear?"

"Not anymore," I muttered. "It used to, but not anymore."

She gave the nod that was like a nervous twitch. "You see," she said. "Nothing can bear there." Then, secure behind her scorn, she added, "But tell me, what's this snow like that you hear so much about?"

Looking up, I studied her closely, sensing my chance, and then I told her, describing at length and with as much drama as I could summon not only what snow in the city was like, but what it would be like here, in her perennial summer kingdom.

"... And you see all these trees you got here," I said. "Well, they'd be bare. No leaves, no fruit, nothing. They'd be covered in snow. You see your canes. They'd be buried under tons of snow. The snow would be higher than your head, higher than your house, and you wouldn't be able to come down into this here gully because it would be snowed under...."

She searched my face for the lie, still scornful but intrigued. "What a thing, huh?" she said finally, whispering it softly to herself.

"And when it snows you couldn't dress like you are now," I said. "Oh no, you'd freeze to death. You'd have to wear a hat and gloves and galoshes and ear muffs so your ears wouldn't freeze and drop off, and a heavy coat. I've got a Shirley Temple coat with fur on the collar. I can dance. You wanna see?"

Before she could answer I began, with a dance called the Truck which was popular back then in the 1930s. My right forefinger waving, I trucked around the nearby trees and around Da-duh's awed and rigid form. After the Truck I did the Suzy-Q, my lean hips swishing, my sneakers sidling zigzag over the ground. "I can sing," I said and did so, starting with "I'm Gonna Sit Right Down and Write Myself a Letter," then without pausing, "Tea For Two," and ending with "I Found a Million Dollar Baby in a Five and Ten Cent Store."

For long moments afterwards Da-duh stared at me as if I were a creature from Mars, an emissary from some world she did not know but which intrigued her and whose power she both felt and feared. Yet something about my performance must have pleased her, because bending down she slowly lifted her long skirt and then, one by one, the layers of petticoats until she came to a drawstring purse dangling at the end of a long strip of cloth tied round her waist. Opening the purse she handed me a penny. "Here," she said half-smiling against her will. "Take this to buy yourself a sweet at the shop up the road. There's nothing to be done with you, soul."

From then on, whenever I wasn't taken to visit relatives, I accompanied Da-duh out into the ground, and alone with her amid canes or down in the gully I told her about New York. It always began with some slighting remark on her part: "I know they don't have anything this nice where you come from," or "Tell me, I hear those foolish people in New York does do such and such. . . ." But as I answered, recreating my towering world of steel and concrete and machines for her, building the city out of words, I would feel her give way. I came to know the signs of her surrender: the total stillness that would come over her little hard dry form, the probing gaze that like a surgeon's knife sought to cut through my skull to get at the images there, to see if I were lying; above all, her fear, a fear nameless and profound, the same one I had felt beating in the palm of her hand that day in the lorry.

Over the weeks I told her about refrigerators, radios, gas stoves, elevators, trolley cars, wringer washing machines, movies, airplanes, the cyclone at Coney Island, subways, toasters, electric lights: "At night, see, all you have to do is flip this little switch on the wall and all the lights in the house go on. Just like that. Like magic. It's like turning on the sun at night."

127

"But tell me," she said to me once with a faint mocking smile, "do the white people have all these things too or it's only the people looking like us?"

I laughed. "What d'ya mean," I said. "The white people have even better." Then: "I beat up a white girl in my class last term."

"Beating up white people!" Her tone was incredulous.

"How you mean!" I said, using an expression of hers. "She called me a name."

For some reason Da-duh could not quite get over this and repeated in the same hushed, shocked voice, "Beating up white people now! Oh, the lord, the world's changing up so I can scarce recognize it anymore."

One morning toward the end of our stay, Da-duh led me into a part of the gully that we had never visited before, an area darker and more thickly overgrown that the rest, almost impenetrable. There in a small clearing amid the dense bush, she stopped before an incredibly tall royal palm which rose cleanly out of the ground, and drawing the eye up with it, soared high above the trees around it into the sky. It appeared to be touching the blue dome of sky, to be flaunting its dark crown of fronds right in the blinding white face of the late morning sun.

Da-duh watched me a long time before she spoke, and then she said very quietly, "All right, now, tell me if you've got anything this tall in that place you're from."

I almost wished, seeing her face, that I could have said no. "Yes," I said. "We've got buildings hundreds of times this tall in New York. There's one called the Empire State Building that's the tallest in the world. My class visited it last year and I went all the way to the top. It's got over a hundred floors. I can't describe how tall it is. Wait a minute. What's the name of that hill I went to visit the other day, where they have the police station?"

"You mean Bissex?"

"Yes, Bissex. Well, the Empire State Building is way taller than that."

"You're lying now!" she shouted, trembling with rage. Her hand lifted to strike me.

"No, I'm not," I said. "It really is, if you don't believe me I'll send you a picture postcard of it soon as I get back home so you can see for yourself. But it's way taller than Bissex."

All the fight went out of her at that. The hand poised to strike

128

me fell limp to her side, and as she stared at me, seeing not me but the building that was taller than the highest hill she knew, the small stubborn light in her eyes (it was the same amber as the flame in the kerosene lamp she lit at dusk) began to fail. Finally, with a vague gesture that even in the midst of her defeat still tried to dismiss me and my world, she turned and started back through the gully, walking slowly, her steps groping and uncertain, as if she were suddenly no longer sure of the way, while I followed triumphant yet strangely saddened behind.

The next morning I found her dressed for our morning walk but stretched out on the Berbice chair in the tiny drawing room where she sometimes napped during the afternoon heat, her face turned to the window beside her. She appeared thinner and suddenly indescribably old.

"My Da-duh," I said.

"Yes, nuh," she said. Her voice was listless and the face she slowly turned my way was, now that I think back on it, like a Benin mask, the features drawn and almost distorted by an ancient abstract sorrow.

"Don't you feel well?" I asked.

"Girl, I don't know."

"My Da-duh, I goin' boil you some bush tea," my aunt, Da-duh's youngest child, who lived with her, called from the shed roof kitchen.

"Who tell you I need bush tea?" she cried, her voice assuming for a moment its old authority. "You can't even rest nowadays without some malicious person looking for you to be dead. Come girl," she motioned me to a place beside her on the old-fashioned lounge chair, "give us a tune."

I sang for her until breakfast at eleven, all my brash irreverent Tin Pan Alley songs, and then just before noon we went out into the ground. But it was a short, dispirited walk. Da-duh didn't even notice that the mangoes were beginning to ripen and would have to be picked before the village boys got to them. And when she paused occasionally and looked out across the canes or up at her trees it wasn't as if she were seeing them but something else. Some huge, monolithic shape had imposed itself, it seemed, between her and the land, obstructing her vision. Returning to the house she slept the entire afternoon on the Berbice chair.

She remained like this until we left, languishing away the mornings on the chair at the window gazing out at the land as if it were already doomed; then, at noon, taking the brief stroll with me through the ground during which she seldom spoke, and afterwards returning home to sleep till almost dusk sometimes.

On the day of our departure she put on the austere, ankle length white dress, the black shoes and brown felt hat (her town clothes she called them), but she did not go with us to town. She saw us off on the road outside her house and in the midst of my mother's tearful protracted farewell, she leaned down and whispered in my ear, "Girl, you're not to forget now to send me the picture of that building, you hear."

By the time I mailed her the large colored picture postcard of the Empire State Building she was dead. She died during the famous '37 strike which began shortly after we left. On the day of her death England sent planes flying low over the island in a show of force—so low, according to my aunt's letter, that the downdraft from them shook the ripened mangoes from the trees in Da-duh's orchard. Frightened, everyone in the village fled into the canes. Except Da-duh. She remained in the house at the window so my aunt said, watching as the planes came swooping and screaming like monstrous birds down over the village, over her house, rattling her trees and flattening the young canes in her field. It must have seemed to her lying there that they did not intend pulling out of their dive, but like the hardback beetles which hurled themselves with suicidal force against the walls of the house at night, those menacing silver shapes would hurl themselves in an ecstasy of self-immolation onto the land, destroying it utterly.

When the planes finally left and the villagers returned they found her dead on the Berbice chair at the window.

She died and I lived, but always, to this day even, within the shadow of her death. For a brief period after I was grown I went to live alone, like one doing penance, in a loft above a noisy factory in downtown New York and there painted seas of sugar-cane and huge swirling Van Gogh suns and palm trees striding like brightly plumed Tutsi warriors across a tropical landscape, while the thunderous tread of the machines downstairs jarred the floor beneath my easel, mocking my efforts.

George

❧ DUDLEY RANDALL

When I was a boy desiring the title of man
And toiling to earn it
In the inferno of the foundry knockout,
I watched and admired you working by my side,
As, goggled, with mask on your mouth and shoulders
    bright with sweat,
You mastered the monstrous, lumpish cylinder blocks,
And when they clotted the line and plunged to the floor
With force enough to tear your foot in two,
You calmly stepped aside.

One day when the line broke down and the blocks reared up
Groaning, grinding, and mounted like an ocean wave
And then rushed thundering down like an avalanche,
And we frantically dodged, then braced our heads together
To form an arch to lift and stack them,
You gave me your highest accolade:
You said: "You not afraid of sweat. You strong as a mule."

Now, here, in the hospital,
In a ward where old men wait to die,
You sit, and watch time go by.
You cannot read the books I bring, not even
Those that are only picture books,
As you sit among the senile wrecks,
The psychopaths, the incontinent.

Miss Rosie

🙂 LUCILLE CLIFTON

When I watch you
wrapped up like garbage
sitting, surrounded by the smell
of too old potato peels
or
when I watch you
in your old man's shoes
with the little toe cut out
sitting, waiting for your mind
like next weeks grocery
I say
when I watch you
you wet brown bag of a woman
who used to be the best looking gal in Georgia
used to be called the Georgia Rose
I stand up
through your destruction
I stand up

Marigolds
&❧ EUGENIA COLLIER

When I think of the home town of my youth, all that I seem to remember is dust—the brown, crumbly dust of late summer—arid, sterile dust that gets into the eyes and makes them water, gets into the throat and between the toes of bare brown feet. I don't know why I should remember only the dust. Surely there must have been lush green lawns and paved streets under leafy shade trees somewhere in town; but memory is an abstract painting—it does not present things as they are, but rather as they *feel*. And so, when I think of that time and that place, I remember only the dry September of the dirt roads and grassless yards of the shanty-town where I lived. And one other thing I remember, another incongruency of memory—a brilliant splash of sunny yellow against the dust—Miss Lottie's marigolds.

Whenever the memory of those marigolds flashes across my mind, a strange nostalgia comes with it and remains long after the picture has faded. I feel again the chaotic emotions of adolescence, illusive as smoke, yet as real as the potted geranium before me now. Joy and rage and wild animal gladness and shame become tangled together in the multicolored skein of 14-going-on-15 as I recall that devastating moment when I was suddenly more woman than child, years ago in Miss Lottie's yard. I think of those marigolds at the strangest times; I remember them vividly now as I desperately pass away the time waiting for you, who will not come.

I suppose that futile waiting was the sorrowful background music of our impoverished little community when I was young. The Depression that gripped the nation was no new thing to us, for the black workers of rural Maryland had always been depressed. I don't know what it was that we were waiting for; certainly not for the prosperity that was "just around the corner," for those were white folks' words, which we never believed. Nor did we wait for hard work and thrift to pay off in shining success as the American Dream promised, for we knew better than that, too. Perhaps we waited for a miracle, amorphous in concept but necessary if one were to have the grit to rise before dawn each day and labor in the white man's vineyard until after dark, or to wander about in the September dust offering one's sweat in return for some meager share of bread. But God was chary with miracles in those days, and so we waited—and waited.

We children, of course, were only vaguely aware of the extent of our poverty. Having no radios, few newspapers, and no magazines, we were somewhat unaware of the world outside our community. Nowadays we would be called "culturally deprived" and people would write books and hold conferences about us. In those days everybody we knew was just as hungry and ill-clad as we were. Poverty was the cage in which we all were trapped, and our hatred of it was still the vague, undirected restlessness of the zoo-bred flamingo who knows that nature created him to fly free.

As I think of those days I feel most poignantly the tag-end of summer, the bright dry times when we began to have a sense of shortening days and the imminence of the cold.

By the time I was 14 my brother Joey and I were the only children left at our house, the older ones having left home for early marriage or the lure of the city, and the two babies having been sent to relatives who might care for them better than we. Joey was three years younger than I, and a boy, and therefore vastly inferior. Each morning our mother and father trudged wearily down the dirt road and around the bend, she to her domestic job, he to his daily unsuccessful quest for work. After our few chores around the tumble-down shanty, Joey and I were free to run wild in the sun with other children similarly situated.

For the most part, those days are ill-defined in my memory, running together and combining like a fresh water-color painting left out in the rain. I remember squatting in the road drawing a picture in the dust, a picture which Joey gleefully erased with one sweep of his dirty foot. I remember fishing for minnows in a muddy creek and watching sadly as they eluded my cupped hands, while Joey laughed uproariously. And I remember, that year, a strange restlessness of body and of spirit, a feeling that something old and familiar was ending, and something unknown and therefore terrifying was beginning.

One day returns to me with special clarity for some reason, perhaps because it was the beginning of the experience that in

134

some inexplicable way marked the end of innocence. I was loafing under the great oak tree in our yard, deep in some reverie which I have now forgotten except that it involved some secret, secret thoughts of one of the Harris boys across the yard. Joey and a bunch of kids were bored now with the old tire suspended from an oak limb which had kept them entertained for awhile.

"Hey, Lizabeth," Joey yelled. He never talked when he could yell. "Hey, Lizabeth, let's us go somewhere."

I came reluctantly from my private world. "Where at, Joey?"

The truth was that we were becoming tired of the formlessness of our summer days. The idleness whose prospect had seemed so beautiful during the busy days of spring now had degenerated to an almost desperate effort to fill up the empty midday hours.

"Let's go see can we find us some locusts on the hill," someone suggested.

Joey was scornful. "Ain't no more locusts there. Y'all got 'em all while they was still green."

The argument that followed was brief and not really worth the effort. Hunting locust trees wasn't fun any more by now.

"Tell you what," said Joey finally, his eyes sparkling. "Let's us go over to Miss Lottie's."

The idea caught on at once, for annoying Miss Lottie was always fun. I was still child enough to scamper along with the group over rickety fences and through bushes that tore our already raggedy clothes, back to where Miss Lottie lived. I think now that we must have made a tragicomic spectacle, five or six kids of different ages, each of us clad in only one garment—the girls in faded dresses that were too long or too short, the boys in patchy pants, their sweaty brown chests gleaming in the hot sun. A little cloud of dust followed our thin legs and bare feet as we tramped over the barren land.

When Miss Lottie's house came into view we stopped, ostensibly to plan our strategy, but actually to reinforce our courage. Miss Lottie's house was the most ramshackle of all our ramshackle homes. The sun and rain had long since faded its rickety frame siding from white to a sullen gray. The boards themselves seemed to remain upright not from being nailed together but rather from leaning together like a house that a child might have constructed from cards. A brisk wind might have blown it down, and the fact that it was still standing implied a kind of enchantment that was stronger than the elements. There it stood, and as far as I know is standing yet—a gray rotting thing with no porch, no shutters, no steps, set on a cramped lot with no grass, not even any weeds—a monument to decay.

In front of the house in a squeaky rocking chair sat Miss Lottie's son, John Burke, completing the impression of decay. John Burke was what was known as "queer-headed." Black and ageless, he sat, rocking day in and day out in a mindless stupor, lulled by the monotonous squeak-squawk of the chair. A battered hat atop his shaggy head shaded him from the sun. Usually John Burke was totally unaware of everything outside his quiet dream world. But if you disturbed him, if you intruded upon his fantasies, he would become enraged, strike out at you, and curse at you in some strange enchanted language which only he could understand. We children made a game of thinking of ways to disturb John Burke and then to elude his violent retribution.

But our real fun and our real fear lay in Miss Lottie herself. Miss Lottie seemed to be at least a hundred years old. Her big frame still held traces of the tall, powerful woman she must have been in youth, although it was now bent and drawn. Her smooth skin was a dark reddish-brown, and her face had Indian-like features and the stern stoicism that one associates with Indian faces. Miss Lottie didn't like intruders either, especially children. She never left her yard, and nobody ever visited her. We never knew how she managed those necessities which depend on human interaction—how she ate, for example, or even whether she ate. When we were tiny children, we thought Miss Lottie was a witch and we made up tales, that we half believed ourselves, about her exploits. We were far too sophisticated now, of course, to believe the witch-nonsense. But old fears have a way of clinging like cobwebs, and so when we sighted the tumble-down shack, we had to stop to reinforce our nerves.

"Look, there she is," I whispered, forgetting that Miss Lottie could not possibly have heard me from that distance. "She's fooling with them crazy flowers."

"Yeh, look at 'er."

Miss Lottie's marigolds were perhaps the strangest part of the picture. Certainly they did not fit in with the crumbling decay of the rest of her yard. Beyond the dusty brown yard, in front of the sorry gray house, rose suddenly and shockingly a dazzling strip of bright blossoms, clumped together in enormous mounds, warm and passionate and sun-golden. The old black witch-woman worked on them all summer, every summer, down on her creaky knees, weeding and cultivating and arranging, while the house crumbled and John Burke rocked. For some perverse reason, we children hated those marigolds. They interfered with the perfect ugliness of the place; they were too beautiful; they said too much that we could not understand, they did not make sense. There was something in the vigor with which the old woman destroyed the weeds that intimidated us. It should have been a comical sight—the old woman with the man's hat on her cropped white head, leaning over the bright mounds, her big backside in the air—but it wasn't comical, it was something we could not name. We had to annoy her by whizzing a pebble into her flowers or by yelling a dirty word, then dancing away from her rage, revelling in our youth and mocking her age. Actually, I think it was the flowers we wanted to destroy, but nobody had the nerve to try it, not even Joey, who was usually fool enough to try anything.

"Y'all git some stones," commanded Joey now, and was met with instant giggling obedience as everyone except me began to gather pebbles from the dusty ground. "Come on, Lizabeth."

I just stood there peering through the bushes, torn between wanting to join the fun and feeling that it was all a bit silly.

"You scared, Lizabeth?"

I cursed and spat on the ground—my favorite gesture of phony bravado. "Y'all children get the stones, I'll show you how to use 'em."

I said before that we children were not consciously aware of how thick were the bars of our cage. I wonder now, though, whether we were not more aware of it than I thought. Perhaps we had some dim notion of what we were, and how little chance we had of being anything else. Otherwise, why would we have been so preoccupied with destruction? Anyway, the pebbles were collected quickly, and everybody looked at me to begin the fun.

"Come on, y'all."

We crept to the edge of the bushes that bordered the narrow road in front of Miss Lottie's place. She was working placidly, kneeling over the flowers, her dark hand plunged into the golden mound. Suddenly "zing"—an expertly-aimed stone cut the head off one of the blossoms.

"Who out there?" Miss Lottie's backside came down and her

head came up as her sharp eyes searched the bushes. "You better git!"

We had crouched down out of sight in the bushes, where we stifled the giggles that insisted on coming. Miss Lottie gazed warily across the road for a moment, then cautiously returned to her weeding. "Zing"—Joey sent a pebble into the blooms, and another marigold was beheaded.

Miss Lottie was enraged now. She began struggling to her feet, leaning on a rickety cane and shouting, "Y'all git! Go on home!" Then the rest of the kids let loose with their pebbles, storming the flowers and laughing wildly and senselessly at Miss Lottie's impotent rage. She shook her stick at us and started shakily toward the road crying, "Black bastards, git 'long! John Burke! John Burke, come help!"

Then I lost my head entirely, mad with the power of inciting such rage, and ran out of the bushes in the storm of pebbles, straight toward Miss Lottie chanting madly, "Old witch, fell in a ditch, picked up a penny and thought she was rich!" The children screamed with delight, dropped their pebbles and joined the crazy dance, swarming around Miss Lottie like bees and chanting, "Old lady witch!" while she screamed curses at us. The madness lasted only a moment, for John Burke, startled at last, lurched out of his chair, and we dashed for the bushes just as Miss Lottie's cane went whizzing at my head.

I did not join the merriment when the kids gathered again under the oak in our bare yard. Suddenly I was ashamed, and I did not like being ashamed. The child in me sulked and said it was all in fun, but the woman in me flinched at the thought of the malicious attack that I had led. The mood lasted all afternoon. When we ate the beans and rice that was supper that night, I did not notice my father's silence, for he was always silent these days, nor did I notice my mother's absence, for she always worked until well into evening. Joey and I had a particularly bitter argument after supper; his exuberance got on my nerves. Finally I stretched out upon the palette in the room we shared and fell into a fitful doze.

When I awoke, somewhere in the middle of the night, my mother had returned, and I vaguely listened to the conversation that was audible through the thin walls that separated our rooms. At first I heard no words, only voices. My mother's voice was like a cool, dark room in summer—peaceful, soothing, quiet. I loved to listen to it; it made things seem alright somehow. But my father's voice cut through hers, shattering the peace.

"Twenty-two years, Maybelle, 22 years," he was saying, "and I got nothing for you, nothing, nothing."

"It's all right, honey, you'll get something. Everybody out of work now, you know that."

"It ain't right. Ain't no man ought to eat his woman's food year in and year out, and see his children running wild. Ain't nothing right about that."

"Honey, you took good care of us when you had it. Ain't nobody got nothing nowadays."

"I ain't talking about nobody else, I'm talking about *me*. God knows I try." My mother said something I could not hear, and my father cried out louder, "What must a man do, tell me that?"

"Look, we ain't starving. I git paid every week, and Mrs. Ellis is real nice about giving me things. She gonna let me have Mr. Ellis' old coat for you this winter—"

"God damn Mr. Ellis' coat! And God damn his money! You think I want white folks' leavings? God damn, Maybelle"—and suddenly he sobbed, loudly and painfully, and cried helplessly and hopelessly in the dark night. I had never heard a man cry before. I did not know men ever cried. I covered my ears with my hands but could not cut off the sound of my father's harsh, painful, despairing sobs. My father was a strong man who would whisk a child upon his shoulders and go singing through the house. My father whittled toys for us and laughed so loud that the great oak seemed to laugh with him, and taught us how to fish and hunt rabbits. How could it be that my father was crying? But the sobs went on, unstifled, finally quieting until I could hear my mother's voice, deep and rich, humming softly as she used to hum to a frightened child.

The world had lost its boundary lines. My mother, who was small and soft, was now the strength of the family; my father, who was the rock on which the family had been built, was sobbing like the tiniest child. Everything was suddenly out of tune, like a broken accordion. Where did I fit into this crazy picture? I do not now remember my thoughts, only a feeling of great bewilderment and fear.

Long after the sobbing and the humming had stopped, I lay on the palette, still as stone with my hands over my ears, wishing that I too could cry and be comforted. The night was silent now except for the sound of the crickets and of Joey's soft breathing. But the room was too crowded with fear to allow me to sleep, and finally, feeling the terrible aloneness of 4 A.M., I decided to awaken Joey.

"Ouch! What's the matter with you? What you want?" he demanded disagreeably when I had pinched and slapped him awake.

"Come on, wake up."

"What for? Go 'way."

I was lost for a reasonable reply. I could not say, "I'm scared and I don't want to be alone," so I merely said, "I'm going out. If you want to come, come on."

The promise of adventure awoke him. "Going out now? Where at, Lizabeth? What you going to do?"

I was pulling my dress over my head. Until now I had not thought of going out. "Just come on," I replied tersely.

I was out the window and halfway down the road before Joey caught up with me.

"Wait, Lizabeth, where you going?"

I was running as if the furies were after me, as perhaps they were—running silently and furiously until I came to where I had half-known I was headed: to Miss Lottie's yard.

The half-dawn light was more eerie than complete darkness, and in it the old house was like the ruin that my world had become—foul and crumbling, a grotesque caricature. It looked haunted, but I was not afraid because I was haunted too.

"Lizabeth, you lost your mind?" panted Joey.

I had indeed lost my mind, for all the smoldering emotions of that summer swelled in me and burst—the great need for my mother who was never there, the hopelessness of our poverty and degradation, the bewilderment of being neither child nor woman and yet both at once, the fear unleashed by my father's tears. And these feelings combined in one great impulse toward destruction.

"Lizabeth!"

I leaped furiously into the mounds of marigolds and pulled madly, trampling and pulling and destroying the perfect yellow blooms. The fresh smell of early morning and of dew-soaked marigolds spurred me on as I went tearing and mangling and sobbing while Joey tugged my dress or my waist crying, "Lizabeth, stop, please stop!"

And then I was sitting in the ruined little garden among the uprooted and ruined flowers, crying and crying, and it was too late

140

to undo what I had done. Joey was sitting beside me, silent and frightened, not knowing what to say. Then "Lizabeth, look."

I opened my swollen eyes and saw in front of me a pair of large calloused feet; my gaze lifted to the swollen legs, the age-distorted body clad in a tight cotton night dress, and then the shadowed Indian face surrounded by stubby white hair. And there was no rage in the face now, now that the garden was destroyed and there was nothing any longer to be protected.

"M-miss Lottie!" I scrambled to my feet and just stood there and stared at her, and that was the moment when childhood faded and womanhood began. That violent, crazy act was the last act of childhood. For as I gazed at the immobile face with the sad, weary eyes, I gazed upon a kind of reality which is hidden to childhood. The witch was no longer a witch but only a broken old woman who had dared to create beauty in the midst of ugliness and sterility. She had been born in squalor and lived in it all her life. Now at the end of that life she had nothing except a falling-down hut, a wrecked body, and John Burke, the mindless son of her passion. Whatever verve there was left in her, whatever was of love and beauty and joy that had not been squeezed out by life, had been there in the marigolds she had so tenderly cared for.

Of course I could not express the things that I knew about Miss Lottie as I stood there awkward and ashamed. The years have put words to the things I knew in that moment, and as I look back upon it, I know that the moment marked the end of innocence. Innocence involves an unseeing acceptance of things at face value, an ignorance of the area below the surface. In that humiliating moment I looked beyond myself and into the depths of another person. This was the beginning of compassion, and one cannot have both compassion and innocence.

The years have taken me worlds away from that time and that place, from the dust and squalor of our lives and from the bright thing that I destroyed in a blind childish striking out at God-knows-what. Miss Lottie died long ago and many years have passed since I last saw her hut, completely barren at last, for despite my wild contrition she never planted marigolds again. Yet, there are times when the image of those passionate yellow mounds returns with a painful poignancy. For one does not have to be ignorant and poor to find that his life is barren as the dusty yards of our town. And I too have planted marigolds.

To Hell with Dying
&❧ ALICE WALKER

"**T**o hell with dying," my father would say. "These children want Mr. Sweet!"

Mr. Sweet was a diabetic and an alcoholic and a guitar player and lived down the road from us on a neglected cotton farm. My older brothers and sisters got the most benefit from Mr. Sweet, for when they were growing up he had quite a few years ahead of him and so was capable of being called back from the brink of death any number of times—whenever the voice of my father reached him as he lay expiring. "To hell with dying, man," my father would say, pushing the wife away from the bedside (in tears although she knew the death was not necessarily the last one unless Mr. Sweet really wanted it to be). "These children want Mr. Sweet!" And they did want him, for at a signal from Father they would come crowding around the bed and throw themselves on the covers, and whoever was the smallest at the time would kiss him all over his wrinkled brown face and begin to tickle him so that he would laugh all down in his stomach, and his moustache, which was long and sort of straggly, would shake like Spanish moss and was also that color.

Mr. Sweet had been ambitious as a boy, wanted to be a doctor or lawyer or sailor, only to find that black men fare better if they are not. Since he could become none of these things he turned to fishing as his only earnest career and playing the guitar as his only claim to doing anything extraordinarily well. His son, the only one that he and his wife, Miss Mary, had, was shiftless as the day is long and spent money as if he were trying to see the bottom of the mint, which Mr. Sweet would tell him was the clean brown palm of his hand. Miss Mary loved her "baby," however, and worked hard to get him the "l'il necessaries" of life, which turned out mostly to be women.

Mr. Sweet was a tall, thinnish man with thick kinky hair going dead white. He was dark brown, his eyes were very squinty and sort of bluish, and he chewed Brown Mule tobacco. He was constantly on the verge of being blind drunk, for he brewed his own liquor and was not in the least a stingy sort of man, and was always very melancholy and sad, though frequently when he was "feelin' good" he'd dance around the yard with us, usually keeling over just as my mother came to see what the commotion was.

Toward all of us children he was very kind, and had the grace to be shy with us, which is unusual in grown-ups. He had great respect for my mother for she never held his drunkenness against him and would let us play with him even when he was about to fall in the fireplace from drink. Although Mr. Sweet would sometimes lose complete or nearly complete control of his head and neck so that he would loll in his chair, his mind remained strangely acute and his speech not too affected. His ability to be drunk and sober at the same time made him an ideal playmate, for he was as weak as we were and we could usually best him in wrestling, all the while keeping a fairly coherent conversation going.

We never felt anything of Mr. Sweet's age when we played with him. We loved his wrinkles and would draw some on our brows to be like him, and his white hair was my special treasure and he knew it and would never come to visit us just after he had had his hair cut off at the barbershop. Once he came to our house for something, probably to see my father about fertilizer for his crops because, although he never paid the slightest attention to his crops, he liked to know what things would be best to use on them if he ever did. Anyhow, he had not come with his hair since he had just had it shaved off at the barbershop. He wore a huge straw hat to keep off the sun and also to keep his head away from me. But as soon as I saw him I ran up and demanded that he take me up and kiss me with his funny beard which smelled so strongly of tobacco. Looking forward to burying my small fingers into his woolly hair I threw away his hat only to find he had done something to his hair, that it was no longer there! I let out a squall which made my mother think that Mr. Sweet had finally dropped me in the well or something and from that day I've been wary of men in hats. However, not long after, Mr. Sweet showed up with his hair grown out and just as white and kinky and impenetrable as it ever was.

Mr. Sweet used to call me his princess, and I believed it. He made me feel pretty at five and six, and simply outrageously devastating at the blazing age of eight and a half. When he came to our house with his guitar the whole family would stop whatever they were doing to sit around him and listen to him play. He liked to play "Sweet Georgia Brown," that was what he called me sometimes, and also he like to play "Caldonia" and all sorts of sweet, sad, wonderful songs which he sometimes made up. It was from one of these songs that I learned that he had had to marry Miss Mary when he had in fact loved somebody else (now living in Chi-ca-go, or De-stroy, Michigan). He was not sure that Joe Lee, her "baby," was also his baby. Sometimes he would cry and that was an indication that he was about to die again. And so we would all get prepared, for we were sure to be called upon.

I was seven the first time I remember actually participating in one of Mr. Sweet's "revivals"—my parents told me I had participated before, I had been the one chosen to kiss him and tickle him long before I knew the rite of Mr. Sweet's rehabilitation. He had come to our house, it was a few years after his wife's death, and was very sad, and also, typically, very drunk. He sat on the floor next to me and my older brother, the rest of the children were grown up and lived elsewhere, and began to play his guitar and cry. I held his woolly head in my arms and wished I could have been old enough to have been the woman he loved so much and that I had not been lost years and years ago.

When he was leaving, my mother said to us that we'd better sleep light that night for we'd probably have to go over to Mr. Sweet's before daylight. And we did. For soon after we had gone to bed one of the neighbors knocked on our door and called my father and said that Mr. Sweet was sinking fast and if he wanted to get in a word before the crossover he'd better shake a leg and get over to Mr. Sweet's house. All the neighbors knew to come to our house if something was wrong with Mr. Sweet, but they did not know how we always managed to make him well, or at least stop him from dying, when he was often so near death. As soon as we heard the cry we got up, my brother and I and my mother and father, and put on our clothes. We hurried out of the house and down the road for we were always afraid that we might someday be too late and Mr. Sweet would get tired of dallying.

When we got to the house, a very poor shack really, we found the front room full of neighbors and relatives and someone met us at the door and said that it was all very sad that old Mr. Sweet Little (for Little was his family name, although we mostly ignored it) was about to kick the bucket. My parents were advised not to take my brother and me into the "death room," seeing we were so young and all, but we were so much more accustomed to the death room than he that we ignored him and dashed in without giving his warning a second thought. I was almost in tears, for these deaths upset me fearfully, and the thought of how much depended on me and my brother (who was such a ham most of the time) made me very nervous.

The doctor was bending over the bed and turned back to tell us for at least the tenth time in the history of my family that, alas, old Mr. Sweet Little was dying and that the children had best not see the face of implacable death (I didn't know what "implacable" was, but whatever it was, Mr. Sweet was not!). My father pushed him rather abruptly out of the way saying, as he always did and very loudly for he was saying it to Mr. Sweet, "To hell with dying, man, these children want Mr. Sweet"—which was my cue to throw myself upon the bed and kiss Mr. Sweet all around the whiskers and under the eyes and around the collar of his nightshirt where he smelled so strongly of all sorts of things, mostly liniment.

I was very good at bringing him around, for as soon as I saw that he was struggling to open his eyes I knew he was going to be all right, and so could finish my revival sure of success. As soon as his eyes were open he would begin to smile and that way I knew that I had surely won. Once, though, I got a tremendous scare, for he could not open his eyes and later I learned that he had had a stroke and that one side of his face was stiff and hard to get into motion. When he began to smile I could tickle him in earnest because I was sure that nothing would get in the way of his laughter, although once he began to cough so hard that he almost threw me off his stomach, but that was when I was very small, little more than a baby, and my bushy hair had gotten in his nose.

When we were sure he would listen to us we would ask him why he was in bed and when he was coming to see us again and could we play with his guitar, which more than likely would be leaning against the bed. His eyes would get all misty and he would sometimes cry out loud, but we never let it embarrass us, for he knew that we loved him and that we sometimes cried too for no reason. My parents would leave the room to just the three of us; Mr. Sweet, by that time, would be propped up in bed with a number of pillows behind his head and with me sitting and lying on his shoulder and along his chest. Even when he had trouble breathing he would not ask me to get down. Looking into my eyes he would shake his white head and run a scratchy old finger all around my hairline, which was rather low down, nearly to my eyebrows, and made some people say I looked like a baby monkey.

My brother was very generous in all this, he let me do all the revivaling—he had done if for years before I was born and so was glad to be able to pass it on to someone new. What he would do while I talked to Mr. Sweet was pretend to play the guitar, in fact pretend that he was a young version of Mr. Sweet, and it always made Mr. Sweet glad to think that someone wanted to be like him—of course, we did not know this then, we played the thing by ear, and whatever he seemed to like, we did. We were desperately afraid that he was just going to take off one day and leave us.

It did not occur to us that we were doing anything special; we had not learned that death was final when it did come. We thought nothing of triumphing over it so many times, and in fact became a trifle contemptuous of people who let themselves be carried away. It did not occur to us that if our own father had been dying we could not have stopped it, that Mr. Sweet was the only person over whom we had power.

When Mr. Sweet was in his eighties I was studying in the university many miles from home. I saw him whenever I went home, but he was never on the verge of dying that I could tell and I began to feel that my anxiety for his health and psychological well-being was unnecessary. By this time he not only had a moustache but a long flowing snow-white beard, which I loved and combed and braided for hours. He was very peaceful, fragile, gentle, and the only jarring note about him was his old steel guitar, which he still played in the old sad, sweet, down-home blues way.

On Mr. Sweet's ninetieth birthday I was finishing my doctorate in Massachusetts and had been making arrangements to go home for several weeks' rest. That morning I got a telegram telling me that Mr. Sweet was dying again and could I please drop everything and come home. Of course I could. My dissertation could wait and my teachers would understand when I explained to them when I got back. I ran to the phone, called the airport, and within four hours I was speeding along the dusty road to Mr. Sweet's

The house was more dilapidated than when I was last there, barely a shack, but it was overgrown with yellow roses which my family had planted many years ago. The air was heavy and sweet and very peaceful. I felt strange walking through the gate and up the old rickety steps. But the strangeness left me as I caught sight of the long white beard I loved so well flowing down the thin body over the familiar quilt coverlet. Mr. Sweet!

His eyes were closed tight and his hands, crossed over his stomach, were thin and delicate, no longer scratchy. I remembered how always before I had run and jumped up on him just anywhere; now I knew he would not be able to support my weight. I looked around at my parents, and was surprised to see that my father and mother also looked old and frail. My father, his own hair very gray, leaned over the quietly sleeping old man, who, incidentally, smelled still of wine and tobacco, and said, as he'd done so many times, "To hell with dying, man! My daughter is home to see Mr. Sweet!" My brother had not been able to come as he was in the war in Asia. I bent down and gently stroked the closed eyes and gradually they began to open. The closed, wine-stained lips twitched a little, then parted in a warm, slightly embarrassed smile. Mr. Sweet could see me and he recognized me and his eyes looked very spry and twinkly for a moment. I put my head down on the pillow next to his and we just looked at each other for a long time. Then he began to trace my peculiar hairline with a thin, smooth finger. I closed my eyes when his finger halted above my ear (he used to rejoice at the dirt in my ears when I was little), his hand stayed cupped around my cheek. When I opened my eyes, sure that I had reached him in time, his were closed.

Even at twenty-four how could I believe that I had failed? that Mr. Sweet was really gone? He had never gone before. But when I looked up at my parents I saw that they were holding back tears. They had loved him dearly. He was like a piece of rare and delicate china which was always being saved from breaking and which finally fell. I looked long at the old face, the wrinkled forehead, the red lips, the hands that still reached out to me. Soon I felt my father pushing something cool into my hands. It was Mr. Sweet's guitar. He had asked them months before to give it to me; he had known that even if I came next time he would not be able to respond in the old way. He did not want me to feel that my trip had been for nothing.

The old guitar! I plucked the strings, hummed "Sweet Georgia Brown." The magic of Mr. Sweet lingered still in the cool steel box.

Through the window I could catch the fragrant delicate scent of tender yellow roses. The man on the high old-fashioned bed with the quilt coverlet and the flowing white beard had been my first love.

The Last Decision

≈ MAYA ANGELOU

The print is too small, distressing me.
Wavering black things on the page.
Wriggling polliwogs all about.
I know it's my age.
I'll have to give up reading.

The food is too rich, revolting me.
I swallow it hot or force it down cold,
and wait all day as it sits in my throat.
Tired as I am, I know I've grown old.
I'll have to give up eating.

My children's concerns are tiring me.
They stand at my bed and move their lips,
and I cannot hear one single word.
I'd rather give up listening.

Life is too busy, wearying me.
Questions and answers and heavy thought.
I've subtracted and added and multiplied,
and all figuring has come to naught.
Today I'll give up living.

On Aging
❧ MAYA ANGELOU

When you see me sitting quietly,
Like a sack left on the shelf,
Don't think I need your chattering.
I'm listening to myself.
Hold! Stop! Don't pity me!
Hold! Stop your sympathy!
Understanding if you got it,
Otherwise I'll do without it!

When my bones are stiff and aching
And my feet won't climb the stair,
I will only ask one favor:
Don't bring me no rocking chair.

When you see me walking, stumbling,
Don't study and get it wrong.
'Cause tired don't mean lazy
And every goodbye ain't gone.
I'm the same person I was back then,
A little less hair, a little less chin,
A lot less lungs and much less wind.
But ain't I lucky I can still breathe in.

Virginia Portrait

꿿 STERLING A. BROWN

Winter is settling on the place; the sedge
Is dry and lifeless and the woods stand bare.
The late autumnal flowers, nipped by frost,
Break from the sear stalks in the trim, neat garden,
And fall unheeded on the bleak, brown earth.

The winter of her year has come to her,
This wizened woman, spare of frame, but great
Of heart, erect, and undefeated yet.

Grief has been hers, before this wintry time.
Death has paid calls, unmannered, uninvited;
Low mounds have swollen in the fenced off corner,
Over brown children, marked by white-washed stones.
She has seen hopes that promised a fine harvest
Burnt by the drought; or bitten by the hoarfrost;
Or washed up and drowned out by unlooked for rains.
And as a warning blast of her own winter,
Death, the harsh overseer, shouted to her man,
Who answering slowly went over the hill.

She, puffing on a jagged slow-burning pipe,
By the low hearthfire, knows her winter now.
But she has strength and steadfast hardihood.
Deep-rooted is she, even as the oaks,
Hardy as perennials about her door.
The circle of the seasons brings no fear,
"Folks all gits used to what dey sees so often";
And she has helps that throng her glowing fire
Mixed with the smoke hugging her grizzled head:

Warm friends, the love of her full-blooded spouse,
Quiet companionship as age crept on him,
Laughter of babies, and their shrewd, sane raising;
These simple joys, not poor to her at all;

151

The sight of smokeclouds pouring from the flue;
Her stalwart son deep busied with "book larnin',"
After the weary fields; the kettle's purr
In duet with the sleek and pampered mouser;
Twanging of dominickers; lowing of Betsey;
Old folksongs chanted underneath the stars. . . .

Even when winter settles on her heart,
She keeps a wonted, quiet nonchalance,
A courtly dignity of speech and carriage,
Unlooked for in these distant rural ways.

She has found faith sufficient for her grief,
The song of earth for bearing heavy years,
She with slow speech, and spurts of heartfelt laughter,
Illiterate, and somehow very wise.

She has been happy, and her heart is grateful.
Now she looks out, and forecasts unperturbed
Her following slowly over the lonesome hill,
Her *'layin' down her burdens, bye and bye.'*

A Summer Tragedy

❧ ARNA BONTEMPS

Old Jeff Patton, the black share farmer, fumbled with his bow tie. His fingers trembled and the high stiff collar pinched his throat. A fellow loses his hand for such vanities after thirty or forty years of simple life. Once a year, or maybe twice if there's a wedding among his kinfolks, he may spruce up; but generally fancy clothes do nothing but adorn the wall of the big room and feed the moths. That had been Jeff Patton's experience. He had not worn his stiff-bosomed shirt more than a dozen times in all his married life. His swallow-tailed coat lay on the bed beside him, freshly brushed and pressed, but it was as full of holes as the overalls in which he worked on weekdays. The moths had used it badly. Jeff twisted his mouth into a hideous toothless grimace as he contended with the obstinate bow. He stamped his good foot and decided to give up the struggle.

"Jennie," he called.

"What's that, Jeff?" His wife's shrunken voice came out of the adjoining room like an echo. It was hardly bigger than a whisper.

"I reckon you'll have to he'p me wid this heah bow tie, baby," he said meekly. "Dog if I can hitch it up."

Her answer was not strong enough to reach him, but presently the old woman came to the door, feeling her way with a stick. She had a wasted, dead-leaf appearance. Her body, as scrawny and gnarled as a string bean, seemed less than nothing in the ocean of frayed and faded petticoats that surrounded her. These hung an inch or two above the tops of her heavy unlaced shoes and showed little grotesque piles where the stockings had fallen down from her negligible legs.

"You oughta could do a heap mo' wid a thing like that'n me—beingst as you got yo' good sight."

"Looks like I oughta could," he admitted. "But ma fingers is gone democrat on me. I get all mixed up in the looking glass an' can't tell wicha way to twist the devilish thing."

153

Jennie sat on the side of the bed and old Jeff Patton got down on one knee while she tied the bow knot. It was a slow and painful ordeal for each of them in this position. Jeff's bones cracked, his knee ached, and it was only after a half dozen attempts that Jennie worked a semblance of a bow into the tie.

"I got to dress maself now," the old woman whispered. "These is ma old shoes an' stockings, and I ain't so much as unwrapped ma dress."

"Well, don't worry 'bout me no mo', baby," Jeff said. "That 'bout finishes me. All I gotta do now is slip on that old coat 'n ves' an' I'll be fixed to leave."

Jennie disappeared again through the dim passage into the shed room. Being blind was no handicap to her in that black hole. Jeff heard the cane placed against the wall beside the door and knew that his wife was on easy ground. He put on his coat, took a battered top hat from the bedpost and hobbled to the front door. He was ready to travel. As soon as Jennie could get on her Sunday shoes and her old black silk dress, they would start.

Outside the tiny log house, the day was warm and mellow with sunshine. A host of wasps were humming with busy excitement in the trunk of a dead sycamore. Gray squirrels were searching through the grass for hickory nuts and blue jays were in the trees, hopping from branch to branch. Pine woods stretched away to the left like a black sea. Among them were scattered scores of log houses like Jeff's, houses of black share farmers. Cows and pigs wandered freely among the trees. There was no danger of loss. Each farmer knew his own stock and knew his neighbor's as well as he knew his neighbor's children.

Down the slope to the right were the cultivated acres on which the colored folks worked. They extended to the river, more than two miles away, and they were today green with the unmade cotton crop. A tiny thread of a road, which passed directly in front of Jeff's place, ran through these green fields like a pencil mark.

Jeff, standing outside the door, with his absurd hat in his left hand, surveyed the wide scene tenderly. He had been forty-five years on these acres. He loved them with the unexplained affection that others have for the countries to which they belong.

The sun was hot on his head, his collar still pinched his throat, and the Sunday clothes were intolerably hot. Jeff transferred the hat to his right hand and began fanning with it. Suddenly the whisper that was Jennie's voice came out of the shed room.

"You can bring the car round front whilst you's waitin'," it said feebly. There was a tired pause; then it added, "I'll soon be fixed to go."

"A'right, baby," Jeff answered. "I'll get it in a minute."

But he didn't move. A thought struck him that made his mouth fall open. The mention of the car brought to his mind, with new intensity, the trip he and Jennie were about to take. Fear came into his eyes; excitement took his breath. Lord, Jesus!

"Jeff . . . O Jeff," the old woman's whisper called.

He awakened with a jolt. "Hunh, baby?"

"What you doin'?"

"Nuthin. Jes studyin'. I jes been turnin' things round'n round in ma mind."

"You could be gettin' the car," she said.

"Oh yes, right away, baby."

He started round to the shed, limping heavily on his bad leg. There were three frizzly chickens in the yard. All his other chickens had been killed or stolen recently. But the frizzly chickens had been saved somehow. That was fortunate indeed, for these curious creatures had a way of devouring "Poison" from the yard and in that way protecting against conjure and black luck and spells. But even the frizzly chickens seemed now to be in a stupor. Jeff thought they had some ailment; he expected all three of them to die shortly.

The shed in which the old T-model Ford stood was only a grass roof held up by four corner poles. It had been built by tremulous hands at a time when the little rattletrap car had been regarded as a peculiar treasure. And, miraculously, despite wind and downpour it still stood.

Jeff adjusted the crank and put his weight upon it. The engine came to life with a sputter and bang that rattled the old car from radiator to taillight. Jeff hopped into the seat and put his foot on the accelerator. The sputtering and banging increased. The rattling became more violent. That was good. It was good banging, good sputtering and rattling, and it meant that the aged car was still in running condition. She could be depended on for this trip.

Again, Jeff's thought halted as if paralyzed. The suggestion of the trip fell into the machinery of his mind like a wrench. He felt dazed and weak. He swung the car out into the yard, made a half turn and drove around to the front door. When he took his hands off the wheel, he noticed that he was trembling violently. He cut off the motor and climbed to the ground to wait for Jennie.

A few minutes later she was at the window, her voice rattling against the pane like a broken shutter.

"I'm ready, Jeff."

He did not answer, but limped into the house and took her by the arm. He led her slowly through the big room, down the step and across the yard.

"You reckon I'd oughta lock the do'?" he asked softly.

They stopped and Jennie weighed the question. Finally she shook her head.

"Ne' mind the do'," she said. "I don't see no cause to lock up things."

"You right," Jeff agreed. "No cause to lock up."

Jeff opened the door and helped his wife into the car. A quick shudder passed over him. Jesus! Again he trembled.

"How come you shaking so?" Jennie whispered.

"I don't know," he said.

"You mus' be scairt, Jeff."

"No, baby, I ain't scairt."

He slammed the door after her and went around to crank up again. The motor started easily. Jeff wished that it had not been so responsive. He would have liked a few more minutes in which to turn things around in his head. As it was, with Jennie chiding him about being afraid, he had to keep going. He swung the car into the little pencil-mark road and started off toward the river, driving very slowly, very cautiously.

Chugging across the green countryside, the small battered Ford seemed tiny indeed. Jeff felt a familiar excitement, a thrill, as they came down the first slope to the immense levels on which the cotton was growing. He could not help reflecting that the crops were good. He knew what that meant, too; he had made forty-five of them with his own hands. It was true that he had worn out nearly a dozen mules, but that was the fault of old man Stevenson, the owner of the land. Major Stevenson had the odd notion that one mule was all a share farmer needed to work a thirty-acre plot. It was an expensive notion, the way it killed mules from overwork, but the old man held to it. Jeff thought it killed a good many share farmers as well as mules, but he had no sympathy for them. He had always been strong, and he had been taught to have no patience with weakness in men. Women or children might be tolerated if they were puny, but a weak man was a curse. Of course, his own children—

Jeff's thought halted there. He and Jennie never mentioned their dead children any more. And naturally he did not wish to dwell upon them in his mind. Before he knew it, some remark would slip out of his mouth and that would make Jennie feel blue. Perhaps she would cry. A woman like Jennie could not easily throw off the grief that comes from losing five grown children within two years. Even Jeff was still staggered by the blow. His memory had not been much good recently. He frequently talked to himself. And, although he had kept it a secret, he knew that his courage had left him. He was terrified by the least unfamiliar sound at night. He was reluctant to venture far from home in the daytime. And that habit of trembling when he felt fearful was now far beyond his control. Sometimes he became afraid and trembled without knowing what had frightened him. The feeling would just come over him like a chill.

The car rattled slowly over the dusty road. Jennie sat erect and silent, with a little absurd hat pinned to her hair. Her useless eyes seemed very large, very white in their deep sockets. Suddenly Jeff heard her voice, and he inclined his head to catch the words.

"Is we passed Delia Moore's house yet?" she asked.

"Not yet," he said.

"You must be drivin' mighty slow, Jeff."

"We might just as well take our time, baby."

There was a pause. A little puff of steam was coming out of the radiator of the car. Heat wavered above the hood. Delia Moore's house was nearly half a mile away. After a moment Jennie spoke again.

"You ain't really scairt, is you, Jeff?"

"Nah, baby, I ain't scairt."

"You know how we agreed—we gotta keep on goin'."

Jewels of perspiration appeared on Jeff's forehead. His eyes rounded, blinked, became fixed on the road.

"I don't know," he said with a shiver. "I reckon it's the only thing to do."

"Hm."

A flock of guinea fowls, pecking in the road, were scattered by the passing car. Some of them took to their wings; others hid under bushes. A blue jay, swaying on a leafy twig, was annoying a roadside squirrel. Jeff held an even speed till he came near Delia's place. Then he slowed down noticeably.

Delia's house was really no house at all, but an abandoned store building converted into a dwelling. It sat near a crossroads, beneath a single black cedar tree. There Delia, a cattish old creature of Jennie's age, lived alone. She had been there more years than anybody could remember, and long ago had won the disfavor of such women as Jennie. For in her young days Delia had been gayer, yellower and saucier than seemed proper in those parts. Her ways with menfolks had been dark and suspicious. And the fact that she had had as many husbands as children did not help her reputation.

"Yonder's old Delia," Jeff said as they passed.

"What she doin'?"

"Jes sittin' in the do'," he said.

"She see us?"

"Hm," Jeff said. "Musta did."

That relieved Jennie. It strengthened her to know that her old enemy had seen her pass in her best clothes. That would give the old she-devil something to chew her gums and fret about, Jennie thought. Wouldn't she have a fit if she didn't find out? Old evil Delia! This would be just the thing for her. It would pay her back for being so evil. It would also pay her, Jennie thought, for the way she used to grin at Jeff—long ago when her teeth were good.

The road became smooth and red, and Jeff could tell by the smell of the air that they were nearing the river. He could see the rise where the road turned and ran along parallel to the stream. The car chugged on monotonously. After a long silent spell, Jennie leaned against Jeff and spoke.

"How many bale o' cotton you think we got standin'?" she said.

Jeff wrinkled his forehead as he calculated.

"'Bout twenty-five, I reckon."

"How many you make las' year?"

"Twenty-eight," he said. "How come you ask that?"

"I's jes thinkin'," Jennie said quietly.

"It don't make a speck o' difference though," Jeff reflected. "If we get much or if we get little, we still gonna be in debt to old man

Stevenson when he gets through counting up agin us. It's took us a long time to learn that."

Jennie was not listening to these words. She had fallen into a trance-like meditation. Her lips twitched. She chewed her gums and rubbed her gnarled hands nervously. Suddenly she leaned forward, buried her face in the nervous hands and burst into tears. She cried aloud in a dry cracked voice that suggested the rattle of fodder on dead stalks. She cried aloud like a child, for she had never learned to suppress a genuine sob. Her slight old frame shook heavily and seemed hardly able to sustain such violent grief.

"What's the matter, baby?" Jeff asked awkwardly. "Why you cryin' like all that?"

"I's jes thinkin'," she said.

"So you the one what's scairt now, hunh?"

"I ain't scairt, Jeff. I's jes thinkin' 'bout leavin' eve'thing like this—eve'thing we been used to. It's right sad-like."

Jeff did not answer, and presently Jennie buried her face again and cried.

The sun was almost overhead. It beat down furiously on the dusty wagon-path road, on the parched roadside grass and the tiny battered car. Jeff's hands, gripping the wheel, became wet with perspiration; his forehead sparkled. Jeff's lips parted. His mouth shaped a hideous grimace. His face suggested the face of a man being burned. But the torture passed and his expression softened again.

"You mustn't cry, baby," he said to his wife. "We gotta be strong. We can't break down."

Jennie waited a few seconds, then said, "You reckon we oughta do it, Jeff? You reckon we oughta go 'head an' do it, really?"

Jeff's voice choked; his eyes blurred. He was terrified to hear Jennie say the thing that had been in his mind all morning. She had egged him on when he had wanted more than anything in the world to wait, to reconsider, to think things over a little longer. Now she was getting cold feet. Actually there was no need of thinking the question through again. It would only end in making the same painful decision once more. Jeff knew that. There was no need of fooling around longer.

"We jes as well to do like we planned," he said. "They ain't nothin' else for us now—it's the bes' thing."

Jeff thought of the handicaps, the near impossibility, of making

159

another crop with his leg bothering him more and more each week. Then there was always the chance that he would have another stroke, like the one that had made him lame. Another one might kill him. The least it could do would be to leave him helpless. Jeff gasped—Lord, Jesus! He could not bear to think of being helpless, like a baby, on Jennie's hands. Frail, blind Jennie.

The little pounding motor of the car worked harder and harder. The puff of steam from the cracked radiator became larger. Jeff realized that they were climbing a little rise. A moment later the road turned abruptly and he looked down upon the face of the river.

"Jeff."

"Hunh?"

"Is that the water I hear?"

"Hm. Tha's it."

"Well, which way you goin' now?"

"Down this-a way," he said. "The road runs 'long 'side o' the water a lil piece."

She waited a while calmly. Then she said, "Drive faster."

"A'right, baby," Jeff said.

The water roared in the bed of the river. It was fifty or sixty feet below the level of the road. Between the road and the water there was a long smooth slope, sharply inclined. The slope was dry, the clay hardened by prolonged summer heat. The water below, roaring in a narrow channel, was noisy and wild.

"Jeff."

"Hunh?"

"How far you goin'?"

"Jes a lil piece down the road."

"You ain't scairt, is you, Jeff?"

"Nah, baby," he said trembling. "I ain't scairt."

"Remember how we planned it, Jeff. We gotta do it like we said. Brave-like."

"Hm."

Jeff's brain darkened. Things suddenly seemed unreal, like figures in a dream. Thoughts swam in his mind foolishly, hysterically, like little blind fish in a pool within a dense cave. They rushed, crossed one another, jostled, collided, retreated and rushed again. Jeff soon became dizzy. He shuddered violently and turned to his wife.

"Jennie, I can't do it. I can't." His voice broke pitifully.

160

She did not appear to be listening. All the grief had gone from her face. She sat erect, her unseeing eyes wide open, strained and frightful. Her glossy black skin had become dull. She seemed as thin, as sharp and bony, as a starved bird. Now, having suffered and endured the sadness of tearing herself away from beloved things, she showed no anguish. She was absorbed with her own thoughts, and she didn't even hear Jeff's voice shouting in her ear.

Jeff said nothing more. For an instant there was light in his cavernous brain. The great chamber was, for less than a second, peopled by characters he knew and loved. They were simple, healthy creatures, and they behaved in a manner that he could understand. They had quality. But since he had already taken leave of them long ago, the remembrance did not break his heart again. Young Jeff Patton was among them, the Jeff Patton of fifty years ago who went down to New Orleans with a crowd of country boys to the Mardi Gras doings. The gay young crowd, boys with candy-striped shirts and rouged-brown girls in noisy silks, was like a picture in his head. Yet it did not make him sad. On that very trip Slim Burns had killed Joe Beasley—the crowd had been broken up. Since then Jeff Patton's world had been the Greenbriar Plantation. If there had been other Mardi Gras carnivals, he had not heard of them. Since then there had been no time; the years had fallen on him like waves. Now he was old, worn out. Another paralytic stroke (like the one he had already suffered) would put him on his back for keeps. In that condition, with a frail blind woman to look after him, he would be worse off than if he were dead.

Suddenly Jeff's hands became steady. He actually felt brave. He slowed down the motor of the car and carefully pulled off the road. Below, the water of the stream boomed, a soft thunder in the deep channel. Jeff ran the car onto the clay slope, pointed it directly toward the stream and put his foot heavily on the accelerator. The little car leaped furiously down the steep incline toward the water. The movement was nearly as swift and direct as a fall. The two old black folks, sitting quietly side by side, showed no excitement. In another instant the car hit the water and dropped immediately out of sight.

A little later it lodged in the mud of a shallow place. One wheel of the crushed and upturned little Ford became visible above the rushing water.

The Bean Eaters
GWENDOLYN BROOKS

They eat beans mostly, this old yellow pair.
Dinner is a casual affair.
Plain chipware on a plain and creaking wood,
Tin flatware.

Two who are Mostly Good.
Two who have lived their day,
But keep on putting on their clothes
And putting things away.

And remembering . . .
Remembering, with twinklings and twinges,
As they lean over the beans in their rented back room that
    is full of beads and receipts and dolls and clothes,
        tobacco crumbs, vases and fringes.

Aging
Discussion Questions

1. Many women figure prominently in these poems and stories. Discuss the contribution made by women to black society and consider the notion of black women as matriarchs. What impact has this had on black family life?

2. What kinds of differences are suggested between the world of grandmothers and that of their grandchildren?

3. Discuss Bambara's Maggie in terms of elderly displacement and right-to-die decisions.

4. Comment on the superstitions described in these stories and on those many of us held as children.

5. Da-duh's visit with her city-oriented grandchild occurs in a Caribbean setting that is probably different from the setting in which we visited our grandparents. Nevertheless, did the story stir any memories?

6. Most children become quiet when "once upon a time" is uttered, the prelude for a story. Although these stories refer to storytelling in a black oral tradition, discuss your own childhood response to stories. Also, consider the modern child and the impact of television as a story source.

7. The idea of aging and death are not easy topics for many. Compare the tone in "George" with that of "Miss Rosie."

8. Do you pass by "bag people" sleeping in the streets without much thought or do you find yourself wondering about their pasts? Have you ever thought about the possibility of becoming a street person?

9. As children, some of us tormented an elderly neighbor. Discuss the behavior of Lizabeth in "Marigolds" toward Miss Lottie. Why are the flowers so important?

10. Many sympathize with the sentiments presented by Maya Angelou in "The Last Decision." Will you prefer to take charge of your final days? Compare this to Angelou's other poem, "On Aging."

11. Do you feel that the figures of Jeff and Jennie Patton ("A Summer Tragedy") are tragic or heroic? Who seems to be the stronger of the two? Discuss Jennie's attitude toward Delia.

12. Brooks' poem, "The Bean Eaters," is visual; it produces a portrait of two old people. Pretend that the work is hanging on a gallery wall. What colors are used? What is the story or what is depicted? What emotions are elicited from you, the viewer?

SECTION III

≈ ≋ ≈

Loss and Grief

I went to the windows then and gently pulled the shades as best I could, I comforted the dying man, making a requiem for him, for myself, and for all the world's people who only know life through death.   FRENCHY HODGES

Introduction

Death is one of the parameters of human existence, the endpoint of the biological process. Foreknowledge of it characterizes our species and evokes from survivors a sense of loss and grief. Although creative interpreters over the ages have provided numerous paintings, stories, and aphorisms about death's abstract nature and inevitability, we remain, nonetheless, uncomfortable with the topic, preferring, as Woody Allen commented, not to be there when it happens.

Black and nonblack impressions of death are shaped by a contrasting array of socioeconomic factors, religious beliefs, and centuries of unrelenting brutality and violence. The stories and poems, set within these overlapping, interconnecting contexts, reveal more than the grieving family members' ability to survive; they reveal personal sensitivities and individual tragedies rarely experienced or understood by nonblacks.

Historically, lynchings, police brutality, and murder have been associated with black communities; except for lynchings, the association persists. Headlines appearing in Miami, Chicago, and Los Angeles are rooted in grim traditions of hatred and frustration, and in painful cultural wounds that continue to fester. The stories and poems in this section can lead readers to a better understanding of

165

the pain, the suffering, and the anger that result from tragic events and can serve as a starting point for healing and reconciliation.

The section opens with James Weldon Johnson's somber poem, "Go Down Death," followed by selections by Langston Hughes and Sterling A. Brown on loss and grief. Both authors use various forms of humor as foils to serious matters such as infidelity, waste of life, injustice, and inequity, motifs of pressing reassertion. In "The Lynching," "Old Lem," "Revolutionary Petunias," "Death in Yorkville," and "Golden Gate," readers witness dangers of irrationality and malevolence that may explain desperate tendencies to turn from overwhelming horror to unexpected humor. For example, the threat implied by "now you listen to me, boy," a phrase commonly used by whites to humiliate African-Americans, is either fearful or funny depending on the circumstances. Late at night in a rural southern community, it would not be funny when history's tragic lessons forced the pulse to race and the mind to envision the scene described so vividly and unforgettably by McKay in "The Lynching":

> The ghastly body swaying in the sun:
> The women thronged to look, but never a one
> Showed sorrow in her eyes of steely blue;
> And little lads, lynchers that were to be,
> Danced round the dreadful thing in fiendish glee.

The gathering of steely-eyed white women and "little lads" dancing around the "dreadful thing" corrupts with breathtaking horror the traditional image of women, and of children dancing innocently and festively around Maypoles in springtime.

The reality of black experience has been circumscribed by oppression, murder, and homicide, so that confusion and ambivalence about the meanings of life and death persist. An oppressed people bows under the imposition of rigid restraints and the lack of positive opportunities. Drug use and homicide—murder and gang shootings—have reached epidemic levels among disenfranchised African-Americans living in settings shaped by socioeconomic imperatives and realities. Education seems useless; poverty is oppressive; and jobs are unattainable.

Like Gwendolyn Brooks's "We Real Cool," Langston Hughes's poem, "Junior Addict," portrays the nightmarish attraction of drugs

166

and the risks—including death—which young black males face in Harlem and elsewhere. No sunrise exists for the boy-child victim in the poem "who sticks a needle in his arm/and seeks an out in other worldly dreams." It is easier after all "to get dope/ than to get a job." Instead of looking west toward sunset, Hughes's poem concludes with an African sunrise, the home where African-Americans, like this dying boy, can return. By looking east, there is an additional implicit link between Africa and prelapsarian innocence—and Christ.

Against this terrifying backdrop, elaborate rituals for grieving become mechanisms for support and survival. Reliance upon fixed entities—God, music, church services—sustain and heal. Funerals, frequent subjects for black writers and artists, become vehicles for managing that which is possible, the ritual of death. If life is regulated by destructive and oppressive forces, African-Americans can try, at least, to control the concluding ceremonies. Funerals, unlike black life, represent freedom and escape from restrictive forces; mourners celebrate loudly and lavishly with words, music, and costume. It is ironic, of course, that death, rather than life, is cause for festivity.

The importance of the funeral is shown in Ann Allen Shockley's story, "The Funeral." A young woman named Melissa is introduced as a foil to the story's subject matter. She has lived with her granny, Miss Eliza, for most of her life, only

> the two of them facing each other in the evenings in the small living room with the shades tightly drawn: Granny rocking slowly back and forth in the ancient rocker with its high straightarrow back, and Melissa, absorbing herself in preparing for the next day which would end like the day before.

Because the funeral represents the most significant event of Granny's life, she has reviewed over and over again with her grandchild specific plans and detailed instructions; fifty cents per week has been paid for burial coverage; scripture passages have been selected for reading; the parlor, where the wake will be held, has been repapered each year in preparation; the satin dress has been chosen for the laying-out; the expensive Cadillac hearse has been stipulated for the "one time" she will ride "in style"; and for music, "Just a Closer Walk with Thee" has been picked to be sung before the preaching. The funeral and its myriad of particulars are central in Granny's mind, and by imposition, foremost in the thoughts of her young granddaughter. Only death and afterlife matter to the impoverished woman; the promise of spiritual salvation provides solace for a lifetime of unrelenting hardship.

The short poem, "As Befits a Man" by Langston Hughes, humorously summarizes what a man's funeral ought to include: ". . . a dozen pretty women/To holler, cry, and moan," "A row of long tall mamas/Fainting, fanning, and crying," ". . . sixteen fish-tail cars/A big brass band" and ". . . a whole truck load of flowers." Val Ferdinand's "Second Line/Cutting the Body Loose" is an account of a colorful New Orleans jazz funeral where "nothing could keep us contained." First-line trumpets are answered with uninhibited shaking and hollering, forcing the amazed narrator to ask appreciatively, "Where did we get all of this from, the marching and dancing and singing and togetherness. . . . Africa can you hear us . . . ?" When the funeral ends, people in the street smile and laugh at each other, suggesting that the energetic ritual has successfully reconciled, however temporarily, the disparate forces of life and death and the difficulties of daily living.

Several selections deal with children's perceptions of death. While we might expect that reactions to death are shared by blacks and nonblacks, racial circumstances can account for overt and subtle distinctions. In one story, "Mother Dear and Daddy," orphaned children realize that acceptance by relatives depends on shading, the lightness or darkness of their skin. The child who resembles his darker father is less desirable to relatives than the one who bears his mother's lighter complexion: "All right Mabel. The fact is, the boys are—well—they're too, well, too much like the father." Cruelties imposed by color-minded families and sibling separation compound the children's pain of loss and provide little hope of comfort.

Several selections similarly focus on the occasion of death as an impetus for reflection. Parents ("A Brown Girl Dead," "We Assume: On the Death of Our Son, Reuben Masai Harper,"), children ("Poem for Granville Ivanhoe Jordan," "Revelation"), and spouses or friends ("Widow Woman," "Praisesong for the Widow") present the range of sentiments induced by loss. Typically, we discover sadness or anger, but as Langston Hughes acknowledges in "Widow Woman" and "As Befits a Man," we also find survival strategies that may include humor. Because the circumstances of death are varied, our expectations about individual responses may be frustrated. Personal reactions to loss in "Widow Woman," for example, are quite different from those presented by Paule Marshall in "Praisesong for the Widow." In the first, a lifetime of anger is released by a mistreated spouse. When you're buried, she says, "That's the one time, pretty papa,/You'll sure stay in your place." Marshall's widow, however, whose grief has been repressed, finally spills forth in a stream of consciousness that reveals the complexities and ambiguities of her marital relationship. Death has stunned both women, but the immediate expression of anger for one and the eventual confrontation with grief for the other permits healing to begin.

In Mike Thelwell's story, "Bright an' Mownin' Star," the human landscape of dreams and emotions is rooted to the historically harsh landscape of rural economics and black suppression. Before Lowe Junior appears, the reader travels "south from Memphis on Highway 49" to the huge tree breaking the monotonously flat horizon. The tree serves as a metaphor for black experiences in the South and for the tensions facing the central character at the time of his grandmother's death. It is an oak, a blackjack oak, its fire-charred torso anchored into the parched, unproductive soil. Its topmost branches reach upward, flourishing "out of the cinders of its own corpse," paralleling Lowe Junior's difficult struggle for survival. When Lowe's grandmother dies, he is encouraged by neighbors to continue to work the barren fields, the quarter section owned by Mr. Peterson and provisioned by Mr. J. D. Odum. His grandmother's familiar and invariable response to "How yo' keepin' Miz Culvah?" was "Porely, thank d' Lawd." If she was the charred and "porely" middle section of the oak, he, like the delicate leaves, would strive higher. Out of death, the phoenix rises; although ignorant and poor, Lowe's courage and determination reach skyward toward dreams of freedom.

Each selection contributes facets of understanding about the experience of death. The fabric is knotted, twisted, uneven, and colorful. The writers with their particular insight present common threads of humanity: its hopes and fears. While we learn a great deal about the effect of death on others, it is likely that the selections raise important questions about relationships in society and our own capacities for loss and grief within personal and public contexts.

169

Go Down Death

🐦 JAMES WELDON JOHNSON

Weep not, weep not,
She is not dead;
She's resting in the bosom of Jesus.
Heart-broken husband—weep no more;
Grief-stricken son—weep no more;
She's only just gone home.

Day before yesterday morning,
God was looking down from his great, high heaven,
Looking down on all his children,
And his eye fell on Sister Caroline,
Tossing on her bed of pain.
And God's big heart was touched with pity,
With the everlasting pity.

And God sat back on his throne,
And he commanded that tall, bright angel standing at his
     right hand:
Call me Death!
And that tall, bright angel cried in a voice
That broke like a clap of thunder:
Call Death!—Call Death!
And the echo sounded down the streets of heaven
Till it reached away back to that shadowy place,
Where Death waits with his pale, white horses.

And Death heard the summons,
And he leaped on his fastest horse,
Pale as a sheet in the moonlight.
Up the golden street Death galloped,
And the hoof of his horse struck fire from the gold,
But they didn't make no sound.
Up Death rode to the Great White Throne,
And waited for God's command.

And God said: Go down, Death, go down,
Go down to Savannah, Georgia,
Down in Yamacraw,
And find Sister Caroline.
She's borne the burden and heat of the day,
She's labored long in my vineyard,
And she's tired—
She's weary—
Go down, Death, and bring her to me.

And Death didn't say a word,
But he loosed the reins on his pale, white horse,
And he clamped the spurs to his bloodless sides,
And out and down he rode,
Through heaven's pearly gates,
Past suns and moons and stars;
On Death rode,
And the foam from his horse was like a comet in the sky;
On Death rode,
Leaving the lightning's flash behind;
Straight on down he came.

While we were watching round her bed,
She turned her eyes and looked away,
She saw what we couldn't see;
She saw Old Death. She saw Old Death.
Coming like a falling star.
But Death didn't frighten Sister Caroline;
He looked to her like a welcome friend.
And she whispered to us; I'm going home,
And she smiled and closed her eyes.

And Death took her up like a baby,
And she lay in his icy arms,
But she didn't feel no chill.
And Death began to ride again—
Up beyond the evening star,
Out beyond the morning star,
Into the glittering light of glory,
On to the Great White Throne.

And there he laid Sister Caroline
On the loving breast of Jesus.

And Jesus took his own hand and wiped away her tears
And he smoothed the furrows from her face,
And the angels sang a little song,
And Jesus rocked her in his arms,
And kept a-saying: Take your rest,
Take your rest, take your rest.
Weep not—weep not,
She is not dead;
She's resting in the bosom of Jesus.

Golden Gate

🕊 LANGSTON HUGHES

"**I**f I was of mind to give a Christmas gift to the Devil," said Simple, leaning on the bar with an empty glass of beer, "I would give him Mississippi, the whole state of Mississippi, police dogs and all."

"You would be too generous with the Devil," I said, "giving him a whole state with all of those sinners in it to torture. He would have a lot of fun."

"I would not want the Devil to have fun with no present I gave him," said Simple. "No! So I better give something to bedevil him. Maybe I'd give him all the roughnecks in Harlem—garbage out the windows, pop bottles, and lighted cigarette butts. I would have the Devil hit on the head with a sack of garbage every time he switched down the streets of hell."

"I would go you one better. For Christmas I would turn the Devil black and let him find out what Jim Crow is like."

"Hell sure must be full of white folks," said Simple, "so if the Devil was black, he would be bound to have a hard time. Suppose he wanted to drive a train and be an engineer, the Railroad Brotherhoods in hell would not let him in the union. Suppose he wanted to get a cup of coffee driving on the highway between the Capital of hell and Baltimore, he would have a hard time. Suppose he wanted to play golf in Alabama, he would be burnt up. To turn him black would be a *real* Un-Merry Christmas for the Devil. But since I am not going to hell myself, why worry about it. I am wondering what it is gonna be like when I get to Glory. There must be white folks up there, too.

"You know," continued Simple. "Last night I drempt I died and went to heaven and Old Governor of Mississippi, Alabama, or Georgia, or wherever he is from, had got there before me, and didn't want to let me in. He was standing at the Golden Gate, right beside Saint Peter, when I come ghosting up.

174

"He said, 'What are you doing here, Jess Semple? Don't you know you have to use the rear entrance?'

" 'What rear entrance?' I says.

" 'The COLORED ENTRANCE,' says Old Governor, 'around the back.'

"I said, 'I did not know heaven was located in the South. I thought it was *up* not *down*. Saint Peter, do you hear the man?'

"Saint Peter said, 'Heaven is so full of white folks now I have no control over it any more.'

"I said, 'How did so many white folks get to heaven, Saint?'

"Old Peter said, 'Jesse B. Semple, I do not know, but they are here.'

" 'I did not realize I was in hell,' I said. 'I thought when I riz through space from my dying bed, I had landed at the Gate of Heaven. Anyway, Peter, is not my sins washed whiter than snow? Am I not white now inside and out?'

"Whereupon, Old Down-home Governor spoke up and said, 'You have to bathe in the River of Life to be washed whiter than snow. The River of Life is in heaven. You are not inside yet, Simple. Therefore, you are still black. White is right, black get back! You are not coming in the front entrance.'

"I said, 'It is too bad I left my weapons down on earth. I am not a Freedom Rider, neither a sit-in kid. The two cheeks I have to turn have done been turned enough. They shall turn no more. You-all better get out of my way and lemme through this Golden Gate.'

"Saint Peter begun to wring his hands. He said, 'I will go call Gabriel. He is one of your folks. He can explain to you how things is up here since the white folks took over.'

"I said, 'Call Gabriel, nothing. If you gonna call anybody, call God!'

" 'God is busy with Vietnam, West Berlin, and NATO,' said Peter.

" 'I did not know God's name was Uncle Sam,' I said. 'Besides, I am as much angel as you, Peter. If you and Old Gov. there don't get out of my way and let me in this gate, I will take my left wing and slap you both down. Then I will take my right wing and whip you good.'

" 'Jesse B., we go in for nonviolence in heaven,' cried Peter.

" 'I am not in heaven, yet,' says I, 'only on the threshold. But if I don't get in, it won't be because I didn't try. Where is Old Governor gone at?'

" 'He has run to call his dogs,' said Peter.

" 'You mean to tell me, you let Southern white folks and their dogs both in heaven?' I asked. 'What is the sky coming to? Earth were bad enough. Maybe the Lord sent for me to clean up heaven. In which case, wait a minute. I will ghost back to earth and round up my boys from Harlem. I will ask them are you willing to die for your rights in heaven as on earth? If so, *die now,* make ghosts out of the Golden Gate. White folks have done got up there and made an American out of St. Peter. They have set up a kennel of police dogs beside the River Jordan. They have put up WHITE ONLY signs at the milk-and-honey counter. Mens, do you intend to stand for this? Whereupon, from their stepladders on every corner in Harlem they will answer, "No!" Peter, I'll bet this Golden Gate will open then. We'll see. We'll see!'

"Whiz-zzz-zz-z! But when I ghosted back to earth, I woke up kicking and sweating, and found that it were nothing but a dream. I were not dead at all—just having nightmares in my sleep. It is a good thing, because had my dream been real, I would of tore up that Golden Gate! Plumb up! White folks can run hell, if they want to, but they better not start no stuff with me in Glory Land."

Maumee Ruth

STERLING A. BROWN

Might as well bury her
    And bury her deep,
Might as well put her
    Where she can sleep.

Might as well lay her
    Out in her shiny black;
And for the love of God
    Not wish her back.

Maum Sal may miss her—
    Maum Sal, she only—
With no one now to scoff,
    Sal may be lonely. . . .

Nobody else there is
    Who will be caring
How rocky was the road
    For her wayfaring;

Nobody be heeding in
    Cabin, or town,
That she is lying here
    In her best gown.

Boy that she suckled—
    How should he know,
Hiding in city holes,
    Sniffing the 'snow'?

And how should the news
    Pierce Harlem's din,
To reach her baby gal,
    Sodden with gin?

To cut her withered heart
    They cannot come again,
Preach her the lies about
    Jordan, and then

Might as well drop her
    Deep in the ground,
Might as well pray for her,
    That she sleep sound. . . .

Sister Lou

❧ STERLING A. BROWN

Honey
When de man
Calls out de las' train
You're gonna ride,
Tell him howdy.

Gather up yo' basket
An' yo' knittin' an' yo' things,
An' go on up an' visit
Wid frien' Jesus fo' a spell.

Show Marfa
How to make yo' greengrape jellies,
An' give po' Lazarus
A passel of them Golden Biscuits.

Scald some meal
Fo' some righdown good spoonbread
Fo' li'l box-plunkin' David.

An' sit aroun'
An' tell them Hebrew Chillen
All yo' stories. . . .

Honey
Don't be feared of them pearly gates,
Don't go 'round to de back,
No mo' dataway
Not evah no mo'.

Let Michael tote yo' burden
An' yo' pocketbook an' evahthing
'Cept yo' Bible,
While Gabriel blows somp'n
Solemn but loudsome
On dat horn of his'n.

Honey
Go straight on to de Big House,
An' speak to yo' God
Widout no fear an' tremblin'.

Then sit down
An' pass de time of day awhile.

Give a good talkin' to
To yo' favorite 'postle Peter,
An' rub the po' head
Of mixed-up Judas,
An' joke awhile wid Jonah.

Then, when you gits de chance,
Always rememberin' yo' raisin',
Let 'em know youse tired
Jest a mite tired.

Jesus will find yo' bed fo' you
Won't no servant evah bother wid yo' room.
Jesus will lead you
To a room wid windows
Openin' on cherry trees an' plum trees
Bloomin' everlastin'.

An' dat will be yours
Fo' keeps.

Den take yo' time. . . .
Honey, take yo' bressed time.

The Lynching

❧ CLAUDE McKAY

His spirit in smoke ascended to high heaven.
His father, by the cruelest way of pain,
Had bidden him to his bosom once again;
The awful sin remained still unforgiven.
All night a bright and solitary star
(Perchance the one that ever guided him,
Yet gave him up at last to Fate's wild whim)
Hung pitifully o'er the swinging char.
Day dawned, and soon the mixed crowds came to view
The ghastly body swaying in the sun:
The women thronged to look, but never a one
Showed sorrow in her eyes of steely blue;
And little lads, lynchers that were to be,
Danced round the dreadful thing in fiendish glee.

Old Lem

❧ STERLING A. BROWN

I talked to old Lem
and old Lem said:
 "They weigh the cotton
 They store the corn
   We only good enough
   To work the rows;
 They run the commissary
 They keep the books
   We gotta be grateful
   For being cheated;
 Whippersnapper clerks
 Call us out of our name
   We got to say mister
   To spindling boys
 They make our figgers
 Turn somersets
 We buck in the middle
   Say, 'Thankyuh, sah.'
   They don't come by ones
   They don't come by twos
   But they come by tens.

 "They got the judges
 They got the lawyers
 They got the jury-rolls
 They got the law
   They don't come by ones
 They got the sheriffs
 They got the deputies
    They don't come by twos
 They got the shotguns
 They got the rope
   We git the justice
   In the end
     And they come by tens.

"Their fists stay closed
Their eyes look straight
    Our hands stay open
    Our eyes must fall
        They don't come by ones
They got the manhood
They got the courage
        They don't come by twos
    We got to slink around
    Hangtailed hounds.
They burn us when we dogs
They burn us when we men
        They come by tens . . .

"I had a buddy
Six foot of man
Muscled up perfect
Game to the heart
        They don't come by ones
Outworked and outfought
Any man or two men
        They don't come by twos
He spoke out of turn
At the commissary
They gave him a day
To git out the county
He didn't take it.
He said 'Come and get me.'
They came and got him
        And they came by tens.
He stayed in the county—
He lays there dead.

        They don't come by ones
        They don't come by twos
        But they come by tens."

183

Revolutionary Petunias

ALICE WALKER

Sammy Lou of Rue
sent to his reward
the exact creature who
murdered her husband,
using a cultivator's hoe
with verve and skill;
and laughed fit to kill
in disbelief
at the angry, militant
pictures of herself
the Sonneteers quickly drew:
not any of them people that
she knew.
A backwoods woman
her house was papered with
funeral home calendars and
faces appropriate for a Mississippi
Sunday School. She raised a George,
a Martha, a Jackie and a Kennedy. Also
a John Wesley Junior.
"Always respect the word of God,"
she said on her way to she didn't
know where, except it would be by
electric chair, and she continued
"Don't yall forgit to *water*
my purple petunias."

Junior Addict

❧ LANGSTON HUGHES

The little boy
who sticks a needle in his arm
and seeks an out in other worldly dreams,
who seeks an out in eyes that droop
and ears that close to Harlem screams,
cannot know, of course,
(and has no way to understand)
a sunrise that he cannot see
beginning in some other land—
but destined sure to flood—and soon—
the very room in which he leaves
his needle and his spoon,
the very room in which today the air
is heavy with the drug
of his despair.

> (Yet little can
> tomorrow's sunshine give
> to one who will not live.)

Quick, sunrise, come—
Before the mushroom bomb
Pollutes his stinking air
With better death
Than is his living here
With viler drugs
Than bring today's release
In poison from the fallout
Of our peace.

> *"It's easier to get dope
> than it is to get a job."*

Yes, easier to get dope
than to get a job—

185

daytime or nightime job,
teen-age, pre-draft,
pre-lifetime job.

Quick, sunrise, come!
Sunrise out of Africa,
Quick, come!
Sunrise, please come!
Come! Come!

Death in Yorkville

🙠 LANGSTON HUGHES

How many bullets does it take
To kill a fifteen-year-old kid?
How many bullets does it take
To kill me?

How many centuries does it take
To bind my mind—chain my feet—
Rope my neck—lynch me—
Unfree?

From the slave chain to the lynch rope
To the bullets of Yorkville,
Jamestown, 1619 to 1963:
Emancipation Centennial—
100 years NOT free.

Civil War Centennial: 1965.
How many Centennials does it take
To kill me,
Still alive?

When the long hot summers come
Death ain't
No jive.

Eulogy for Alvin Frost

&ოᲖ AUDRE LORDE

I.

Black men bleeding to death inside themselves
inside their fine strong bodies
inside their stomachs
inside their heads
a hole
as large as a dum-dum bullet
eaten away from the inside
death at 37.

Windows are holes to let in the light
in Newark airport at dawn I read
of your death by illumination
the carpets are dark and the windows are smoky
to keep out the coming sun
I plummet down through a hole in the carpet
seeking immediate ground for my feet to embrace
my toes have no wisdom no strength
to resist
they curl in a spasm of grief
of fury uprooted
It is dawn in the airport and nothing is open
I cannot even plant you a tree
the earth is still frozen
I write a card saying
machines grew the flowers I send
to throw into your grave.

On occasion we passed in the hallway
usually silent and hurried but fighting
on the same side.
You congratulate me on my latest book
in a Black Caucus meeting
you are distinguished
by your genuine laughter

188

and you might have been my long lost
second grade seat-mate named Alvin
grown into some other magic
but we never had time enough
just to talk.

I I.

From an airplane heading south
the earth grows slowly greener
we pass the first swimming pool
filled with blue water
this winter is almost over
I don't want to write a natural poem
I want to write about the unnatural death
of a young man at 37
eating himself for courage in secret
until he vanished
bleeding to death inside.
He will be eulogized in echoes
by a ghost of those winters
that haunt morning people
wearing away our days like smiling water
in southern pools
leaving psychic graffiti
clogging the walls of our hearts
carving out ulcers inside our stomachs
from which we explode
or bleed to death.

I I I.

The day after your burial
John Wade slid off his chair
onto the carpet in the student cafeteria
and died there on the floor
between Abnormal Psychology and a half-finished
cup of black coffee.
Cafeteria guards rushed him out
the back door between classes

189

and we never knew until a week later
that he had even been ill.

I am tired of writing memorials to black men
whom I was on the brink of knowing
weary like fig trees
weighted like a crepe myrtle
with all the black substance poured into earth
before earth is ready to bear.
I am tired of holy deaths
of the ulcerous illuminations the cerebral accidents
the psychology of the oppressed
where mental health is the ability
to repress
knowledge of the world's cruelty.

I V.

Dear Danny who does not know me
I am
writing to you for your father
whom I barely knew
except at meetings where he was
distinguished
by his genuine laughter
and his kind bright words
Danny son of Alvin
please cry
whenever it hurts
remember to laugh
even when you do battle
stay away from coffee and fried plastic
even when it looks like chicken
and grow up
black and strong and beautiful
but not too soon.

We need you
and there are so few
left.

We Real Cool

🐦 GWENDOLYN BROOKS

> The Pool Players.
> Seven at the Golden Shovel.

We real cool. We
Left school. We

Lurk late. We
Strike straight. We

Sing sin. We
Thin gin. We

Jazz June. We
Die soon.

Free at Last
(excerpt from *Meridian*)

≈ ALICE WALKER

A DAY IN APRIL, 1968

Long before downtown Atlanta was awake, she was there beside the church, her back against the stone. Like the poor around her, with their meager fires in braziers against the April chill, she had brought fried chicken wrapped in foil and now ate it slowly as she waited for the sun. The nearby families told their children stories about the old days before black people marched, before black people voted, before they could allow their anger or even their exhaustion to show. There were stories, too, of Southern hunts for coons and 'possums among the red Georgia hills, and myths of strong women and men, Indian and black, who knew the secret places of the land and refused to be pried from them. As always they were dressed in their very Sunday best, and were resigned; on their arms the black bands of crepe might have been made of iron.

They were there when the crowd began to swell, early in the morning. Making room, giving up their spots around the entrance to the church, yet still pressing somehow forward, with their tired necks extended, to see, just for a moment, just for a glimpse, the filled coffin.

They were there when the limousines began to arrive, and there when the family, wounded, crept up the steps, and there when the senators running for President flashed by, and there when the horde of clergy in their outdone rage stomped by, and there when the movie stars glided, as if slowly blown, into the church, and there when all these pretended not to see the pitiable crowd of nobodies who hungered to be nearer, who stood outside throughout the funeral service (piped out to them like scratchy Muzak) and shuffled their feet in their too tight shoes, and cleared their throats repeatedly against their tears and all the same helplessly cried.

Later, following the casket on its mule-drawn cart, they began to sing a song the dead man had loved. "I come to the gar-den *a-lone*. . . . While the dew is still on the *ro-ses* . . . ." Such an old favorite! And neutral. The dignitaries who had not already slipped away—and now cursed the four-mile walk behind the great dead man—opened their mouths eagerly in genial mime. Ahead of Meridian a man paraded a small white poodle on a leash. The man was black, and a smiler. As he looked about him a tooth encased in patterned gold sparkled in his mouth. On the dog's back a purple placard with white lettering proclaimed "I have a dream."

Then she noticed it: As they walked, people began to engage each other in loud, even ringing, conversation. They inquired about each other's jobs. They asked after members of each other's families. They conversed about the weather. And everywhere the call for Coca-Colas, for food, rang out. Popcorn appeared, and along their route hot-dog stands sprouted their broad, multicolored umbrellas. The sun came from behind the clouds, and the mourners removed their coats and loosened girdles and ties. Those who had never known it anyway dropped the favorite song, and there was a feeling of relief in the air, of liberation, that was repulsive.

Meridian turned, in shame, as if to the dead man himself.

"It's a black characteristic, man," a skinny black boy tapping on an imaginary drum was saying. "We don't go on over death the way whiteys do." He was speaking to a white couple who hung on guiltily to every word.

Behind her a black woman was laughing, laughing, as if all her cares, at last, had flown away.

Requiem for Willie Lee

👀 FRENCHY HODGES

I teach you know, and it was summer, one of the few times we get to be like children again. Summers we pack up and go somewhere that only rich folk year-round can afford. And if we can only afford a day and a night, we take what we can get and do not count the loss. For twenty-four hours we groove fine on the dollar we have to spend, and in my purse with the credit cards was exactly eighteen dollars: a ten, a five, and three ones.

El Habre is a rustic resort area halfway between Los An and Sanfran. Not a swanky place, but fronting two miles of the most beautiful oceanic view, the jungle-beach is splattered with endless numbers of summer-camp type cabins whitewashed and dingy gray measuring about nine by nine and most of them claiming five sleeping places. Crowded with beds, they can only be used for sleeping. Such is El Habre.

But El Habre has one thing more. El Habre has one of the most popular clubhouses in the world and people who have no intention of ever seeing the cabins—some never even knowing they exist—come to enjoy the fun, the food, and the fine show of stars. So, one lazy summer afternoon near the end of my vacation, Gaile (my hostess) and I and her little girl Donaile set out in my trusty old Mercedes for remote El Habre.

Now we, like many people, didn't know of the need for reservations and we experienced a foreboding of the wait to come when we saw the acres and acres of cars in the Temporary Guests' parking lot. We parked and were ushered by red-coated attendants through a multi-turnstile entrance to a waiting room as we cracked private jokes about the three of us and the only occasional dark faces in evidence among the sea of white. The waiting room was a comfortable no-nonsense place with white straight-backed chairs placed everywhere. There were perhaps a hundred people or more. Only three others were black, an older couple looking for all the world like contented grandparents, which in fact they were, as we

194

learned from the restless little boy of about four who was with them. To my right were two hippie couples making jokes and telling stories about places they'd been and things they'd done. Most of the people were encouraging them to keep up this light show by laughing animatedly at every joke and story punch line. I was sorta enjoying them myself, exchanging "ain't-they-sick" glances with Gaile as we kept a wary eye on Donaile across the room playing with the little grandboy.

Somewhere in the middle of all this, the door burst open and in came Willie Lee, tall, lean, reed-slender, country-sun-and-rain-black, and out of place. In his right hand was a little girl's. With his left he closed the door. He then thrust this hand to some hidden place in the bosom of his black denim jacket and stood for a moment deliberately surveying the room. Though he had a pleasant mischievous schoolboy face, he seemed to be about twenty-two or three. Right away I knew him. Well, not *him,* but from some wellspring of intuition I knew into him and sensed some sinister intent enter that room in the winsome grin and bold arresting gaze that played around the room.

Silence played musical chairs around the group and the hippies were *it,* ending a story that was just begun. All eyes were on the man and the child at the door.

He swaggered Saturday-night-hip-style to a seat across the room from Gaile and me, sat, and the little girl leaned between his knees looking smug and in-the-know about something she knew and we did not. Willie Lee his name was, he said, but somewhere later I heard the child call him Bubba.

Oh, Willie Lee, where did you come from and why are you here where you don't belong with that do-rag on your head, and those well-worn used-to-be-bright-tan riding boots on your feet, and that faded blue sweat shirt and those well-worn familiar-looking faded dungarees? Willie Lee, why did you come here and I know it's a gun or a knife in your jacket where your left hand is and you ain't gonna spoil my last-of-summer holiday!

"What do you think?" *sotto voce,* I said to Gaile.

"Methinks the deprived has arrived," *sotto voce,* her reply.

From the time he entered, he took over.

"Don't let me stop nothing, gray boys," he said to the storytellers. "We just come to have some fun. Yeah! Spread around the goodwill!" He threw back his head and laughed.

That was when I noticed fully the little girl. She was watching him, laughing to him like she knew what was to come and was deliciously waiting, watching him for the sign. She seemed to be about nine. He stuck out his hand and carefully looked at his watch.

"Yeah!" he said, stretching out his legs from some imaginary lounge chair. "Whatcha say, Miss Schoolteacher?" He laughed, looking boldly amused at me.

Years of teaching and I knew him. Smart, a sharp mind, very intelligent and perceptive but reached by so many forces before me, yet coming sometimes and wanting something others had not given, others who didn't know how, some not knowing he needed, grown in the street and weaned on corners, in alleys, and knowing only a wild creative energy seeking something all humans need. I knew him, looked in his eyes and perceived the soul lost and wandering inside.

"I say forget it, Willie Lee. That's what I say."

A momentary look of recognition crossed his face and when he realized what we both knew, he laughed a laugh of surprise that even here some remnant of his failed past jumped out to remind him of the child he'd been, yet appreciating too, I think, that here it was he in charge, not I.

Gaile had tensed as I spoke. "Come here a minute, Baby," she called to Donaile, but the child was already on her way to her mother, and quickly positioned herself between her legs. She stood facing this newly arrived pair and stared at them. The little girl, Willie's sister he said, made a face at the smaller child who then hid her face in her mother's lap. Still, I looked at Willie Lee. Then I looked away, regretting having acknowledged his person only to have that acknowledgement flung laughingly back in my face, and I resolved to have no more to say to him but to try and figure out what his plan was and how to escape it unharmed.

Again, he must have read my mind.

"Folks," he said, "my sister and I just come to have a little fun. She's had a little dry run of what to expect, and it's coming her birthday and I told her, 'Donna,' I say, 'I'ma let you have a little piece of the action up at El Habre.' She'll be seven next week, you know, and well, it's good to learn things while you young." He laughed again.

Then he turned to a flushed-looking man sitting on his left.

"Hey, Pops, how's business on Wall Street?" That laugh again.

The poor man looked for help around the room and finding none in the carefully averted eyes, finally perceived Willie Lee waiting soberly for his answer.

"Nnnnn-not in the ssss-stockmarket," he said, to which Willie Lee guffawed.

I found myself looking intently at that laughing face, trying to figure out what to do and how to do it. I reviewed the entrance from the parking lot. We'd come through a turnstile such as large amusement parks have and we'd been ushered to this side room to wait for reservations. Now where were those uniformed ushers who'd directed us here? One had come and called out a party of five about forty minutes ago. I decided to give up my waiting position and be content to read about this fiasco in tomorrow's paper.

So deciding, I stood up resolutely, took Donaile's hand and said to Gaile, "Let's go," and started for the door. The whole room stumbled from its trance to begin the same pilgrimage.

Coldly, "Stop where you are, *everybody!*" he said, arresting us, and we turned to look at him standing and calmly holding a gun.

Defeated, I dropped the child's hand and stood there watching the others return to their original seats.

You will not hurt me, Willie Lee. I stood still, looking at him.

"Slim, you and the sister can go if you want to," he said looking levelly at me. Dreamlike I saw a little lost boy sitting in my class, wanting something—love maybe—but too lost, misguided and misbegotten and too far along on a course impossible to change and too late if we but knew how.

"Thank you," I said, and Gaile and I went out the door, each of us holding one of Donaile's hands.

Something was wrong at the turnstiles, and the sky had turned cloudy and dark. Instead of the neatly dressed ushers we'd seen coming in, there were two do-rags-under-dingy-brim-hatted fellows wearing old blue denims and black denim jackets calmly smoking in the graying day.

When they saw us, I felt the quick tension as cigarettes were halted in midair.

"Where y'all going, Sistuhs?" the short pudgy one said.

"We got tired of waitin' and *he* said we could go," I answered, standing still and looking at them intently.

They looked at each other a moment.

197

Then, "I think y'all better wait a while longer," the tall droopy-eyed one said.

Some sixth sense told me we'd be safer inside, and then I saw the bulge of the gun at the pudgy one's side sticking from the waist of his pants.

"You're probably right," I said, and with studied casualness, we turned and went back to the room we'd just left.

Things had started to happen inside. Willie Lee was brandishing the little black and sinister gun as he methodically went to each person collecting any valuables people were wearing and money from pockets and bags.

"Get your money out, Slim," he said to me as we came back inside.

Distinctly, I remember returning to my seat, locating my billfold, extracting eight dollars—the five and three ones, thinking I'd not give any more than I *had* to and holding the three ones in my hand and stashing the five in my skirt pocket.

He was snatching watches from wrists and rings from fingers and making people empty their pockets and purses to him and putting these things in a dingy little laundry bag with a drawstring. People seemed dazed in their cooperation while the little girl, Donna, carted booty from all over the room in wild and joyful glee. The room was hot and deathly quiet. Then her hand was in my skirt pocket and she was gone to him and his bag with my three singles and the five.

Gaile was just sitting there and Donaile was leaning quietly between her legs. And I was thinking. Where is everybody? What have they done to them? We'd heard nothing before *he* came. Then I heard something. I heard the sirens and my mouth dropped open. Oh, no! Don't come now. I sat wishing they had not come just then with Willie's job unfinished and the child in the throes of her wild pre-birthday glee!

Then he was standing in front of me.

"I'm sorry, Slim, but you see how it is!" he said with amused resolution.

He grabbed the not-on-Wall-Street man, pushed him roughly toward the door.

"Okay, everybody out," he said.

Things got confusing then. Outside we vaguely heard shouts

and what I guess was gunfire, and not the holiday fireworks it sounded like. We all went rushing to the door. The door got jammed, then was not. More shots were heard and screams and cries. Outside, amid rushing legs, a turnstile smoker lay groaning and bleeding on the ground. The child Donna ran screaming to where he groaned and lay. Holding tight to Donaile's hand, Gaile and I ran toward the turnstile amid wild and crowded confusion. Then someone was holding me.

"Let me go!"

"Bitch, come with me!" a mean voice said. "You too, Bitch, and bring the kid!" This to Gaile.

We were shoved and pushed into the rear seat of a Scaporelli's Flower Delivery station wagon. Crowded next to us were the two hippie girls clinging to each other and crying. The back doors were slammed, and Willie Lee hustled the pleading Wall Street man in the front seat, jumping in behind him. And Droopy-Eye of the turnstile jumped in the driver's seat, and started the car. Donaile was crying and clinging to Gaile. The course we took was bizarre and rash because people were running everywhere. And still more people were running from the gilded entrance of the El Habre Clubhouse to scatter confusedly along the course we sped. Too many people scattered along this fenced-in service drive where running people and a racing car should never be. He tried to dodge them at first, blowing his horn, but they would not hear and heed, so soon he was knocking them down, murdering his way toward a desperate freedom. The blond hippie girl began to heave and throw up on her friend. I closed my eyes begging the nightmare end. And then I smelled the flowers. Looking back, I saw them silently sitting there.

I looked at the back of Willie Lee's head, where he, hunched forward, gun in hand, tensely peered ahead.

"Willie Lee, it just won't work." I kept my eyes on the back of his head.

"Shut up, Bitch," Droopy-Eye said.

Willie Lee looked back to me.

"Man, that's Miss Schoolteacher. She knows *everything*," he exaggerated. "Slim, it'll work 'cause *you* part of our exit ticket now, since Ol' Sam here brought y'all in."

"Willie Lee, give it up," I said.

"Man, let's dump the dizzy bitch! I was just grabbing anybody," he excused himself. Then as an afterthought, "I never did like schoolteachers no way."

Then up ahead they saw the gate.

"Hey, Sam, crash that gate. No time to stop," Willie said, peering behind.

"Man, ain't no cops gonna run down no people. You got time to open that gate!" This from a man who'd run people down.

Willie Lee peered again through the flowers at the road behind.

"Willie Lee, the road will end when you reach the gate. It's a dirt road then where you have to go slow, unless," I added, "you're ready to die and meet your maker."

"Damn, this bitch think she know everything!" Droopy-Eye said while Willie Lee just looked at me.

Donaile was crying still. Gaile was too. Wall Street was now quietly sitting there, just sitting and staring straight ahead. The hippie girls were crying.

I turned around and looked behind. The running people had receded in the distance, framed in stage-like perspective by the big El Habre Clubhouse where we'd been going to enjoy an afternoon show. And tomorrow my vacation would end, if my life didn't end today.

Droopy-Eye stopped the car and Willie Lee got out and opened the gate. Now began dust and sand as the station wagon plowed too fast down the gravelly, dusty road. Down before us, we could see the ocean's white-capped waves. And between us and the ocean was the circular courtyard flanked by four or five small buildings and one other building larger than the rest.

"The road will end at those buildings," I said. "What you gonna do then, Willie Lee?"

"I'ma chunk yo' ass in the ocean, Bitch, if you don't shut up."

I kept looking levelly at Willie Lee. He kept hunched forward looking down the slowly ending road. We reached the courtyard entrance, a latticed, ivy-covered archway, and Droopy drove the station wagon through.

"Oh, shit, the road do end!" Droopy moaned as he stopped the car.

When the motor was cut, we heard the ocean's waves, and back in the distance, the people running and screaming behind. Why are they coming this way, I wondered, remembering the time we kids ran home to our burning house. They must be cabin dwellers, I thought.

"What now, Willie Lee?" I said.

Willie and Droopy jumped out of the car.

"Okay, everybody out!" Willie directed.

When Wall Street, the last, had finally climbed out, Willie shouted, "Okay, Slim, y'all take off. Sam, you take Wall Street, and the two girls come with me." And they began to hustle the three toward the bigger building with the cafeteria sign.

Thank you, Willie Lee, for letting me free. Gaile and Donaile ran toward the woods where the cabins were and where beyond was the busy sea. As I ran behind them, I looked back to see Sam and Willie crashing in the cafeteria door, dragging and pushing the man and the girls inside, just as a Wonder Bread truck began to enter the courtyard from behind. It was filled with guns-ready police. I screamed to Gaile to wait for me.

When we'd reached the bottom of the hill, we heard shouting and gunfire. We ran on cutting right to a service path that led through the green woods lush with undergrowth. About every fifty feet on either side of the path were the cabins, whitewashed, dank and gray. Running and running, stopping some to breathe and rest and to try and soothe the terrified child. *You shouldn't have come here, Willie Lee, bringing your sister to see you fail.* Soon we heard others coming, loud and excited in the tragedy of this day.

Why couldn't you stop, Willie Lee, when it started going wrong and kept on going that way? You're not a fool, because I know you from each year you've been in my classes, and when I've tried to teach you, reach you, touch you, love you, you've snarled "Take your hands off me" and I've kept myself to myself and tried my best to forget every one of you and this afternoon at El Habre was part of my plan to get as far away from you as I can and here you are set on tearing up my turf. Will I never get away from you?

Once while I stopped resting, some people passed.

"They killed the one with the droopy-eyes," they said, "but the other was only wounded and got away."

"He's coming this way, they say."

Then another: "I got my gun in the cabin. When I git it, I'ma help hunt'im and I hope I get to blow'im away."

"They say he's looking for his girlfriend, a teacher or somebody that got away."

Willie Lee, why are you looking for me? Why don't you give yourself up and die? Will I never get away from you?

"Gaile, I've got to go find him," I said. "You take Donaile and try to get away."

I didn't stay for her protest but started walking resolutely back over the path we'd come. The day was dark and the woods were dark and the clouds were dark in the sky. I met and passed people who looked curiously at me. He is looking for me, I thought, and maybe they wondered, thought they knew. I had visions of him knocking people down, shooting anyone trying to stop him, keep him from having his way. Still, why *was* he looking for me? And then I knew. For the same reason I was now looking for him. He was my student who'd failed and I was the teacher who'd failed him. Not for hostage, not for harm, but to die! To die near me who knew him. Well, not *him,* but knew into him just the same. He, who's going to die. Is dying. And now he knows. And I'm the only person who knows him and can love the little boy hurting inside.

His jacket was gone and so was his do-rag and blood was caked in his straightened unkempt hair. His eyes unseeing, he peered ahead and stumbled dying past me.

"Willie Lee," I called his name.

He stopped and in slow motion, semi-crouched, gun half-raised, he turned, peering at me through time. In the green-gray light, I opened wide my arms and silently bade him come. He dropped his gun and came paining into my arms.

It was another world then. People continued to run by bumping us as they did. Glancing about, I saw a cabin nearby.

"Let's go in here," I said.

"Yeah, this what I want," he said. "Someplace to stop."

I looked inside and saw the cabin was bare except for the beds. I climbed through the door and helped him in, leading him to the one double bed. Two singles above and one single below on the side.

"What is this place?" he asked in wonder as our eyes grew accustomed to the darker inside. Drab even in this darkened day.

"This is one of the resort cabins," I said. "Part of El Habre too."

"What do they *do* here?" he asked.

"Sun and swim and sleep," I said. "Hear the ocean on the beach below?"

"And for this, shit, people *pay?*" He gestured around the room in unbelieving wonder.

"Yes," I said, "for this, *Shit,*" I looked to him and was held by his waiting eyes, "people pay. For the sun and the earth and the good growing things and the moon, and the dawn and the dew, people take their hard-earned bread and come here and stay and pay. *They pay!*"

Until then, I had been calm. *Steady, Teach, or you'll lose again.* I softer added, *"We pay. We all pay."*

He was quiet then and dropped his head. He looked at his hands and then at his feet. Then he looked at me.

Soberly, "Well, I spoiled it for them today, didn't I? I spoiled it today real bad," he chuckled, "didn't I?" Then he threw back his head and laughed and laughed.

And I threw back my head and just laughed and laughed hugging him.

"Yes, you did!" I said. "Yes, you really did!"

Perhaps our laughter called the people. And there they were outside the cabin windows peering and laughing in. I went to the windows then and gently pulled the shades and as best I could, I comforted the dying man, making a requiem for him, for myself, and for all the world's people who only know life through death.

Widow Woman

ᑫ LANGSTON HUGHES

Oh, that last long ride is a
Ride everybody must take.
Yes, that last long ride's a
Ride everybody must take.
And that final stop is a
Stop everybody must make.

When they put you in the ground and
They throw dirt in your face,
I say put you in the ground and
Throw dirt in your face,
That's one time, pretty papa,
You'll sure stay in your place.

You was a mighty lover and you
Ruled me many years.
A mighty lover, baby, cause you
Ruled me many years—
If I live to be a thousand
I'll never dry these tears.

I don't want nobody else and
Don't nobody else want me.
I say don't want nobody else
And don't nobody else want me—

Yet you never can tell when a
Woman like me is free!

As Befits a Man

&. LANGSTON HUGHES

I don't mind dying—
But I'd hate to die all alone!
I want a dozen pretty women
To holler, cry, and moan.

I don't mind dying
But I want my funeral to be fine:
A row of long tall mamas
Fainting, fanning, and crying.

I want a fish-tail hearse
And sixteen fish-tail cars,
A big brass band
And a whole truck load of flowers.

When they let me down,
Down into the clay,
I want the women to holler:
Please don't take him away!
    Ow-ooo-oo-o!
Don't take daddy away!

Second Line/Cutting the Body Loose
VAL FERDINAND a.k.a. KALAMU YA SALAAM

Me, Ike and Pat with Bertha just behind us silently walked on down the street moving real slowly with the band. The cornet was held high in the air and had a piece of purple (faded purple or maybe even sunbleached royal blue) ribbon tied beneath the second valve. They were playing hard with their jaws puffed out and we walked beside them. I was trying to catch who was playing what notes but I could only hear the melodies comingling, fusing and becoming indistinguishable one from another. The band marched solemnly slow.

We stepped slowly and the saxophone began sounding like Albert Ayler in his meditative moments, low and deep, full of shaking vibrato and immense feeling. The keening saxophone was a mournful sound. The player was old but the sound was surprisingly strong, especially coming out of a tarnished silver tenor that had keys held together with red rubber bands and body-heated air blown through its curves, the breath of a fifty-nine-year-old "negro" man, his fingers working in concert with his breathing to produce this sound. He eyed me over his glasses, white and black marching cap slightly tilted, keeping the sun out of his eyes.

We were turtle-marching our way out to wide Orleans Avenue and going past the city's old auditorium and an empty lot where reverend somebody-or-the-other was in town holding revival services at night in what looked like an old circus tent. The tent's sides were rolled up and a few tobacco-colored folding chairs lay stacked against the white-painted center pole.

We could see Jerome up ahead, his body dipping on the beats as the old men played their dirge. I was watching Jerome march, his long body immersed in the flood of bloods dancing to some cemetery. Jerome had danced with death prancing at his side innumerable times before during the freedom rides and sit-ins when he was with CORE—his raggity head jerking, trying to relax beneath the cruel crack of the nightstick, visibly flinching to bear the pain.

Now he was bent at the waist, mostly his chest was moving, and he was doing a step that was probably as close to shuffling as he had ever come in his life. Later, after it was over, beads of sweat would surface, popping out from the dark of his unshaded head.

"Where ya at?"

"Hey man-an."

"How you feel?"

"Feels good. Good. Feel damn good."

And then our paths which had just crossed would have uncrossed and I would wonder just how good he was really feeling, would wonder if he had discontinued using the medication he had to take to ease the Mississippi hurt that still stung his body long, long after every hamburger stand was integrated, or "desegregated," as he would probably say. You could tell it was Jerome up there rocking back, lurching forward and weaving in and out. Even though you couldn't see his face, you could tell it was Jerome just from the way his head looked (that is, you could tell him if you knew him 'cause you would never forget the way his head looked, it looked like that). Anyway, Jerome was up front marching. Jerome marched like how they march in church, dignified as they wanted to be and yet still at the same time, very, very down. The procession rounded corners slowly, at a gentle tilt, like a waiter with a heavy tray full of food weaving expertly through a crowded dining room.

"They gon cut the body loose!"

One short brother with a big mustache was running up and down the second liners explaining that they wasn't going to have to go all the way to the cemetery on account of they was going to cut the body loose. This meant that the hearse would keep on going and the band and the second liners and the rest of the procession was going to dance on back to some bar not too far away.

"They gon cut the body loose yall."

The marshal, out in front of the hearse, was draped in a blue-black suit that was a little too big and too long but which was all the better to dance with. He wore yellow socks and brown shoes as a crazy combination of his own. After the body was cut loose, the steps he invented, with his hat flipped jauntily over his forearm, were amazing contortions of knees, shins and flying feet. He executed those moves with the straightest, bored, nonchalant, don't-give-a-damn look I have ever seen on anybody's face what was doing as much work as he was doing under this merciless hot sun.

He had somebody by him fanning and wiping his face after every series of grief-inspired movements. He looked so sad to be dancing so hard and making so many others of us smile as we watched him and tried to imitate some of his easier and more obvious moves but couldn't. He was the coolest person in that street marching toward a bar two or three blocks away under a two-thirty p.m. New Orleans summer sun. The coolest.

So we stood in a line and the second liners were shouting, "Open it up, open it up," meaning for the people in front to get out the way so the hearse could pass with the body. After the hearse was gone, we turned the corner and danced down to a bar where two of the younger trumpeters engaged in a short duel at the bar house door. The older of the two won 'cause he not only had the chops to blow high and strong but he had the fingers and the knowledge that let you know he knew what he was doing when he began whipping out those wild runs. You can't really describe it all especially when we were marching and it seemed that all the horns were going for themselves but were really together. And free, wide open, shouting. Nowhere else in this country were people dancing in the streets after someone had died. Nowhere else was the warm smell of cold beer on tap a fitting conclusion for the funeral of a friend. Nowhere else was death so pointedly belittled. One of us dying was only a small matter, an occasion for the rest of us to make music and dance. Nothing could keep us contained. With this spirit and this music in us, black people would never die, never die, never.

Like a sudden urge to regurgitate and with the intensity of an ejaculation, an explosive sound erupted from the crowd. People spontaneously answered the traditional call of the second line trumpet.

"Are you still alive!"

"YEAH!"

"Do we like to live!"

"YEAH!"

"Do you want to dance?"

"YEAH!"

"Well damn it, let's go!"

And the trumpet broke into a famous chorus that was maybe a hundred years old.

"Ta-dant Dant Dant

Dant Dant Dant
Ta-dant Dant Dant, Dant
Dant, daDant"

An old bass drummer with a black coat hanger in one hand and a damp drum mallet in the other, his biceps knotted up beneath a sweat-drenched, white Arrow dress shirt, was beating the cadence of his ancestors. A beat. A sound that set us jumping like beads of perspiration leaping from the grey head of an elderly cook onto the top of a greasy, hot, cast-iron hotel stove.

"BaBOOM, BaBOOM
BabubuBOOM
BaBOOM BaBOOM

BabubuBOOM" the drummer was saying, the drum skin vibrating real tough, the band's name painted on the head a blur of motion.

The trumpeter was taunting us now and the older people were jumping from their front porches as we passed them, and they were answering that blaring hot high taunt with unmistakable fires blazing in their sixty-year-old black eyes. They too danced as we passed them. They did the dances of their lives, the dances they used to celebrate how old they had become and what they had seen getting to their whatever number years. The dances they used to defy death. The hip shakings, whose function was to lure men, demonstrate their loving abilities and make babies. A sixty-year-old woman shook her hips and clapped her hands high over her head as our noisemaking passed her porch. She was up on her feet; a small child, perhaps her granddaughter whom she was caring for, was looking at her, and ma-mi, or grand ma-maw, or aunt T., or whatever she was called was on her feet dancing, nimbly dancing for maybe a whole minute or so. Not too long but nevertheless dancing strong.

We were all ecstatic. We could see the bar. We knew it was ending, we knew we were almost there and defiantly we danced harder anyway. We hollered back even that much louder at the trumpeter as he squeezed out the last brassy blasts his lungs could throw forth. The end of the funeral was near, just as the end of life was near for some of us but it did not matter. When we get there, we'll get there. Meanwhile, the drums were talking and we were listening to the old code, the bamboula beat,

"BaBOOM (tah) BaBOOM (tah)

BOOMBOOM BOOM
BaBOOM (tah) BaBOOM (tah)
BOOMBOOM BOOM"

We was looking good. Black people be looking good dancing in the street. One of us dropped an umbrella and lots of us went down real low like you do the duck walk but dancing and circling all around that umbrella, legs shot out straight and stiff, but steady stepping in time.

Another was prostrate, like in a push-up position, worshipping the god of earthiness. This was the alligator, the ancient Egyptian symbol for Abyssinian folk. It was a mean position, mouth inches above the earth, extremities stretched, an up and down and side-ways sway, sort of like churning butter, but this was better. His palms didn't mind the heat of the concrete. The echo of the prone brother's voice praying in this ancient way was joined by shouted approval. The alligator was a mighty dance, thank you Lord.

I looked up at another brother who was on top of a broke car that was sitting on the side of the street, and he was doing something that might be what the original funky butt was like. I saw another brother, at least three feet above the tallest head, what looked like he was dancing in mid-air till I saw his right foot was on a telephone pole stake, and he had a black umbrella in his left hand, a gold tooth in his mouth, a red bandana with white polka dots around his neck, green work clothes on and two fingers of his right hand, only two fingers, wrapped around a stake above his head. He shook what for and screamed like he had discovered flight. I spied another brother, his shirt off, stomach muscles tight from daily lifting soggy shovels full of dirt under the drooping supervisory eye of some white civil servant well past his physical prime who was "boss man" on this team for the city sewage and water board department. The tight stomached brother had on clean pressed khaki pants and semi-soft brown suede loafers. He was bent forward engrossed with shaking his butt up to the skies. Jehovah, can you understand this?

Where did we get all of this from, the marching and dancing and singing and togetherness, and those beats and ringing melo-dies? Africa, can you hear us, do you know us, do you know our second line? Africa can you feel us, our palms clapping time to-gether, our feet slapping the asphalt and our throats pouring forth our vibrant cheers? Africa. Can you feel us? We can feel you, ancient and subconsciously, but intimately there. We jump with your spirits in us.

Our crowd didn't care what each other smelled like. We were all here for the same purpose. Whether it was wine or listerine on your breath didn't matter as long as you were breathing, as long as you were shouting out. And it didn't really matter if you used the latest deodorant when you raised your arms to dance and wave umbrellas in the sun. And who cared what was on your feet as long as you kicked them high in the air and allowed yourself to rise and fall with that beat.

I looked at some of the white people who were there walking away after the band had gone inside, looked at them walking up the street away from all of that Blackness, walking in the sun and looking so out of place, looking at best curious, at worst like vultures, always outside this action even when they were in the middle of the happenings. I looked at the tourists who had stumbled on something "super," and the bearded one over there who writes about all of this with a knowledge he claims (in private to his awed friends and amazed editor) to be based on authentic personal field work and specially cultivated friendship with a number of the Black revelers. I looked at them going home to wait for another nigger to die, or be killed, so they could come again and I wasn't even mad. I wasn't mad, not even about the cameras and tape recorders carried by Ph.D.s-to-be, machines strapped to their bodies. It was just a lot better to be there as a necessary processional participant instead of being a voyeur or a dilettante looking for another experience to trophy in conversation with envious friends.

Ike danced his ass off and Kush, who never usually missed a second line, got there late. Kush asked who had died and we told him we didn't know. We really didn't know, even though we had seen a small, gold-framed picture being held out of the front window of the hearse by some relative as it passed by us. We didn't even know what instrument the brother had played.

But we knew it was important to be there. I should say we felt it was important to be there because there is so much we don't really know. We don't really know or understand how all of this hooks up, its meaning. But we feel its importance and smile at it and go with it 'cause it's good. Dancing is good. Music is good. Shaking in the sun is good. Shouting and second lining together is good. So we go with it and are never disappointed by being together like this.

The trumpeter was doing his crazy runs again and people were courteously pushing to get into the bar, but they were letting the marshal, the distant relatives and the band go in first. The two trumpeters were the last of the band to go in. At the doorway they turned to blow their parting shots at us. And a duel began.

People hollered out after the notes of whichever trumpeter they favored had gone ringing out, riding high over the telephone wires. I was laughing 'cause the older brother was winning. His last run had almost nearly followed the twisting quick kind of flight of a mocking bird catching mosquito hawks at dawn except say that bird would have had to been as big as an ostrich or something to match how huge a sound the brother had. The loser ducked his head and started turning toward the barroom door behind him.

The peak of the older man's top lip was pink from the pressure of playing trumpet umpteen-many years at different funerals and dances and lawn parties and hotels. He had been playing that horn a long, long time. I saw him smile as he had just bested young brotherman who looked like he was only nineteen or twenty.

"Can you beat that?" his eyes said. His weathered face broke out smiling. He had just played some kind of horn. Everybody felt like laughing with him remembering the clarion calls he had put down. We laughed. We all felt good. Some of us hummed. "Can you beat that, Ha-ha. Not today you can't, youngblood. But maybe another day you will, but not today. I'm old but I got what you got to get old to get. Can you beat that? Not today. Ha-ha. Yeah." Love was in his eyes, musta been love, his arm was around the young brother's shoulders and they was grinning in each other's face, lips wide, noses inches apart, hats way back on their heads, two horns held down by their thighs as they stepped cross the bar threshold together. Can't beat that.

The funeral ended with us smiling and laughing at each other in the street.

Cotton Alley

❧ PEARL CRAYTON

Cotton Alley ain't the right kind of name for a stretch where folk live. A person hates to tell anybody his address is on a street with that name, it just sounds too common. Most folk who hear the word "alley" think of something cheap and nobody wants folk to think he lives in a cheap place, even if he does. A person's got to have some pride somewhere about him, but it's hard to have any living in a place called Cotton Alley.

That's the way we are, all of us who lived on Cotton Alley—a bunch of black folk living in a quarter of dingy little shot-gun houses far enough away from the better part of town, some trying hard to have a little pride and too many not trying at all. Mister Sam was one of those who didn't try, and when he did take a notion to, he paid a big price for it.

Cotton Alley, and what we who lived there were to the rest of the world, and one policeman, got all tangled up together one Saturday evening and did something bad to Mister Sam—hurt him real bad—but he's out of it now. It hurt me too, and it's still hurting me.

Things are better for my people now; we're free to go anywhere we want to go and do any kind of work we're smart enough to do; so it's best to forget about all the troubles we've been through and work together to do something for our country like President Kennedy said we should do. Anybody with a dime's worth of sense can see that this is the best thing to do; ain't nobody got any business going around crying about something that happened twenty-nine years ago, yet every now and then that old nightmare memory from those days before the War rise up in my mind and I cry. There just ain't no sense in me troubling my mind about what happened to Mister Sam; I want to forget! Lord knows, I've tried to forget, but I can't!

Mister Sam wasn't any kin to me and I didn't care a cent about him. He just wasn't the kind of man folk take a liking to. Every

213

Saturday after he got his paycheck, he'd stop by the honky-tonk and drink too much wine, then he'd come home and fight Miss Pee-wee, his common-law wife; and their little girl, Lucy Mae, would stand on their porch and cry. Sometimes when Mister Sam got the best of Miss Pee-wee, she'd run off up to Mister Mose Johnson's house and call the police. They'd come and take Mister Sam to jail and call up his boss-man, who'd tell them to turn Mister Sam aloose, and in about an hour he'd come home and eat supper. He was just another one of the bad things we had to put up with on Cotton Alley.

All the church-going folk kept away from Mister Sam on account of his drinking, and all the sporting folk kept away from him on account of he worked on the garbage truck and didn't ever smell right. Besides that, he couldn't read or write, and some folk claimed he had fits. There could have been plenty of folk living on Cotton Alley who liked Mister Sam but didn't any of them ever show it while I was around. I didn't make pretend I liked him either; I got a bigger kick out of poking fun at how bad he smelled. Then one Saturday evening came when he stood up in the yard behind the house where he lived, swinging an old half-rotten plank at two policemen, panting and hollering, "Ah ain't gonna let y'all hit me on mah head wit dat black-jack again, white folk!," and his bad smell didn't seem funny to me anymore. Mister Sam looked too much all by himself standing there with nothing but that policeman's trigger-finger between him and death. But the funny thing was that he didn't look any different to me than he had looked every day that I'd seen him. He'd always been that much all by himself, I just hadn't paid any attention to it until that evening.

Blood was running from a cut on the side of Mister Sam's head, getting mixed up with his sweat. Every now and then he'd wipe that side of his face on his shoulder real quick, not slowing down the swing of the plank as he did so. That was too hot a day for anybody to be getting all worked up like he was doing. The sun was going down but it had been so hot all day that the heat of it was still in the ground and in the wood of the houses and in the old tin cans and bottles and slop-jars laying around in the back yard. All that heat brought out the smell of everything in that back yard that didn't smell good—the two old toilets that everybody on the block used but nobody cleaned; the sloppy place under the water faucet that always dripped; the old rusty zinc tubs of garbage with flies singing over them; the wet places around the back doors of the houses where the women threw their dish water. The big bunch of folk who were standing around looking at Mister Sam and the policemen made it seem hotter. There were too many of them and they were too quiet, everything was too quiet—which made what Mister Sam and the policemen said sound louder than was natural.

"Now you drop that plank, boy, now you drop that plank right now," one policeman was saying in a lazy-sounding hillbilly drawl, holding his pistol on Mister Sam with one hand and holding out the other hand like he was looking for Mister Sam to stop swinging the plank and give it to him. He'd said those same words more times than he had fingers and toes, and Mister Sam was still swinging the plank at him.

"Aw, Mike, you're playing with that nigger," the other police-man who had come in the black car said. "Come on, let's take that plank from this nigger and take him in, it's getting close to supper time, I'm hungry!" He was standing off to the side with both hands on his hips, looking real sassy, his face all frowned up like he'd been smelling that back yard too long.

Lucy Mae was standing on their back steps crying and calling, "Daddy . . . daddy . . . daddy . . . daddy . . . ," calling Mister Sam like she had something to tell him, but he didn't pay any attention to her.

"What happened?" somebody who came up behind me asked in a whisper.

"Sam did some sassy talking to them laws 'n one of 'em hit 'im over th' head 'n he runned back here 'n started acting a fool," someone whispered back.

I wanted to say, "That ain't the way it happened," but when I turned my head and saw that it was Miss Viney who'd done the answering I knew better than dispute her word. Miss Viney was the best shouter at our church, a loudly professed "soldier in the army of the Lord" who went around fighting sin right and left, and she was over-average good at bringing punishment upon children who sassed grown folk. I held back what I wanted to say, but holding it made me feel bad inside. Now when I remember how it was, I wish that I had turned around and said to Miss Viney, "I saw the whole thing. I was standing by Mister Sam's porch when those policemen came to arrest him and I heard every word they said. That police-man standing over there with his hands on his hips called Mister

215

Sam a nigger and Mister Sam told him, 'Don' call me no nigger, Cap'n, 'cause Ah ain't no nigger, I'se a 'Merican man jes' like you is.' That's all he said and that little old sassy-looking policeman hit him over the head with his black-jack." Looking back, I don't see how I could have been so scared of a whipping that I wouldn't speak up for Mister Sam.

"Now you listen to me, boy, I'm getting tired of fooling around with you," the policeman called Mike said in a voice that was too lazy to sound mean. He didn't act like he was in a great big hurry to take Mister Sam to jail—maybe because he knew it wouldn't do any good. He had come and arrested Mister Sam plenty of times before and he'd always had to come back and do it again in a couple of weeks. "Boy, don't you know that old plank you have there ain't no match for this here pistol? Besides, there's two of us, you can't whip us both by yourself, don't you know that? Now you stop this foolishness and put that plank down." He was trying to talk some sense into Mister Sam's head and maybe wait until his arms got tired from swinging that plank.

"Ef Ah throw 'way mah pretecksun y'all gonna beat me up wit dem black-jacks, Cap'n," Mister Sam said, panting like a tired dog but still swinging the plank. "Ef y'all promise me ya'll ain't gonna beat me up wit dem black-jacks, Ah'll put dis plank down." It seemed like Mister Sam wanted to put the plank down but he had went and made a big show of standing up for himself in front of all of us, so he didn't want to give in without getting the policemen to give in a little too. He must have had a notion to try to pretend he had some pride.

The policeman called Mike didn't answer right off, like he was making up his mind about what kind of answer to give Mister Sam. Right away I crossed my fingers and closed my eyes and started to wish real hard that he'd promise like Mister Sam asked, because Mister Sam was trying to have a little pride for the first time in his life and he should let him have his pride. He was ugly and black and he didn't have much sense but *he was an American* and an American had a right to have some pride. But before I got the wish straight in my mind, that little old sassy looking policeman was hollering, "Aw no, Mike! No promises! We can't make any promises at all! No!"

I opened my eyes and saw him waving his hands and shaking his head like he was trying to head off somebody from walking into

216

a wasp nest. I took a quick look at the other policeman's face and at Mister Sam's face and they both looked let-down. They had their eyes on that little sassy looking policeman. Didn't either of them seem to know what to do next; it seemed to me they were looking for him to tell them and that put him in charge.

A cold and ugly Something move up behind me. I'd been around it enough before to know that it was just old Scared creeping up on me. I wanted to walk off so I wouldn't see what I was scared I was going to see but I stood there and watched Mister Sam pay the full price for his pride.

A Feeling inside of me held me there, an ugly Feeling that had come on me a long, long time before, way back when I first found out that there was more than one color of folk in the world and I was of the color that didn't fare so well, the color that all other colors looked down on. I had pushed this Feeling to the back of my mind because in church our preacher claimed that God loved black folk as much as He loved white folk, and in school our teacher claimed that everybody born in our country were Americans and all Americans were equal to our country's laws, so all the while I was in church or school I could keep that Feeling in the back of my mind, but every time I saw a bus driver make a person my color go sit in the back of the bus, or I had to drink water from a fountain marked for my color, or I had to sit up-the-steps in the picture show where everybody my color had to sit, or I passed by City Park and saw children other colors playing on ground I couldn't walk on and swinging in swings I couldn't touch, or I wanted to go any place folk my color weren't allowed to go or I heard somebody call a person my color "nigger," that old feeling rubbed inside of me. It was rubbing me then, hurting my belief that what my preacher and teacher said was right, hurting me all over.

"If we make a promise to this here nigger, all these other niggers standing around here are gonna go all over town bragging about how he got the best of us and, after that, every time one of us go and try to arrest a nigger he'll grab up a stick and make us promise him something! Aw, Mike, you don't know these niggers, you give them an inch and they'll take a mile! You've got to handle a nigger like he's a nigger and he'll stay in his place! Now you watch me, I'll show you how to handle a nigger!"

That little old sassy looking policeman started moving towards Mister Sam real slowly with both his hands held up as high as his

217

shoulders. "You see, I don't have anything in my hands," he said to Mister Sam. "I'm coming to take that plank away from you!" Then he looked over his shoulder and said to us standing around, "You all see, I don't have anything in my hands, now do I? Do I have anything in my hands?" He stood dead still, waiting for one of us to answer.

It was plain that he wanted one of us to agree with him so that we'd be on his side against Mister Sam. He had the rest of the world on his side, it didn't make sense for him to want us too. Us and him and his guns and all the world against Mister Sam was just too much! All my insides wanted to holler out, "Somebody ought to be on Mister Sam's side," but my throat was too choked up with being scared for the sound to come out. My eyes jumped from one face to the other of the folk standing around in the back yards, looking for somebody to say something or do something to help Mister Sam. It seemed to me that while that policeman was standing still waiting for one of us to answer him, somebody standing around there could say something to Mister Sam to get him to throw down that plank and save himself. Maybe all he needed was for one of us to say something to him, but I just didn't know who would do the saying.

My daddy was standing over by the corner of our house still dressed in the coveralls he worked in at the sawmill. It just happened that when my eyes jumped to him he was looking at me and I thought at him with all my heart and soul, *Say something to help Mister Sam, daddy,* but either he didn't get it, or he got it and didn't know what to say, or he was scared to say anything because he dropped his head and got all wrapped up in an old tin can that was laying by his foot. He kicked it and watched it roll off to the edge of the grass, then he kicked what maybe was a rock on the ground. Maybe it was just the ground he kicked. He didn't look at me anymore.

Right then, I knew that I needed to be all grown up so that I could say something to make that policeman understand that Mister Sam was an American man just like he'd told him he was and he had a right to stand up and tell folk to not call him a nigger because he was an American man! I needed to be grown up so that I could do *something* to stop the bad thing I was scared was going to happen so that I could help myself hold on to believing that Mister

218

Sam and all of us black folk *were Americans* because that was all the pride I had!

"Do I have anything in my hands?" the policeman was asking.

"No, suh, you shore don't," Miss Viney's voice came from behind me.

Everybody turned and looked at her with the kind of looks that went with cussing but didn't anybody say anything. My hands went into fists all by themselves but I knew that I couldn't let them hit her. Very slowly, I made my fingers uncurl, holding back being mad, hurting my insides holding it back.

"All right, nigger, I'm coming to take that plank from you with my bare hands," the policeman said, moving slowly towards Mister Sam again. "You can act a fool and hit me if you want to. If you're fool enough to hit a policeman you're the biggest fool in town!"

"Don' come up on me, Cap'n," Mister Sam said, backing back, so scared his eyes were bucked as big as saucers. "Don' come up on me, Ah say!"

The policeman reached out his hand real quick to grab the plank and it hit his hand. He jumped clean off the ground and hollered like he'd been shot, grabbing the hit hand with his other one and shaking them above his head. He really clowned for a while, he hollered so loud that I could hardly hear the shot from the other policeman's pistol.

Mister Sam was laying on the ground with his head in the sloppy place under the water faucet and his feet kicking up dust. Then all of a sudden he was too still. The policeman called Mike went to him and squatted beside him. He took Mister Sam's hand in his and held it for a long time, feeling on his wrist. Then he laid one of his ears on Mister Sam's chest and let it lay there for a long time, listening. He raised his hand for us to be quiet, even though nobody was saying anything—wasn't either one of us hardly breathing. He turned his head and laid his other ear on Mister Sam's chest and listened so long that I wanted to holler, "CAN'T YOU SEE HE'S DEAD!"

After a while he looked up at all of us standing around, turning his head slowly from one side to the other, looking at us all, his breath moving his chest coming out of him, his face looking like he'd come upon something he didn't want to believe and he was looking for somebody to tell him it wasn't so. Then his eyes got to

Lucy Mae and he couldn't turn them away. She was still standing on their back steps, crying and calling Mister Sam, calling his name louder and faster, "Daddy! Daddy! Daddy! Daddy!," screaming his name.

Somebody went to Lucy Mae and took her inside the house and got her quieted down, but I could still hear her crying. The sound of it was too sad for me; I ran away from that sound but it followed me. I had run a long, long ways before it came to me that the sound was coming from inside of me; it was my own crying. It's still inside of me. Everytime I pass by a street named Alley and see a bunch of folk my color living in dingy little houses not fit for poodles, I can see Mister Sam again, buying a little pride with his life, and I just can't keep from crying.

Lucielia Louise Turner
(excerpt from *The Women of Brewster Place*)

え GLORIA NAYLOR

The sunlight was still watery as Ben trudged into Brewster Place, and the street had just begun to yawn and stretch itself. He eased himself onto his garbage can, which was pushed against the sagging brick wall that turned Brewster into a dead-end street. The metallic cold of the can's lid seeped into the bottom of his thin trousers. Sucking on a piece of breakfast sausage caught in his back teeth, he began to muse. Mighty cold, these spring mornings. The old days you could build a good trash fire in one of them barrels to keep warm. Well, don't want no summons now, and can't freeze to death. Yup, can't freeze to death.

His daily soliloquy completed, he reached into his coat pocket and pulled out a crumpled brown bag that contained his morning sun. The cheap red liquid moved slowly down his throat, providing immediate justification as the blood began to warm in his body. In the hazy light a lean dark figure began to make its way slowly up the block. It hesitated in front of the stoop at 316, but looking around and seeing Ben, it hurried over.

"Yo, Ben."

"Hey, Eugene, I thought that was you. Ain't seen ya round for a coupla days."

"Yeah." The young man put his hands in his pockets, frowned into the ground, and kicked the edge of Ben's can. "The funeral's today, ya know."

"Yeah."

"You going?" He looked up into Ben's face.

"Naw, I ain't got no clothes for them things. Can't abide 'em no way—too sad—it being a baby and all."

"Yeah. I was going myself, people expect it, ya know?"

"Yeah."

"But, man, the way Ciel's friends look at me and all—like I was filth or something. Hey, I even tried to go see Ciel in the hospital, heard she was freaked out and all."

"Yeah, she took it real bad"

"Yeah, well, damn, I took it bad. It was my kid, too, ya know. But Mattie, that fat, black bitch, just standin' in the hospital hall sayin' to me—to me, now, 'Whatcha want?' Like I was a fuckin' germ or something. Man, I just turned and left. You gotta be treated with respect, ya know?"

"Yeah."

"I mean, I should be there today with my woman in the limo and all, sittin' up there, doin' it right. But how you gonna be a man with them ball-busters tellin' everybody it was my fault and I should be the one dead? Damn!"

"Yeah, a man's gotta be a man." Ben felt the need to wet his reply with another sip. "Have some?"

"Naw, I'm gonna be heading on—Ciel don't need me today. I bet that frig, Mattie, rides in the head limo, wearing the pants. Shit—let 'em." He looked up again. "Ya know?"

"Yup."

"Take it easy, Ben." He turned to go.

"You too, Eugene."

"Hey, you going?"

"Naw."

"Me neither. Later."

"Later, Eugene."

Funny, Ben thought, Eugene ain't stopped to chat like that for a long time—near on a year, yup, a good year. He took another swallow to help him bring back the year-old conversation, but it didn't work; the second and third one didn't either. But he did remember that it had been an early spring morning like this one, and Eugene had been wearing those same tight jeans. He had hesitated outside of 316 then, too. But that time he went in . . .

Lucielia had just run water into the tea kettle and was putting it on the burner when she heard the cylinder turn. He didn't have to knock on the door; his key still fit the lock. Her thin knuckles gripped the handle of the kettle, but she didn't turn around. She knew. The last eleven months of her life hung compressed in the air between the click of the lock and his "Yo, baby."

The vibrations from those words rose like parasites on the air waves and came rushing into her kitchen, smashing the compression into indistinguishable days and hours that swirled dizzily before

222

her. It was all there: the frustration of being left alone, sick, with a month-old baby; her humiliation reflected in the caseworker's blue eyes for the unanswerable "you can find him to have it, but can't find him to take care of it" smile; the raw urges that crept, uninvited, between her thighs on countless nights; the eternal whys all meshed with the explainable hate and unexplainable love. They kept circling in such a confusing pattern before her that she couldn't seem to grab even one to answer him with. So there was nothing in Lucielia's face when she turned it toward Eugene, standing in her kitchen door holding a ridiculously pink Easter bunny, nothing but sheer relief. . . .

"So he's back." Mattie sat at Lucielia's kitchen table, playing with Serena. It was rare that Mattie ever spoke more than two sentences to anybody about anything. She didn't have to. She chose her words with the grinding precision of a diamond cutter's drill.

"You think I'm a fool, don't you?"

"I ain't said that."

"You didn't have to," Ciel snapped.

"Why you mad at me, Ciel? It's your life, honey."

"Oh, Mattie, you don't understand. He's really straightened up this time. He's got a new job on the docks that pays real good, and he was just so depressed before with the new baby and no work. You'll see. He's even gone out now to buy paint and stuff to fix up the apartment. And, and Serena needs a daddy."

"You ain't gotta convince me, Ciel."

No, she wasn't talking to Mattie, she was talking to herself. She was convincing herself it was the new job and the paint and Serena that let him back into her life. Yet, the real truth went beyond her scope of understanding. When she laid her head in the hollow of his neck there was a deep musky scent to his body that brought back the ghosts of the Tennessee soil of her childhood. It reached up and lined the inside of her nostrils so that she inhaled his presence almost every minute of her life. The feel of his sooty flesh penetrated the skin of her fingers and coursed through her blood and became one, somewhere, wherever it was, with her actual being. But how do you tell yourself, let alone this practical old woman who loves you, that he was back because of that. So you don't.

223

You get up and fix you both another cup of coffee, calm the fretting baby on your lap with her pacifier, and you pray silently—very silently—behind veiled eyes that the man will stay.

Ciel was trying to remember exactly when it had started to go wrong again. Her mind sought for the slender threads of a clue that she could trace back to—perhaps—something she had said or done. Her brow was set tightly in concentration as she folded towels and smoothed the wrinkles over and over, as if the answer lay concealed in the stubborn creases of the terry cloth.

The months since Eugene's return began to tick off slowly before her, and she examined each one to pinpoint when the nagging whispers of trouble had begun in her brain. The friction on the towels increased when she came to the month that she had gotten pregnant again, but it couldn't be that. Things were different now. She wasn't sick as she had been with Serena, he was still working—no it wasn't the baby. It's not the baby, it's not the baby—the rhythm of those words sped up the motion of her hands, and she had almost yanked and folded and pressed them into a reality when, bewildered, she realized that she had run out of towels.

Ciel jumped when the front door slammed shut. She waited tensely for the metallic bang of his keys on the coffee table and the blast of the stereo. Lately that was how Eugene announced his presence home. Ciel walked into the living room with the motion of a swimmer entering a cold lake.

"Eugene, you're home early, huh?"

"You see anybody else sittin' here?" He spoke without looking at her and rose to turn up the stereo.

He wants to pick a fight, she thought, confused and hurt. He knows Serena's taking her nap, and now I'm supposed to say, Eugene, the baby's asleep, please cut the music down. Then he's going to say, you mean a man can't even relax in his own home without being picked on? I'm not picking on you, but you're going to wake up the baby. Which is always supposed to lead to: You don't give a damn about me. Everybody's more important than me—that kid, your friends, everybody. I'm just chickenshit around here, huh?

All this went through Ciel's head as she watched him leave the stereo and drop defiantly back down on the couch. Without saying a word, she turned and went into the bedroom. She looked down on the peaceful face of her daughter and softly caressed her small cheek. Her heart became full as she realized, this is the only thing I have ever loved without pain. She pulled the sheet gently over the tiny shoulders and firmly closed the door, protecting her from the music. She then went into the kitchen and began washing the rice for their dinner.

Eugene, seeing that he had been left alone, turned off the stereo and came and stood in the kitchen door.

"I lost my job today," he shot at her, as if she had been the cause.

The water was turning cloudy in the rice pot, and the force of the stream from the faucet caused scummy bubbles to rise to the surface. These broke and sprayed tiny starchy particles onto the dirty surface. Each bubble that broke seemed to increase the volume of the dogged whispers she had been ignoring for the last few months. She poured the dirty water off the rice to destroy and silence them, then watched with a malicious joy as they disappeared down the drain.

"So now, how in the hell I'm gonna make it with no money, huh? And another brat comin' here, huh?"

The second change of the water was slightly clearer, but the starch-speckled bubbles were still there, and this time there was no way to pretend deafness to their message. She had stood at that sink countless times before, washing rice, and she knew the water was never going to be totally clear. She couldn't stand there forever—her fingers were getting cold, and the rest of the dinner had to be fixed, and Serena would be waking up soon and wanting attention. Feverishly she poured the water off and tried again.

"I'm fuckin' sick of never getting ahead. Babies and bills, that's all you good for."

The bubbles were almost transparent now, but when they broke they left light trails of starch on top of the water that curled around her fingers. She knew it would be useless to try again. Defeated, Ciel placed the wet pot on the burner, and the flames leaped up bright red and orange, turning the water droplets clinging on the outside into steam.

Turning to him, she silently acquiesced. "All right, Eugene, what do you want me to do?"

He wasn't going to let her off so easily. "Hey, baby, look, I don't care what you do. I just can't have all these hassles on me right now, ya know?"

"I'll get a job. I don't mind, but I've got no one to keep Serena, and you don't want Mattie watching her."

"Mattie—no way. That fat bitch'll turn the kid against me. She hates my ass, and you know it."

"No, she doesn't, Eugene." Ciel remembered throwing that at Mattie once. "You hate him, don't you?" "Naw, honey," and she had cupped both hands on Ciel's face. "Maybe I just loves you too much."

"I don't give a damn what you say—she ain't minding my kid."

"Well, look, after the baby comes, they can tie my tubes—I don't care." She swallowed hard to keep down the lie.

"And what the hell we gonna feed it when it gets here, huh—air? With two kids and you on my back, I ain't never gonna have nothin'." He came and grabbed her by the shoulders and was shouting into her face. "Nothin', do you hear me, nothin'!"

"Nothing to it, Mrs. Turner." The face over hers was as calm and antiseptic as the room she lay in. "Please, relax. I'm going to give you a local anesthetic and then perform a simple D&C, or what you'd call a scraping to clean out the uterus. Then you'll rest here for about an hour and be on your way. There won't even be much bleeding." The voice droned on in its practiced monologue, peppered with sterile kindness.

Ciel was not listening. It was important that she keep herself completely isolated from these surroundings. All the activities of the past week of her life were balled up and jammed on the right side of her brain, as if belonging to some other woman. And when she had endured this one last thing for her, she would push it up there, too, and then one day give it all to her—Ciel wanted no part of it.

The next few days Ciel found it difficult to connect herself up again with her own world. Everything seemed to have taken on new textures and colors. When she washed the dishes, the plates felt peculiar in her hands, and she was more conscious of their smoothness and the heat of the water. There was a disturbing split second between someone talking to her and the words penetrating sufficiently to elicit a response. Her neighbors left her presence with slight frowns of puzzlement, and Eugene could be heard mumbling, "Moody bitch."

She became terribly possessive of Serena. She refused to leave her alone, even with Eugene. The little girl went everywhere with Ciel, toddling along on plump uncertain legs. When someone asked to hold or play with her, Ciel sat nearby, watching every move. She found herself walking into the bedroom several times when the child napped to see if she was still breathing. Each time she chided herself for this unreasonable foolishness, but within the next few minutes some strange force still drove her back.

Spring was slowly beginning to announce itself at Brewster Place. The arthritic cold was seeping out of the worn gray bricks, and the tenants with apartment windows facing the street were awakened by six o'clock sunlight. The music no longer blasted inside of 3C, and Ciel grew strong with the peacefulness of her household. The playful laughter of her daughter, heard more often now, brought a sort of redemption with it.

"Isn't she marvelous, Mattie? You know she's even trying to make whole sentences. Come on, baby, talk for Auntie Mattie."

Serena, totally uninterested in living up to her mother's proud claims, was trying to tear a gold-toned button off the bosom of Mattie's dress.

"It's so cute. She even knows her father's name. She says, my da da is Gene."

"Better teach her your name," Mattie said, while playing with the baby's hand. "She'll be using it more."

Ciel's mouth flew open to ask her what she meant by that, but she checked herself. It was useless to argue with Mattie. You could take her words however you wanted. The burden of their truth lay with you, not her.

Eugene came through the front door and stopped short when he saw Mattie. He avoided being around her as much as possible. She was always polite to him, but he sensed a silent condemnation behind even her most innocent words. He constantly felt the need to prove himself in front of her. These frustrations often took the form of unwarranted rudeness on his part.

Serena struggled out of Mattie's lap and went toward her father and tugged on his legs to be picked up. Ignoring the child and cutting short the greetings of the two women, he said coldly, "Ciel, I wanna talk to you."

Sensing trouble, Mattie rose to go. "Ciel, why don't you let me take Serena downstairs for a while. I got some ice cream for her."

"She can stay right here," Eugene broke in. "If she needs ice cream, I can buy it for her."

Hastening to soften his abruptness, Ciel said, "That's okay, Mattie, it's almost time for her nap. I'll bring her later—after dinner."

"All right. Now you all keep good." Her voice was warm. "You too, Eugene," she called back from the front door.

The click of the lock restored his balance to him. "Why in the hell is she always up here?"

"You just had your chance—why didn't you ask her yourself? If you don't want her here, tell her to stay out," Ciel snapped back confidently, knowing he never would.

"Look, I ain't got time to argue with you about that old hag. I got big doings in the making, and I need you to help me pack." Without waiting for a response, he hurried into the bedroom and pulled his old leather suitcase from under the bed.

A tight, icy knot formed in the center of Ciel's stomach and began to melt rapidly, watering the blood in her legs so that they almost refused to support her weight. She pulled Serena back from following Eugene and sat her in the middle of the living room floor.

"Here, honey, play with the blocks for Mommy—she has to talk to Daddy." She piled a few plastic alphabet blocks in front of the child, and on her way out of the room, she glanced around quickly and removed the glass ashtrays off the coffee table and put them on a shelf over the stereo.

Then, taking a deep breath to calm her racing heart, she started toward the bedroom.

Serena loved the light colorful cubes and would sometimes sit for an entire half-hour, repeatedly stacking them up and kicking them over with her feet. The hollow sound of their falling fascinated her, and she would often bang two of them together to re-create the magical noise. She was sitting, contentedly engaged in this particular activity, when a slow dark movement along the baseboard caught her eye.

A round black roach was making its way from behind the

couch toward the kitchen. Serena threw one of her blocks at the insect, and, feeling the vibrations of the wall above it, the roach sped around the door into the kitchen. Finding a totally new game to amuse herself, Serena took off behind the insect with a block in each hand. Seeing her moving toy trying to bury itself under the linoleum by the garbage pail she threw another block, and the frantic roach now raced along the wall and found security in the electric wall socket under the kitchen table.

Angry at losing her plaything, she banged the block against the socket, attempting to get it to come back out. When that failed, she unsuccessfully tried to poke her chubby finger into the thin horizontal slit. Frustrated, tiring of the game, she sat under the table and realized she had found an entirely new place in the house to play. The shiny chrome of the table and chair legs drew her attention, and she experimented with the sound of the block against their smooth surfaces.

This would have entertained her until Ciel came, but the roach, thinking itself safe, ventured outside of the socket. Serena gave a cry of delight and attempted to catch her lost playmate, but it was too quick and darted back into the wall. She tried once again to poke her finger into the slit. Then a bright slender object, lying dropped and forgotten, came into her view. Picking up the fork, Serena finally managed to fit the thin flattened prongs into the electric socket.

Eugene was avoiding Ciel's eyes as he packed. "You know, baby, this is really a good deal after me bein' out of work for so long." He moved around her still figure to open the drawer that held his T-shirts and shorts. "And hell, Maine ain't far. Once I get settled on the docks up there, I'll be able to come home all the time."

"Why can't you take us with you?" She followed each of his movements with her eyes and saw herself being buried in the case under the growing pile of clothes.

"'Cause I gotta check out what's happening before I drag you and the kid up there."

"I don't mind. We'll make do. I've learned to live on very little."

"No, it just won't work right now. I gotta see my way clear first."

"Eugene, please." She listened with growing horror to herself quietly begging.

"No, and that's it!" He flung his shoes into the suitcase.

229

"Well, how far is it? Where did you say you were going?" She moved toward the suitcase.

"I told ya—the docks in Newport."

"That's not in Maine. You said you were going to Maine."

"Well, I made a mistake."

"How could you know about a place so far up? Who got you the job?"

"A friend."

"Who?"

"None of your damned business!" His eyes were flashing with the anger of a caged animal. He slammed down the top of the suitcase and yanked it off the bed.

"You're lying, aren't you? You don't have a job, do you? Do you?"

"Look, Ciel, believe whatever the fuck you want to. I gotta go." He tried to push past her.

She grabbed the handle of the case. "No, you can't go."

"Why?"

Her eyes widened slowly. She realized that to answer that would require that she uncurl that week of her life, pushed safely up into her head, when she had done all those terrible things for that other woman who had wanted an abortion. She and she alone would have to take responsibility for them now. He must understand what those actions had meant to her, but somehow, he had meant even more. She sought desperately for the right words, but it all came out as—

"Because I love you."

"Well, that ain't good enough."

Ciel had let the suitcase go before he jerked it away. She looked at Eugene, and the poison of reality began to spread through her body like gangrene. It drew his scent out of her nostrils and scraped the veil from her eyes, and he stood before her just as he really was—a tall, skinny black man with arrogance and selfishness twisting his mouth into a strange shape. And, she thought, I don't feel anything now. But soon, very soon, I will start to hate you. I promise—I will hate you. And I'll never forgive myself for not having done it sooner—soon enough to have saved my baby. Oh, dear God, my baby.

Eugene thought the tears that began to crowd into her eyes were for him. But she was allowing herself this one last luxury of brief mourning for the loss of something denied to her. It troubled her that she wasn't sure exactly what that something was, or which one of them was to blame for taking it away. Ciel began to feel the overpowering need to be near someone who loved her. I'll get Serena and we'll go visit Mattie now, she thought in a daze.

Then they heard the scream from the kitchen.

The church was small and dark. The air hung about them like a stale blanket. Ciel looked straight ahead, oblivious to the seats filling up behind her. She didn't feel the damp pressure of Mattie's heavy arm or the doubt that invaded the air over Eugene's absence. The plaintive Merciful Jesuses, lightly sprinkled with sobs, were lost on her ears. Her dry eyes were locked on the tiny pearl-gray casket, flanked with oversized arrangements of red-carnationed bleeding hearts and white-lilied eternal circles. The sagging chords that came loping out of the huge organ and mixed with the droning voice of the black-robed old man behind the coffin were also unable to penetrate her.

Ciel's whole universe existed in the seven feet of space between herself and her child's narrow coffin. There was not even room for this comforting God whose melodious virtues floated around her sphere, attempting to get in. Obviously, He had deserted or damned her, it didn't matter which. All Ciel knew was that her prayers had gone unheeded—that afternoon she had lifted her daughter's body off the kitchen floor, those blank days in the hospital, and now. So she was left to do what God had chosen not to.

People had mistaken it for shock when she refused to cry. They thought it some special sort of grief when she stopped eating and even drinking water unless forced to; her hair went uncombed and her body unbathed. But Ciel was not grieving for Serena. She was simply tired of hurting. And she was forced to slowly give up the life that God had refused to take from her.

After the funeral the well-meaning came to console and offer their dog-eared faith in the form of coconut cakes, potato pies, fried chicken, and tears. Ciel sat in the bed with her back resting against the headboard; her long thin fingers, still as midnight frost on a frozen pond, lay on the covers. She acknowledged their kindnesses with nods of her head and slight lip movements, but no sound. It was as if her voice was too tired to make the journey from the diaphragm through the larynx to the mouth.

Her visitors' impotent words flew against the steel edge of her pain, bled slowly, and returned to die in the senders' throats. No one came too near. They stood around the door and the dressing table, or sat on the edges of the two worn chairs that needed upholstering, but they unconsciously pushed themselves back against the wall as if her hurt was contagious.

A neighbor woman entered in studied certainty and stood in the middle of the room. "Child, I know how you feel, but don't do this to yourself. I lost one, too. The Lord will . . ." And she choked, because the words were jammed down into her throat by the naked force of Ciel's eyes. Ciel had opened them fully now to look at the woman, but raw fires had eaten them worse than lifeless—worse than death. The woman saw in that mute appeal for silence the ragings of a personal hell flowing through Ciel's eyes. And just as she went to reach for the girl's hand, she stopped as if a muscle spasm had overtaken her body and, cowardly, shrank back. Reminiscences of old, dried-over pains were no consolation in the face of this. They had the effect of cold beads of water on a hot iron—they danced and fizzled up while the room stank from their steam.

Mattie stood in the doorway, and an involuntary shudder went through her when she saw Ciel's eyes. Dear God, she thought, she's dying, and right in front of our faces.

"Merciful Father, no!" she bellowed. There was no prayer, no bended knee or sackcloth supplication in those words, but a blasphemous fireball that shot forth and went smashing against the gates of heaven, raging and kicking, demanding to be heard.

"No! No! No!" Like a black Brahman cow, desperate to protect her young, she surged into the room, pushing the neighbor woman and the others out of her way. She approached the bed with her lips clamped shut in such force that the muscles in her jaw and the back of her neck began to ache.

She sat on the edge of the bed and enfolded the tissue-thin body in her huge ebony arms. And she rocked. Ciel's body was so hot it burned Mattie when she first touched her, but she held on and rocked. Back and forth, back and forth—she had Ciel so tightly she could feel her young breasts flatten against the buttons of her dress. The black mammoth gripped so firmly that the slightest increase of pressure would have cracked the girl's spine. But she rocked.

And somewhere from the bowels of her being came a moan from Ciel, so high at first it couldn't be heard by anyone there, but the yard dogs began an unholy howling. And Mattie rocked. And then, agonizingly slow, it broke its way through the parched lips in a spaghetti-thin column of air that could be faintly heard in the frozen room.

Ciel moaned. Mattie rocked. Propelled by the sound, Mattie rocked her out of that bed, out of that room, into a blue vastness just underneath the sun and above time. She rocked her over Aegean seas so clean they shone like crystal, so clear the fresh blood of sacrificed babies torn from their mother's arms and given to Neptune could be seen like pink froth on the water. She rocked her on and on, past Dachau, where soul-gutted Jewish mothers swept their children's entrails off laboratory floors. They flew past the spilled brains of Senegalese infants whose mothers had dashed them on the wooden sides of slave ships. And she rocked on.

She rocked her into her childhood and let her see murdered dreams. And she rocked her back, back into the womb, to the nadir of her hurt, and they found it—a slight silver splinter, embedded just below the surface of the skin. And Mattie rocked and pulled— and the splinter gave way, but its roots were deep, gigantic, ragged, and they tore up flesh with bits of fat and muscle tissue clinging to them. They left a huge hole, which was already starting to pus over, but Mattie was satisfied. It would heal.

The bile that had formed a tight knot in Ciel's stomach began to rise and gagged her just as it passed her throat. Mattie put her hand over the girl's mouth and rushed her out the now-empty room to the toilet. Ciel retched yellowish-green phlegm, and she brought up white lumps of slime that hit the seat of the toilet and rolled off, splattering onto the tiles. After a while she heaved only air, but the body did not seem to want to stop. It was exorcising the evilness of pain.

Mattie cupped her hands under the faucet and motioned for Ciel to drink and clean her mouth. When the water left Ciel's mouth, it tasted as if she had been rinsing with a mild acid. Mattie drew a tub of hot water and undressed Ciel. She let the nightgown fall off the narrow shoulders, over the pitifully thin breasts and jutting hipbones. She slowly helped her into the water, and it was like a dried brown autumn leaf hitting the surface of a puddle.

And slowly she bathed her. She took the soap, and, using only

233

her hands, she washed Ciel's hair and the back of her neck. She raised her arms and cleaned the armpits, soaping well the downy brown hair there. She let the soap slip between the girl's breasts, and she washed each one separately, cupping it in her hands. She took each leg and even cleaned under the toenails. Making Ciel rise and kneel in the tub, she cleaned the crack in her behind, soaped her pubic hair, and gently washed the creases in her vagina— slowly, reverently, as if handling a newborn.

She took her from the tub and toweled her in the same manner she had been bathed—as if too much friction would break the skin tissue. All of this had been done without either woman saying a word. Ciel stood there, naked, and felt the cool air play against the clean surface of her skin. She had the sensation of fresh mint coursing through her pores. She closed her eyes and the fire was gone. Her tears no longer fried within her, killing her internal organs with their steam. So Ciel began to cry—there, naked, in the center of the bathroom floor.

Mattie emptied the tub and rinsed it. She led the still-naked Ciel to a chair in the bedroom. The tears were flowing so freely now Ciel couldn't see, and she allowed herself to be led as if blind. She sat on the chair and cried—head erect. Since she made no effort to wipe them away, the tears dripped down her chin and landed on her chest and rolled down to her stomach and onto her dark pubic hair. Ignoring Ciel, Mattie took away the crumpled linen and made the bed, stretching the sheets tight and fresh. She beat the pillows into a virgin plumpness and dressed them in white cases.

And Ciel sat. And cried. The unmolested tears had rolled down her parted thighs and were beginning to wet the chair. But they were cold and good. She put out her tongue and began to drink in their saltiness, feeding on them. The first tears were gone. Her thin shoulders began to quiver, and spasms circled her body as new tears came—this time, hot and stinging. And she sobbed, the first sound she'd made since the moaning.

Mattie took the edges of the dirty sheet she'd pulled off the bed and wiped the mucus that had been running out of Ciel's nose. She then led her freshly wet, glistening body, baptized now, to the bed. She covered her with one sheet and laid a towel across the pillow— it would help for a while.

And Ciel lay down and cried. But Mattie knew the tears would end. And she would sleep. And morning would come.

234

From **The Learning Tree***
❧ GORDON PARKS

Dawn arrived painfully slow, and Newt, as if in a trance, lay gazing out the window through the dank lace curtains. He watched the sky pale as the sun climbed to the foggy horizon and brightened the upper reaches. His mind, with unaccountable calm, explored the reality of this hour over the deep, uneven snoring of Roy and Pete, sleeping beside him.

Their mother was dead, he knew, but it was hard to believe. Suddenly he wondered if, somewhere up there in the pale blue nothingness, her soul—free of tortured body and earthly things— was already floating silently about, knowing at last the real purpose of its sojourn on a complex and troubled earth. What if she found that all the praying and religious rites were just a lot of folly; that her soul floated with no more righteousness or dignity than that of Doc Cheney, Big Mabel, or even Captain Tuck? What a shock it would be to her?

He now thought uneasily of such a possibility, and he couldn't help but feel that this was more than likely the case—and the feeling shamed him. Then he softened his shame with the reasoning that if such were true, she would never begrudge anyone such equality. Whatever judgment settled upon her, he thought, would surely be the best that eternity could possibly extend.

As Newt dressed quietly, the sun burned through the fog, warming the wet rooftops, drying the leaves and grass. And the moist cool earth took in the heat and in return gave forth little curlings of cloud that quickly disappeared in the clean morning air.

He entered the dining room and looked around. Everything was just about the same, except the door which the shot had blasted. Stepping to it, he ran his fingers over the splintered surface.

* Because this excerpt is taken from a larger work of the same title, there are references to previous experiences, violence (a common theme in the southern town where Newt and his family reside), and previously introduced characters.

Daylight leaked through it now, and a sudden fright gripped him, for he realized that this destruction was actually meant for Rende. Remembering the gun against his father's head, he shivered and stepped back involuntarily (this could've been Poppa's skull), then he moved warily across to his mother's room. They had already taken her to the undertaker's.

The odor of camphor and medicine still hung in the air, and a bouquet of withered posies lay on the rocking chair in the corner of the room. The sheets had been removed, and the mattress was doubled upon the sagging springs. Above the antique dresser hung an oval-shaped photograph of his father and mother, framed in a polished, worn wood. It had been taken their wedding day, and both stared straight ahead—unmindful of this faraway moment when their last child would stand silent, alone and uncertain in this room of death.

Almost in every sense, Newt had come to link death with violence. Even his mother's passing, he thought, couldn't escape a brush with it. Nearly everyone he had known intimately, and who had ceased to live, met their demise in bloodshed. And it was probably for this reason that he feared death so much—and this fear, he reasoned, was childish. His mother's easy, tranquil and unflinching acceptance of death enhanced his respect for her. Now, this morning, it was creating within him a near-fanatical desire to rid himself of this stigma that had dogged his soul since the day of Doc Cheney's death.

Turning from the room, he channeled his thoughts into an imaginary rectangular hole that someday would be his grave. And his whole being reacted against the eternal blackness, the unending airlessness, the unchangeable recumbent position of his body— never to eat, taste, feel, speak or hear again. He shuddered. Now he envisaged the others reposing about him, acre after acre; worm-bored coffin sides, everlasting decay, dust piling forever upon eternal dust—entombed in the still, suffocating blackness.

Why, then, was life given, and for no logically explained reason taken away again? He recalled the rolling, wearisome voice of Pastor Broadnap. "—From dust you came and to dust you must returneth!" Newt remembered his authoritatively hollering such things over Big Mabel's coffin. He remembered, too, his swing about the pulpit, frock coat flying, sweat dripping, screaming of immortality— "of the spirit, of the soul"—not the good, solid body.

Newt opened the front door and stepped out on the porch. As his bare feet moved over the clammy boards, he heard the creaking beneath them and noted that they would soon have to be replaced. Sunlight bathed the edge of the porch, so he went to stand there, warming his body in the brilliant glow.

Morning eased into afternoon, evening, night, restless sleep— then there was morning again. The gray, simple casket arrived in the early afternoon. It was placed in the parlor by the window, resting on six silver wheels, and by late evening the room had become filled with flowers.

Twice during the day Newt went to look at his mother, once with his father and then with Prissy and Pete. Prissy cried, but he didn't; and as the three of them walked from the coffin, he placed his arms consolingly about her shoulders—this for the very first time in his life. And she cuddled to his touch. It gave him a good feeling, a good, big-brother and close-family feeling; one that demanded swift growing up, in mind and body alike. His entire body and his mind reacted to this demand, and he seemed to grow on the spot, feeling the expansion in his muscles, his thighs and belly—and heart. On impulse, he said to himself, "I've got to prove somethin'— to myself."

"What'd you say?"

"Nothin'. Just thinkin', Prissy. Just thinkin'."

Later, walking through the backyard toward the hog pens, he had a certain notion, and as he worked this notion grew. He would sleep this night on the floor beside his mother's coffin, in the very presence of death. If during the night his fear left forever, the purpose would be served. It if remained. . . . His thoughts juggled the possibility for a few seconds, then he shrugged it off. "Mornin' holds the answer," his voice sighed to the crimson evening, "mornin' holds the answer."

As night raced upon him, all else—funeral plans, mourning, telegrams, arriving kinfolk—passed as would trifling scenes in a powerful drama. He was caught in an impulse that denied significance to anything but that impulse. And though he existed in the land of the living, his mind was unrelated to it.

By one-thirty in the morning he was lying in his bed hearing nothing but the deep, unrhythmed sleep of the household; his heart pounding, the finger of fear touching it, the challenge calling from the dark room where his mother's body lay. The reality of the moment grasped him like steel claws. Dreamlike, he rose as if pulled from the bed and draped a blanket about his shoulders. The immense underground of death took its place in his mind, but he moved on toward the room through the ever-so-quiet darkness. Reaching the parlor door, he stopped, breathing heavily. He felt that he had awaited this moment all his life, and now that it had arrived, he could not fail it. He pushed the door open gently, paused, then stepped in—leaving the door ajar behind him. In the dimness he could see the shape of the coffin. His heart sank, and he wanted to run from the room; but he realized he had to go through with it after coming this far. Sweat dripped from his armpits, and he could feel the moisture in the palms of his hands. He made another small step toward the coffin (the lid's down), one more step—driplets of sweat coursed down the sides of his face. He gently eased up the lid, shivered, trembled, looked. The dark form of his mother lay deep in the cushion of crinkly white. (I made it, Momma—I made it—give me strength to stay on—give me strength.) Bracing himself, he took a final steady, muscle-taut, teeth-grinding look, dropped the blanket to the floor, spread it, lay upon it, jerked it about him, closed his eyes tightly—sealing off all blackness except that of his own inner being. After a while the heartbeat slowed, the trembling eased. He commenced the struggle with sleep. Though his eyes were closed, all the counterparts of fear tried forcing their way into his vision; but he helped his mind form the image of his mother as it had existed in reality, before death—and he held onto that image with great tenacity. (. . . I ain't afraid . . . I ain't afraid. . . .) An owl hooted in the nearby woods; crickets chirped in brittle unending chorus; and in this hour Newt heard the forlorn cry of the whippoorwill. (I ain't afraid no more, Momma . . . I ain't afraid. . . .) He was easing into weariness now. (I ain't afraid. . . .) At last, as if in answer to his courage, sleep came. Before long, he was snoring softly. His dreams, unafraid.

Here, Jack Winger found his son in early morning. At first, the sight of Newt curled up on the floor alongside the open coffin shook him. But he quickly understood. He knew his son better than his son thought. And the look of peace on the boy's face signified something more important than his just sleeping there. He started to rouse him and put out his hand, then suddenly drew it back, tiptoed out and softly closed the door. Then he went through the foggy morning to appease the hunger of his squealing hogs.

". . . Ashes to ashes . . . dust to dust . . . from dust we came and to dust we returneth." The petals of the broken rose fell from Pastor Broadnap's fingers, twisted and dipped in blurred confusion before Newt's tear-filled eyes, then came to rest on Sarah Winger's coffin " . . . may this beloved mother and wife rest, forever, in peace. May God have mercy on this family . . . Amen."

Newt felt his Uncle Rob's hand ease to his shoulder, pressing home the end of the rites. Grief engulfed him as he stood staring into his mother's open grave. (Goodbye, Momma—I won't forget your dream.)

"Come on, son—let's go," Rob said.

"Okay, Uncle Rob, I just want to stay a little longer."

"It's all right, boy. Take your time." Rob waited as the others started filing out toward the waiting cars.

Newt's eyes swept the grave for the last time, continued on to two chalk-white headstones, lined up stiffly to the left of his mother's final resting place. Time and weather had worn the once crisp lettering:

Clarinda Winger	Miller Winger
Born May 12, 1901	Born December 16, 1897
Died May 12, 1901	Died June 14, 1909

A warm gentle breeze licked his ear. He turned at its touch and took Rob's hand and they walked away. As he neared the car, he noticed two workmen sitting beneath a giant oak tree. Picks and shovels lay at their sides, and they were eating from tin lunch pails. (. . . grave diggers . . . they'll be coverin' Momma soon's we leave. . . .) The thought began overpowering him, and he screamed inside. He hurried Rob the last few yards to the car, helped him in beside his father and slammed the door.

"Everything all right, boy?" Jack asked.

"Yessir, Poppa. Everything's all right now."

The big black funeral limousine moved slowly through the huge wrought-iron gate, turned onto the highway and rolled smoothly into high gear. Newt heard its tires singing on the hot macadam, drowning out the stifling silence of anguish and sorrow. He closed his eyes and his thoughts, slumped down into the seat and completely surrendered his body to the car's gentle, surging motion.

The following day Newt began packing for his trip north. As he neatly arranged his meager belongings, Beansy sat on the dining room floor, his back to the wall, harboring a regret at Newt's leaving.

"Hate to see you go, Newt. Won't be the same round here without you. But it's prob'ly best this way."

"Maybe yes. Maybe no." Newt paused and gazed blankly at the candy-striped pajamas in his hand. "Who can say—I'll miss you and the fellas—but I'll be comin' back for visits—and who knows, maybe you can come see me before long. It ain't really like we won't never see each other again." He pressed and held his weight upon some wrinkled overalls.

"Wonder what it's like up where you're goin', Newt?"

Newt folded his gray bell-bottomed pants on top of the overalls. "I don't know for sure. Clara and Lou say you don't have to sit in the buzzard's roost at the picture shows, and you can even eat in some of the white places and play on white school teams like everybody else."

"You think that's just a lotta talk?"

"Don't know."

A grin stretched Beansy's rubbery, fat face. "What about the white girls, Newt?"

"I ain't worried about *them* none. I ain't for kickin' 'em out if they get in bed with me. But like Roy says, 'All behinds feel the same in the dark.' "

Clara strutted in and stood above them, her hands wet with washing suds. "Newt, you ain't takin' those bell-bottom pants nowhere."

"What's wrong with 'em?"

"You just ain't takin' 'em, that's all." She picked up the end of one of the spreading legs. "Why, that cold air'd get up under them things and freeze your tail off. You're goin' north, boy—not south." She wiped the suds off on her dress. "Take 'em out now, like I say." She switched off to the kitchen.

"Crapmafittle," Newt said under his breath, exchanging grins with Beansy. He glanced toward the kitchen, took the pants, hid them in brown wrapping paper and squeezed the package in at the very bottom of the pasteboard suitcase.

"She's gonna be bossy, Newt."

"Her growl's worse'n her bite. Anyway, I'll be on my own soon's I get myself a job." Roy had given him two shirts and a tie. He cocked his head to one side and proudly observed the presents and placed them on top of the pile. He exhaled deeply, then pushed the bag into the corner. "That's about all I can do now—finish the rest in the mornin'."

"Prissy gonna live with you?"

"No. She's gonna be with Lou, but we'll be in the same neighborhood. Poppa and Pete are gonna stay here for a while. They may come up later."

"What time we meetin' the gang over at the river?"

"About four," Newt said, "I went over to the hospital to say goodbye to Earl this mornin'."

Aware now of their possibly never seeing each other again, Newt and Beansy casually ambled into the open, and for the next half hour they sat quietly on the edge of the porch, swatting flies, pitching rocks, whittling sticks—their thoughts saddened by the waning hours of comradeship.

"'Bout time to meet Jappy. He'll be at Logan's Grove at a quarter to four," Newt said.

"Where's Skunk?"

"Cuttin' grass—be over later."

Mother Dear and Daddy

&⋅ JUNIUS EDWARDS

They came in the night while we slept. We knew they were coming, but not when, and we expected to see them when they did. We never thought that they would come at night. When we got up, well, when John, my brother, got up (he was always getting up early), when he got up, he looked out of the window and ran and jumped back in bed and shook me and called my name.

"Jim, Jim, they here. They here already. Wake up, Jim. They—"

"Hey, quit shaking me. I been woke long time."

"They here," he ran to the window. "Come on look."

He didn't have to tell me "come on look" because I was at the window when he got there, almost, anyway. They had come all right; we could see the cars parked in the yard, like big cats crouching, backs hunched, ready to attack.

"I'll go tell Mary, then," John said, and bolted out of the room as fast as you could blow out a coal oil lamp.

While he was out telling our three sisters, I stood there at the window and counted the cars. There were five in all, besides our car, and they were all black and shiny as my plate whenever I got through eating red beans and rice. Our car sat over there by itself, dusty and dirty as one of those bums that come by all the time wanting a meal.

I stood there, leaning on the windowsill, with my right foot on top of my left foot, scratching my left foot with my toes, and looking at our car. I could feel my eyes burning, burning, and the tears coming and washing the burns, and me sucking my tongue because of the burning and trying not to make a sound. My body went cold and inside it I could feel something surging up; not like being sick, this surging came up my whole body, my arms, too, and ended with my eyes burning. I fought to hold it back, keep it buried. Even when I was alone, I always fought it, always won and kept it down, even at times when it was sudden and fast and got to my eyes and burned like hot needles behind my eyelids, hot needles with legs running around trying to get past my eyelids and spill out on my cheeks, even then I kept it down.

I had fought it for two weeks and I was good at it and getting better. Maybe I was good at it because of that first day. I had not fought it then. I had let it come, right in front of Aunt Mabel, I let it come, not trying to stop it, control it; I let it come.

"What we going to do?" I asked Aunt Mabel, after it had come, had shaken me and left me as empty as an unfilled grave. "What we going to do, Aunt Mabel?"

"Lord knows, son. Lord knows," Aunt Mabel said, sitting in her rocker, moving, slow, back and forth, looking down at me, on my knees, my arms resting on her huge right thigh and my head turned up to her, watching that round face, her lips tight now, her head shaking side to side, and her eyes clouded, and me not understanding her answer, but thinking I should and not daring to ask again and feeling the question pounding my brain: What we going to do? What we going to do?

"The Lord giveth and the Lord taketh away."

But, what we going to do? I could not understand Aunt Mabel. I did not know what her mumbling about the Lord had to do with this. All I knew was she had just told me Mother Dear and Daddy were dead. Mother Dear and Daddy were dead. Mother Dear and Daddy would not come back. Mother Dear and Daddy wouldn't take us home again. What we going to do?

"I want to go home. I want to go home," I screamed and got to my feet and ran to the door, realizing it was Aunt Mabel calling my name. I ran out to the yard where John and our sisters played, and right past them. I did not feel my feet move; I did not feel I owned a body. I wanted to get home. And hearing Aunt Mabel call my name, seeing houses, cars, people, trees, like one big thing made of windows, walls, wheels, heads, branches, arms and legs and behind that one big thing, our house, with our car out front, and our yard and our tree, and then the big thing was gone and I was at our house, running up the steps across the porch, as fast as I could, straight to the screened door, wham! and I lay on my back on the porch looking up at the screen, at the imprints made in it by my head and hands and my right knee. I got right up and started banging on the door, trying to twist the knob.

"Mother Dear! Daddy! Mother Dear! Daddy!" I called as loud

as I could and kept banging on the door. Then, I ran to the back door and called again and banged and kicked the door. They did not come.

They would not come.

"Mother Dear! Daddy! It's me. Let me in. Open the door!"

They would not come.

I ran to the front, out to the street and turned and looked up to their room and saw the shades were drawn just as they were drawn when Mother Dear and Daddy took us over to Aunt Mabel's house to stay for the weekend while they went away fishing with cousin Bob.

I cupped my hands up to my mouth.

"Mother Dear. Daddy. Mother Dear! Daddy!"

I called, and called again and all the while I kept my eyes glued on that window, waiting. Any moment now, any second now, now, *now,* waited to see that white shade zoom up and then the window, and then Mother Dear and Daddy, both together, lean out, smiling, laughing, waving, calling my name, now, now, *now.*

They did not come.

They would not come. The shade stood still, stayed still, with the sun shining on it through the window pane; stayed still, as if the sun were a huge nail shooting through the pane and holding it down. It did not go up. It would not go up.

They would not come.

I knew it. Suddenly, just like that, snap, I knew they would not come; could not come. The shades would stay still. I knew they would not come. I lowered my hands, my eyes darting from shaded window to shaded window, around the yard, under the house, searching, for what? I did not know, and then there was the car. My eyes were glued to the car, and I started over to it, slowly at first, and then I ran and I stopped short and pressed my head up against the glass in the front door beside the steering wheel. The glass was hot on my nose and lips and forehead, and burned them, but I did not care, I pressed harder, as if by doing so I could push right through the glass, not breaking it, but melting through it. Then, I felt as though I *was* inside, in my favorite spot up front with Daddy, and in back were Mother Dear and John and our sisters; Daddy whistling and the trees going by and the farms and green, green, green, and other cars and Daddy starting to sing and all of us joining him singing "Choo-choo Train to Town," even Jo Ann and Willie

Mae, who had not learned the words yet, singing, singing, and ending laughing and feeling Daddy's hand on my head.

"Jim," I turned from the window, and it was Aunt Mabel's hand on my head.

"Come on, son." She took my right hand and led me up the street as if I were a baby just starting to walk.

"What we going to do, Aunt Mabel?"

"You got to be brave, Jim. You the oldest. You got to look out for your brother and sisters."

I decided then that I would not let my brother and sisters see me cry, ever. I was twelve years old and the oldest and I had to take care of them.

"When can we go back home, Aunt Mabel?"

"I guess we ought to move over to your house while we wait for the family to get here," Aunt Mabel said. "It's bigger than mine and your clothes there."

I looked up at Aunt Mabel. I had not expected her to move back with us. I wanted only we children to move back home.

When we got back to Aunt Mabel's house, I told John about the automobile accident and that Mother Dear and Daddy were dead. John was only eight, but he understood and he cried and I understood just how he felt, so I left him alone.

The next day we moved back to our house. Aunt Mabel, too. Every time one of our sisters would ask for Mother Dear and Daddy we always said they were gone away. They were too young to understand about death.

Aunt Mabel told me that our Uncles and Aunts and Grandparents were coming. I didn't know any of them. I remembered Christmas presents from them and Mother Dear and Daddy talking about them, but I had never seen them.

"They're good folks," Aunt Mabel said, "and it won't make no difference which one you all go to live with."

"But, Aunt Mabel. We going to stay home."

"You can't, son. You all too young to stay here by yourself and I can't take care of you."

"I can take care of us, Aunt Mabel. I'm the oldest. I can take care of us."

Aunt Mabel smiled. "Bet you could, too. But you all need somebody to be a Mama and a Papa to you. You all got to go live with one of your Aunts and Uncles."

245

I knew right away that Aunt Mabel was right. I told John about it and we started trying to guess where we would go. The family was scattered all over, mostly in big cities like New York, Philadelphia and Boston. Our Grandfather on Daddy's side was in Texas. John and I couldn't decide what we liked best: Texas and horses or big cities and buildings. We talked about it every day while we waited for them to come, and now they were here.

I left the window and started to get dressed. John ran back into the room.

"Them won't wake up."

"They can sleep, then," I said. "Let's go see where the cars came from."

We got dressed and ran out to the yard and looked at the license plates. There were two from New York, two from Pennsylvania and one from Massachusetts.

"None of them from Texas," I said.

"Which one you like best?" asked John.

"That one," I said, pointing to the one from Massachusetts. I liked it because it was the biggest one. The five of us could get in it without any trouble at all.

We examined each car carefully for an hour and then Aunt Mabel called us and told us to come in the house.

"They all here," she said, "all that's coming, I guess. Now, you all be good so they'll like you."

I followed Aunt Mabel into the living room. I could feel John right behind me, up close, and I could hear his breathing.

"Here the boys," Aunt Mabel announced, and walked across the room and sat down.

John and I stopped at the door. Our sisters were lined up, side by side, in the middle of the room, smiling. I had heard voices before we came into the room, but now, there was silence and all eyes were on us. They sat in a half circle in straight back chairs, near the walls around the room. I looked at them. I stared at each face. Aunt Mabel and our sisters were the only smiling faces I saw. I didn't know about John, but right at that moment, I was scared. I wanted to turn and run away as fast as I could. I felt as if I had committed the worst crime and those faces hated me for it. Besides Aunt Mabel, there were five men and five women, all dressed in black. Each man had a black line above his upper lip. The two men who were fat had thick black lines and the other three had thinner ones. I didn't like the lines. Daddy never wore one and I always thought his face was cleaner and friendlier and happier than other men I had seen who wore them.

I noticed the features of these people right away. They were all like Mother Dear, Aunt Mabel and our sisters, and they were pink rose. I knew they were Mother Dear's relatives. Daddy didn't have any brothers or sisters and he used to tell John and me whenever we got into a fight with each other that we should be kind to each other because we were brothers and it was good to have a brother and that he wished he had had brothers and sisters. Mother Dear had plenty of brothers and sisters. She had three brothers, and I knew them right away as the three men who weren't fat, and three sisters, Aunt Mabel, of course, and the two women who sat beside the fat men.

I stood there looking, staring at those faces that looked as if they had just taken straight castor oil. I looked at John, now standing at my right. He stood there with his mouth hanging open and his eyes straight ahead. I could tell he was scared and as soon as I knew he was scared, I wasn't scared any more and I wanted to tell him not to be scared because I wasn't going to let anything happen to him. Just when I was about to tell him, Aunt Mabel broke the silence.

"Come on over here next to your sisters," she said.

We shuffled over to where our sisters were and stood there like slaves on auction.

"They good children," Aunt Mabel said. "No trouble at all."

The others still kept quiet, except for whispers among themselves.

"Say your names, boys," Aunt Mabel said.

"James," I said.

"John," said John.

"We call James, Jim," Aunt Mabel said, and smiled at me.

I looked at her. It was all right for her to call me Jim. Mother Dear and Daddy called me Jim. I looked back at those faces. I didn't want *them* to call me Jim.

"Well," Aunt Mabel said to them, "you all going to tell the boys your names?"

They introduced themselves to us, not smiling, not changing those castor oil expressions. Apparently they had already introduced themselves to our sisters.

"Mabel," one of the fat men said, "why don't you get these kids out of here so we can talk."

"Jim, you and the children go into the dining room," Aunt Mabel said, and when we were going, she added, "And close the door."

We went into the dining room and I closed the door. Our sisters sat down in the middle of the floor and played. John stood over them, watching, but when he saw me with my ear to the door, he came over and joined me. We faced each other with our heads pressed up against the door and we listened. The only voice I could recognize was Aunt Mabel's.

"Carol and I have thought this thing over and we can see our way clear to take the girls," one of the men said.

"Now, wait a minute, Sam," another man said. "We thought we'd take *one* of the girls, at least."

Then, for a minute it sounded as if they were all trying to get a word in. They talked all at the same time, even yelled. It sounded as if everyone wanted a girl.

"Lord have mercy. You mean you going to split them up? You mean they won't be together?"

"Five kids? Frankly, we can't afford two, but we'd be willing to take the three girls."

There was another minute of all of them trying to speak at the same time, at the top of their voices, each one wanting a girl.

"Why don't you all talk like people? I don't like to see them split up, but I guess five is too many for anybody, specially when they not your own."

"Then you understand that they'll have to be separated? There's no other way, and since we already have a son, we thought we would take one of the girls."

"Well," Aunt Mabel said, "look like to me all you all want a girl. I didn't hear nobody say nothing about the boys, yet."

There was silence. John and I pressed harder against the door. John's mouth was open, his bottom lip hanging, and he was staring at me hard. I could tell he was scared and I must have looked scared to him so I closed my own mouth and tried to swallow. There was nothing to swallow and I had to open my mouth again and take a deep breath.

"Come to think of it, you all didn't say one word to them boys," Aunt Mabel said. "Why don't you all want boys?"

248

"We have a boy."

"We do, too."

"Girls are easier."

"Boys are impossible."

"Lord have mercy."

"Listen, Mabel, you don't understand the situation."

"Don't get on your high horse with me. Talk plain."

"All right, Mabel. The fact is, the boys are—well—they're too, well, too much like the father."

"What?"

"You heard me. I know that's why *we* don't want one, and it's probably why the others here don't want one and it's no use avoiding it."

"Is that right? Is that why you all don't want one, too?" Aunt Mabel asked.

There was silence.

"Lord have mercy. I never heard such a thing in all my life. Your own sister's children, too."

"You don't understand, Mabel."

"No, I don't. Lord knows I don't. What you all doing up there? Passing? Huh? That what you doing? No. No. You couldn't be doing that. Even if you wanted to, you couldn't be doing that. You not that light that you can pass, none of you all. Lord have mercy. They too black for you. Your own sister's children."

John looked down at his hands, at the back of his hands and then at me and down at our sisters and at his hands again.

"I never thought I'd live to see the day my own flesh and blood would talk like that, and all the trouble in the world. My own sisters and brothers," Aunt Mabel said.

"Mabel, you've been here in this town all your life. This town isn't the world. You don't know how it is."

John rubbed the back of his hand on his pants and looked at it again.

I kept listening.

"It's hard enough like it is without having these boys, having to always explain about them. You can see that, Mabel. Look at us, how light we are. We'd always have to explain to everyone they're our dead sister's boys and people who we don't explain to will jump to all kinds of conclusions. Socially, we'd be out, too. No, Mabel. That's just the way it is and we can't do a thing about it. I, for one, have certain standards I want to live up to and having these boys won't help."

"I never thought it. I never thought it."

"That's the way it is, Mabel. Those boys will do none of us any good."

John went over to where our sisters played and stood over them, examining them.

Aunt Mabel said: "So that's how come you didn't want her to get married. That's how come you tried to get her away from here."

John kneeled down and touched each one of our sisters. He looked at them and at his hand, at them and at his hand, and then to me. Then, his eyes became shiny and he started batting his eyes and the sides of his face grew, his cheeks puffed way out, his mouth closed tight. He fought it all he could and I knew it was useless, he would not succeed. I could feel the same thing happening to me, but I held it back and concentrated on him, watched his swelling face until it exploded and thinking he might yell out, I rushed to him and got down on my knees and held him, held him close, just as Daddy would have, with my left arm around his back and my right hand behind his head, holding his head to my chest and felt his body shaking like a balloon when you let out the air and I listened to him groan like a whipped dog. I didn't say one word to him. I couldn't. I let him cry and I held him and watched our sisters and they suddenly realized he was crying and they came to us and helped me hold him and tried to get him to tell why he cried and when he would not tell they asked me and when I would not tell they stood there holding both of us until John got control of himself. He sat back on his heels and sobbed and the girls stepped back and watched him. I stood up and watched all of them. The girls stood there and watched him and waited, their faces alert, ready to run to him and help him. It was as if they knew, now, this was not a physical wound that made him cry, not a twisted arm, a stubbed toe, or a beating, and certainly not a cry that would make them laugh and yell "cry baby" at him. It was as if they knew it was a wound they had never had and that it was deeper than skin.

I heard the voices in the living room, louder now, and wilder, so I started back to my place at the door, but before I got there, John lost control again. We got to him at the same time and tried to hold him, but this time he pushed us away, fought us off, and got to his feet and ran into the living room. I got to my feet as fast as I could and ran after him into the living room. He was screaming now and when I ran into the living room, I stopped short at what I saw. John had run in and jumped in the lap of the first man he came to and he was there on his knees in the man's lap screaming and pounding the man's chest and face. The man pushed him off and John fell to the floor on his back and got right up and jumped in the man's lap again, still screaming, and pounded the man's chest and face with both his little fists.

"John, John, John!" I yelled, and ran to him and pulled him out of the man's lap, just in time, too, because the man swung at him back handed, but I had John down and the man missed. John, still screaming, kicking, struggled with me, trying to get away from me so he could get back to the man.

"John, John!" I yelled, shaking him, trying to make him hear me. "John, John!" but I could see he wasn't listening to me even though he was looking straight at me as I stood in front of him holding both of his arms and shouting his name. He only screamed.

Suddenly, I started walking backwards from him, holding his arms still, pulling him along with me until we were in the center of the room and then I smiled at him. "Come on, John, come on, John," I said, and laughed, laughed hard, looking into his eyes, I kept it up, laughed loud and harder still and felt my body shake from it. Then I saw John's face change, first a smile, then he broke into a laugh, too. I stared into his eyes and we laughed. We laughed. We laughed. We laughed. We threw our heads back and we laughed. We held each other's hands and danced round and round and laughed. Our sisters came and joined our dance. We formed a circle, all of us laughing, laughing, and we danced round and round. We were the only people in the world. We danced round and round and laughed and laughed.

"Hey," I said. "Choo-Choo Train, Choo-Choo Train" and they joined me:

"Choo-choo train, choo-choo train
We going to take that choo-choo train
Choo-choo train to town
Choo-choo train
Choo-choo train"

251

Round and round, "Choo-choo train" louder and louder I sang, "CHOO-CHOO TRAIN, CHOO-CHOO TRAIN, CHOO-CHOO TRAIN TO TEXAS" round and round "choo-choo train" until I realized what I had said and I screamed happily and said it again and again until they caught on and said it too. We went faster and faster and said it louder and louder sounding like a Choo-choo Train: TEXAS, TEXAS, TEXAS, TEXAS, TEXAS ...

A Brown Girl Dead

ᴥ COUNTEE CULLEN

With two white roses on her breasts,
    White candles at head and feet,
Dark Madonna of the grave she rests;
    Lord Death has found her sweet.

Her Mother pawned her wedding ring
    To lay her out in white;
She'd be so proud she'd dance and sing
    To see herself tonight.

We Assume: On the Death of Our Son, Reuben Masai Harper

ðø MICHAEL S. HARPER

We assume
that in 28 hours,
lived in a collapsible isolette,
you learned to accept pure oxygen
as the natural sky;
the scant shallow breaths
that filled those hours
cannot, did not make you fly—
but dreams were there
like crooked palmprints on
the twin-thick windows of the nursery—
in the glands of your mother.

We assume
the sterile hands
drank chemicals in and out
from lungs opaque with mucus,
pumped your stomach,
eeked the bicarbonate in
crooked, green-winged veins,
out in a plastic mask;

A woman who'd lost her first son
consoled us with an angel gone ahead
to pray for our family—
gone into that sky
seeking oxygen,
gone into autopsy,
a fine brown powdered sugar,
a disposable cremation:

We assume
you did not know we loved you.

Poem for Granville Ivanhoe Jordan
November 4, 1890–December 21, 1974
Dedicated to Stephen Henderson

❧ JUNE JORDAN

I

At the top of your tie
the dressy maroon number
with one/small
gravy stain
remaining

the knot is now too narrow for your neck

a ridiculous a dustfree/shiny box confines
your arms and legs
accustomed to a boxer's hunch a wrestler's hauling
energies at partial rest

3 or 4 A.M. a thousand nights
who stubbornly retrieved your own
into
illumination
     bright beyond blindfiling of
     a million letters at the Post Office which
     never forwarded even one
     of a hundred
     fantasies
     your kitchenkept plans
keeping you awake

West Indian in kitchen exile
alone between the days
and studying the National Geographic Magazines
white explorations and
excitement

in the places you were forced to leave

      no shoes
      no teeth

but oxlike shoulders
and hazel eyes that watered
slightly
from the reading you did teach yourself to do

West Indian in kitchen exile
omnivorous consumer of thick
kitchen table catalogs
of seeds for sale
for red
bright flowers

seeds

slick and colorful
on the quick
lush pages
advertising pear and
apple trees
or peaches
in first bloom

      who saved for money orders
      for the flowers
      for the trees
      who used a spade
      and shovel
      heavily and well
      to plant the Brooklyn backyard
      innocent of all
      the succulent
      the gorgeous schemes
      you held between your fingers
      like a simple
      piece of paper

Jesus, Daddy
what did you expect

an orange grove
a eucalyptus
roses
from the cities that despised the sweet calypso
of your trust?

II

Who stole the mustache from your face?
It's gone.
Who took it away?
Why did you stop there

      on your knees

at eighty four

      a man

down on your knees

      in inconceivable but willing
      prayer/your life
      God's baby in gray hair

What pushed you from your own two feet?

      my father

III

To this you have come

      a calm a concrete pit

contains your corpse
above the spumespent ending of the surf

against the mountain trees and fertile pitch
of steeply clinging dirt

> *"Sleep on Beloved*
> *Take Thy Rest"*

the minister
eyes bare beneath the island light
intones a feeling mumbo jumbo

> *"ashes to ashes*
> *dust to dust"*

the village men
wrists strained to lumped up veins and cartilage
(from carrying the casket)
do not pray
they do not sing

> *"A-bide with me,*
> *fast falls the eventide"*

It's afternoon
It's hot
It's lit by sun that cannot be undone

by death

Revelation

⪛ CAROLE C. GREGORY

I

An old woman in me walks patiently to the hospital,
I felt ridiculous,
I was mad about my life,
it was never in harmony with Momma's,
and now her 300 pressure pushed life every which a way,
I couldn't stand her god,
I wanted to hurt her spoiled sons,
but I smiled and fed Momma potatoes, peaches,
the softest food I could find,
why didn't I give her the tobacco she asked for?

II

Momma had cut through,
I flew home Christmas and heard her
talking about Harriet Tubman on a Seagram's calendar
and asking didn't Sojourner Truth look like Grandma?
a little darker though,
not talking no Jesus to me,
she had exchanged the Christian truth for the real truth
and just asked if I'd fix the tree.
The white man that molested your brother's grandchild
who was playing Mary in the Nativity play,
you understood him too late.
Only nine and five, sisters walking home from school
into a slum once a neighborhood of choir members, garden
    keepers
coming home they faced his knife and sucked his desire,
their father searches to kill the man.

At the hospital
I watch the room fill with those faithful lovers—
grandmothers with no switches in their hands,
silent about your brother's grandgirls,

always silent about sex,
glad to see me even though I am too grown for my own good,
they had rehearsed the Nativity play
the same as nothing had happened,
expecting the molested child to say Mary's lines.

III

Momma, a unselfish woman,
soft-voiced and brown in an apron
and setting a table with the Lord's Prayer,
once a child sharecropper whose father was driven
from the land to the Ohio steel mills,
Momma grew up not liking artificial flowers,
married, bore children, watched her husband leave,
she loved the end of winter,
birds pulling Spring out as worms,
the earth in her fingers planting red morning glories,
petunias, sunflowers decorating our yard,
braiding our hair, proud of my brothers,
she held her head up as we moved into the projects.

IV

My brother, a Central State graduate in elementary
        education,
shot heroin while teaching his sixth grade class,
he started his habit in Black Power meetings
denouncing mothers like Momma as apolitical women.
For years Momma hid his secret,
one Christmas I slept on the sofa,
at 3:00 am in the morning
my youngest brother came in and overcharged
the other for heroin,
their fight waking me.

At coffee the sunrise,
I questioned Momma til she dug out
her son's needle.
"No," my brother said, "I am not on,"

later that day he was fighting with
our younger brother.
I saw Momma run between them
at the top of the stairs,
Momma screaming, "You should say brother, that's enough,"
all three of them falling down the stairs,
Momma's head landing at my feet.

In the new year the mothers
walked to the Mayor's office
with the name and address of the drug dealers,
next week the dealers moved to another address.

V

I felt rough from the needs that took me away,
weakened from comfortable white minds,
afraid to come home so broken,
afraid to lose you, Momma
confused and painful like my brother's arms,
but contemptuous of his needle.
I walk to the store for a pop,
Arabs own the corner store now,
we still stand outside.

I grow older,
agreeing with my Uncle, no new kidney,
"I want your mother to pass sweetly,"
and the fear spreads more,
til everybody saw me and said I was fine
and looked so good
and when am I coming back to stay.

From Praisesong for the Widow

?❧ PAULE MARSHALL

The lights from the surrounding balconies caught the sheen of the tears against her blackness. The tropical night resonated with the sound of her grief. For the first time in the four years since Jerome Johnson's death, she was mourning for him, finally shedding the tears that had eluded her even on the day of his funeral.

Bent over almost double on the side of the recliner, Avey Johnson mourned—not his death so much, but his life.

His life: that massive unstinting giving of himself which had gone on for more than forty years.

His life: that the struggle had been so unrelenting. "When you come this color, it's uphill all the way," he would say, striking the back of one dark hand with the other—hard, punishing little blows that took his anger out on himself. Or, with even greater vehemence, out on his own: "The trouble with half these Negroes out here is that they spend all their time blaming the white man for everything. He won't give 'em a job. Won't let 'em in his schools. Won't have 'em in his neighborhood. Just won't give 'em a break. He's the one keeping 'em down. When the problem really is most of 'em don't want to hear the word 'work.' If they'd just cut out all the good-timing and get down to some hard work, put their minds to something, they'd get somewhere." Holding them solely responsible. When she reminded him of the countless times he had been refused despite all his efforts, his reply would be swift. Naive. He had been young and naive. He hadn't understood back then that it was *their* companies, *their* firms, *their* offices, *their* country,* and therefore, theirs the power to give or deny, to say yes or no. Naive. But he had learned his lesson. He had come to understand one thing: That we had to have our own! "That's what most of these Negroes out here still haven't gotten through their heads. Instead of marching and protesting and running around burning down everything in the hope of a handout, we need to work and build our own, to have our own. Our own! Our own!" Shouting it at her.

262

Lashing out periodically at her, himself, his own and at that world which had repeatedly denied him, until finally the confusion, contradiction and rage of it all sent the blood flooding his brain one night as he slept in the bed next to hers.

His life: that it had ended with a stranger's cold face laughing in Mephistophelian glee behind his in the coffin . . .

And Avey Johnson mourned Jay, sobbing wildly now, the tears raining down on her gloved hands gripping the pocketbook on her lap. This was a much larger grief, a far greater loss, and as if in recognition of this the plaintive voice of the sea in the darkness eight stories below rose up to mourn with her.

Jay's death had taken place long before Jerome Johnson's. There had been nothing to mark his passing. No well-dressed corpse, no satin-lined coffin, no funeral wreaths and flowers. Jay had simply ceased to be. He had vanished without making his leaving known.

When had it happened? She remembered that Tuesday in the winter of '45. Just moments before he had steeled himself and stepped forward, gathering her to him, she had sensed him, hadn't she, slowly backing away from her and Sis, easing toward the door to the hall behind him, a man eager to be gone.

Perhaps he had left after all. While she had stood in the arms of the tearful man who had stepped forward, Jay might have slipped quietly out of the room, down the five flights of stairs and up Halsey Street out of their lives, leaving Jerome Johnson to do what he perhaps felt he had neither the strength nor the hear for. . . .

And in leaving he had taken with him the little private rituals and pleasures, the playfulness and wit of those early years, the host of feelings and passions that had defined them in a special way back then, and the music which had been their nourishment. All these had departed with him that Tuesday night. Her tears flowing, Avey Johnson mourned them.

They were things which would have counted for little in the world's eye. To an outsider, some of them would even appear ridiculous, childish, *cullud*. Two grown people holding a pretend dance in their living room! And spending their Sunday mornings listening to gospels and reciting fragments of old poems while eating coffee cake! A ride on a Jim Crow bus each summer to visit the site of an unrecorded, uncanonized miracle!

Such things would matter little to the world. They had nonetheless been of the utmost importance. Dimly, through the fog of her grief, Avey Johnson understood this. Not important in themselves so much as in the larger meaning they held and in the qualities which imbued them. Avey Johnson could not have spelled out just what these qualities were, although in a way that went beyond words, that spoke from the blood, she knew. Something vivid and affirming and charged with feeling had been present in the small rituals that had once shaped their lives. They had possessed qualities as transcendent as the voices on the radio each Sunday, and as joyous as their embrace could be at times in that narrow bedroom.

And they had expressed them—these simple things—in the most fundamental way! They had been as much a part of them as Jay's wing-flared nose and his seal-brown color, and her high-riding Bantu behind (Gulla gold he used to call it, his hand coming to rest there) and the deep earth tones of her skin.

Moreover (and again she only sensed this in the dimmest way), something in those small rites, an ethos they held in common, had reached back beyond her life and beyond Jay's to join them to the vast unknown lineage that had made their being possible. And this link, these connections, heard in the music and in the praisesongs of a Sunday: "*. . .I bathed in the Euphrates when dawns were/young . . . ,*" had both protected them and put them in possession of a kind of power. . . .

All this had passed from their lives without their hardly noticing. There had been no time. Their exhaustion at the end of each day had been too great. Running with the blinders on they had allowed that richness, protection and power to slip out of the living room, down the stairs and out of the house, where it had vanished, along with Jay, in the snowy wastes of Halsey Street.

"*Too much!*" Her sudden outcry caused the darkness on the balcony to fly up for a moment like a flock of startled birds.

"*Too much!*" Loud, wrenching, issuing from her very center, it was a cry designed to make up for the silence of years.

Too much! She found herself thinking suddenly of the Christmas she had spent with Sis and her family in Los Angeles the year after Jerome Johnson's death. That Christmas morning her youngest grandson, who was just turning three at the time, had sat crying amid the scores of presents he had received, all because he had not been given a toy xylophone he had fallen in love with when out shopping with her and his mother the day before. He had been promised it to keep him quiet and the matter had been forgotten. But he had remembered, and he had sat crying inconsolably next to the Christmas tree that morning and kicking from around him the shiny new tricycle and train set, the Corgi cars and the walking space man and all the rest. She had been appalled at his behavior, and had secretly accused Sis of having spoiled him. Now, three years later, on an island thousands of miles away, she found herself wanting to applaud his outburst. She understood suddenly what it must be like for a child to find itself surrounded by a wealth of Christmas toys but finding no pleasure in them because the one it wanted most wasn't there. This might be nothing more than a toy xylophone, as in her grandson's case, or one of those paper pin-wheels from the five-and-dime store she had loved as a little girl, whose colored vanes would whirr into singing life when she held it up to the wind. Something that simple, yet containing all the magic in the world.

Too much! They had behaved, she and Jay, as if there had been nothing about themselves worth honoring!

Too much! Couldn't they have done differently? Hadn't there perhaps been another way? Questions which scarcely had any shape to them flooded her mind, and she struggled to give them form. Would it have been possible to have done both? That is, to have wrested, as they had done over all those years, the means needed to rescue them from Halsey Street and to see the children through, while preserving, safeguarding, treasuring those things that had come down to them over the generations, which had defined them in a particular way. The most vivid, the most valuable part of themselves! They could have done both, it suddenly seemed to her, bowed over in tears there on the hotel balcony. She and Jay could have managed both. What would it have taken? What would it have called for? The answers were as formless as the questions inundating her mind. They swept through her in the same bewilder-ing flood of disconnected words and images. All of it the bursting forth of a river that had long been dammed up. Awareness. It would have called for an awareness of the worth of what they possessed. Vigilance. The vigilance needed to safeguard it. To hold it like a jewel high out of the envious reach of those who would either destroy it or claim it as their own. And strength. It would have taken strength on their part, and the will and even cunning necessary to withstand the glitter and the excess. To take only what was needed and to run. And distance. Above all, a certain distance of the mind and heart had been absolutely essential. . . ." Her body she always usta say might be in Tatem, but her mind, her mind was long gone with the Ibos . . ."

Too much! What kind of bargain had they struck? How much had they foolishly handed over in exchange for the things they had gained?—an exchange they could have avoided altogether had they been on their guard!

Too much! " . . . the trouble with *these* Negroes out here . . ."; ". . . that's the only way *these* Negroes around here will ever begin to make any progress. . . ." Speaking of his own in the harsh voice that treated them as a race apart. She used to wince in the beginning hearing him, and she had even objected on occasion. But had she been any better? Hadn't she lived through most of the sixties and the early seventies as if Watts and Selma and the tanks and Stoner guns in the streets of Detroit somehow did not pertain to her, denying her rage, and carefully effacing any dream that might have come to her during the night by the time she awoke the next morning. Years!—she had spent nearly a decade avoiding the headlines and pictures on the front pages of the newspapers and the nightly television newscasts. There was the time Marion had telephoned her collect from the Poor People's March in Washington, and she had almost refused to accept the call she had been so annoyed. Why? Because in the second or two between the time the operator asked if she would accept the charges and her reply, she seemed to hear in the background the great hungry roar of the thousands encamped in the mud near the Lincoln Memorial, the sound reaching out to draw her into its angry vortex, to make her part of their petition. And not only that. She had also seen, in a sudden vivid flash, the poor half-crazed woman from Halsey Street, who would sometimes, it seemed, herding the man home from the bars of a Saturday morning, make the five-story leap to their bedroom. And there, standing over her in the bed would berate her in one breath for the superior airs she gave herself ("I see you lookin' the other way when you pass by . . ."), and in the next breath, plead with her to be remembered. Marion's call had brought the woman vividly to mind. What had happened to her and her children? Where were they today? Unsettling thoughts that had made her so annoyed with Marion and her Poor People's March she had wanted to refuse her call.

"What's she doing down there anyway?" Jerome Johnson had wanted to know afterwards. (He and Marion hardly spoke to each other.) "When did she ever have to go without three square meals a day?"

Too much! They were getting to look, even to sound alike, their friends had started teasing them. As often happens when two people have been married a long time, she and Jerome Johnson, their friends insisted, had grown to resemble each other—the same mannerisms, the same facial expression almost, the rather formal way they held themselves. They could almost pass for twins!

Too much! "Jerome Johnson," she had taken to calling him in the privacy of her thoughts, no longer able to think of him as "Jay." But hadn't she, in the same formal way, also started referring to herself as Avey Johnson? Hadn't she found it increasingly difficult as the years passed to think of herself as "Avey" or even "Avatara"? The woman to whom those names belonged had gone away, had been banished along with her feelings and passions to some far-off place—not unlike the old Eskimo woman in the strange recurring vision that had troubled her for a time after that trip to the Laurentians, who had been cast out to await her death alone in the snow. The names "Avey" and "Avatara" were those of someone who was no longer present, and she had become Avey Johnson even in her thoughts, a woman whose face, reflected in a window or mirror, she sometimes failed to recognize.

Too much! At her funeral, when Sis and Annawilda and Marion were led forward to view her body for the last time, they might sense, they might even glimpse, gazing down at her, the pale outline of another face superimposed on hers like a second skin, a thin-lipped stranger's face, alive and mocking. And to their further puzzlement, to their horror, they might hear, echoing above them in the church, the sound of someone laughing in cold glee. . . .

Suddenly, with a cry that again startled the darkness holding the wake with her on the balcony, Avey Johnson was lunging out. It was the same abrupt and threatening movement that had sent her surging forward over Jerome Johnson's bier that day in the church. This time, though, there was no one to restrain her, so that the moment she sprang forward still seated on the edge of the recliner, her gloved fist came up, and she struck the wall of air just in front of her. Over and over, in a rage of tears, she assaulted the dark and empty air, trying with each blow to get at the derisive face she saw projected there. Her own face was tear-streaked and distorted in the light reaching it from the surrounding balconies, and she could be heard uttering the same murderous, growl-like sound as on the Lido yesterday, when she had snatched her skirt and fled from the skeletal old man in the bikini.

Repeatedly she sent her fist smashing out. Her hat slid to a crazy angle over her ear from the force of her blows. The constant lunging out soon sent the pocketbook on her lap crashing to the floor, where its contents came spilling out as the catch sprung open. Eventually, the violence of her blows brought her sliding off the edge of the chair and down to the floor on her knees. And still she continued to pound away at the face she alone could see, bathed in furious tears, growling, repeating her angry litany: *"Too much!"*

Finally, all the strength went out of her, and still on her knees, she slumped forward until her forehead was almost touching the floor. She remained like this—prostrate before the darkness, a backslider on the threshing floor, at the mourner's bench. *"Come/Won't you come . . . ?"* her great-aunt had pleaded silently with her in the dream. *"Come/Will you come . . . ?"*

What lights there had been were all but extinguished by the time Avey Johnson finally struggled to her feet. Slowly, her pocketbook forgotten, she groped her way across the darkened balcony toward the sliding glass door to the room, suddenly a feeble old woman with a painful lower back and stiff noisy joints, muttering incoherently to herself: "Too much . . . !" Time might have played a trick on her while she was on the balcony, and brought her to the senile end of her days in the space of a few hours. The years telescoping, she might have lived out the rest of her life in a single evening.

Inside, she didn't bother to search for the light switch. She had no wish to encounter herself in one of the mirrors there. It was bad enough to feel in her bones the old woman she had become hobbling off to her grave. Nor did she bother to undress once she felt her way across the unfamiliar room to the bed.

When was the last time she had slept in her clothes? It came to her almost immediately, her life passing in swift review, her mind leapfrogging back over the years.

268

It had been a New Year's Eve not long after they had moved to Halsey Street, just months before Jay went in the army. They had gone with friends to a dance at the Renny; and afterwards, nearing dawn, their group had stopped off at Dickie Wells for the ritual chicken and waffles. Given the hour, their friends had urged them to sleep over. Or they could have gone and stayed with her mother, who still lived in the apartment on Seventh Avenue where Avey had been born.

But she and Jay had wanted to usher in the new year in their own bed, so that sunrise had found them taking the long train ride to Brooklyn. By the time they reached Halsey Street and climbed the five flights of stairs, it had been all they could do just to pull off their coats, toss aside their gloves and shoes and turn on the kerosene burner they kept in the room before falling exhausted across the bed.

That afternoon when they awakened she had started to undress, only to have Jay stop her. He had done it himself, slowly removing each piece of her clothing and laying it on a nearby chair, his hands and lips caressing each new place he bared before continuing; talking his talk. Leaving her briefly he slipped across the room to swing open the closet door with the full-length mirror on the inside and to turn up the burner; then, hurrying back, he resumed the undressing.

He removed everything that day except her party hat, a conical affair held on by a thin elastic band under her chin, and with the year, 1941, printed in iridescent numbers across the front; a magical Merlin's hat which she had worn at a rakish angle all evening.

It was not to remain there long. In their playfulness at the beginning, they heard the elastic band give a snap, and laughing watched the hat tumble from the bed and roll across the floor until it came to rest with the peak pointing to the reflection of their tangled bodies in the mirror . . .

Avey Johnson shucked the gloves off her hands with such violence the fingers turned inside out. The hat slanted to one side on her head found itself being hurled into the nether darkness of a corner. The plush carpeting failed to completely muffle the thud of the shoes she flung down one after the other. With the last of her strength she reached under her dress and, fumbling, unhooked the long-line girdle. (Her hair-shirt Marion insisted on calling it.) That was all she could manage before collapsing onto the bed.

"Too much! Too much! Too much!" Raging as she slept.

Bright an' Mownin' Star

❧ MIKE THELWELL

Traveling south from Memphis on Highway 49, one crosses over the last rolling hill and the Mississippi Delta stretches before you like the sea, an unbroken monotony of land so flat as to appear unnatural. So pervasive is this low-ceilinged, almost total flatness that one loses all other dimensions of space and vision. An endless succession of cotton and soybean fields surround the road.

A few weather-greyed shacks, stark, skeletal and abrasively ugly perch in a precarious oasis hacked out in the narrow, neutral strip between the road and the encroaching fields. Contemptuous of weather, time and gravity, they stand apparently empty, long-abandoned and sheltering nothing but the wind. Then some appear, no different in point of squalor and decrepitude from the others, except that people stand before them.

At one point a single huge tree, off in a cotton field a distance, breaks the horizon. It is the first tree of any size that has appeared. This tree is an oak that bears small, gnarled acorns so bitter that there is no animal that will eat them. Its wood is very hard, but is knotty, faulted, and with a grain so treacherous and erratic that it cannot easily be worked. It is used for nothing more durable than a weapon. In this region they are called blackjacks, from the sootlike darkness of the bark, and find utility mainly in conversation as a metaphor of hardness, "tougher'n a blackjack oak."

This one is unusual beyond its mere presence and size, having both name and history. Its appearance, too, is unusual. The trunk and lower limbs are fire-charred to a dull black. These limbs are leafless and dead, but the topmost branches in the center of the tree continue to grow. In a strange inharmony the living oak flourishes out of the cinders of its own corpse. White folks call this tree the Nigger Jack, while Negroes speak of it hardly at all, save on those Sundays when the tree becomes the central symbol in some hell-fire sermon, for it is widely known that the flames that burned the oak

270

roasted the bodies of slaves judged dangerous beyond redemption or control.

Once, it is said, some young black men from the county, returned from defeating the Kaiser, resolved to fell and burn the tree. On the night before this event was to take place, a huge and fiery cross was seen to shine at the base of the tree, burning through the night and into the next day.

For many years—the space of three generations—the land around this tree has lain fallow, producing annually only a tangled transient jungle of rabbit grass and myriad nameless weeds, for no Negro could be found who might be bribed, persuaded, or coerced into working there.

Lowe Junior grunted deep in his chest as the heavy, broad-bladed chopping hoe hit into the dry black earth. He jerked it up, sighted on the next clump of wire-grass and weeds, and drove the hoe-blade into the furrow just beyond the weeds, and with the same smooth motion pulled the blade towards his body and slightly upwards, neatly grubbing out the intruder in a little cloud of dust, without touching the flanking cotton plants.

"Sho do seem like the grass growin' faster'n the cotton." He leaned on the hoe handle and inspected the grubbed-up weed. "Hit be greener an' fatter'n the cotton evrahtime. Heah hit is, middle o' June, an hit ain't sca'cely to mah knee yet." He ran his glance over the rows of stunted plants, already turning a dull brownish green, then squinted down the row he was chopping, estimating the work left. He saw much "grass" wrestling its way around and between the cotton. "Finish dishyer after dinner," he said, noting that the sun had already cleared the tip of the blackjack oak which stood some ten rows into the middle of the field. Dragging his hoe he started towards the tree's shade.

Lowe Junior was tall, a gaunt, slightly-stooped figure as he shambled with the foot-dragging, slightly pigeon-toed, stiff-backed gait that a man develops straddling new-turned furrows while holding down the jerking, bucking handle of a bull-tongue plow. His boots and the dragging hoe raised a fine powder of dust around his knees. When he reached the tree he leaned his tool against the trunk and stretched himself. He moved his shoulders, feeling the pull of the overalls where the straps had worn into his flesh during the morning's work. Holding the small of his back, he arched his middle forward to ease the numb, cramping ache that hardly seemed to leave the muscles in his back. Then he straightened up and stood for a while looking out over his cotton.

Then Lowe Junior turned to the tree and took a pail which hung from one of the broken stubs. He touched the blackened trunk, running his hands over the rough cinders. "Thet fiah oney toughed yo' up, thass all . . . an there ain't nothin' wrong with thet." There was something familiar, almost affectionate, in his voice and action. When he first started working this section, he had carefully avoided the tree, sitting on the hot earth in the rows to eat and rest. But he had become accustomed to the tree now, was grateful for its shade, and he found himself accepting it as the only other living thing he encountered during the day. After all, he assured himself, "Hit cain't be no harm to no tree, fo' a certain fack."

He eased himself down ponderously, almost painfully, like a man too old or too fat, and began to eat. In the pail were butter beans boiled with country peppers, wild onions, and slabs of salted fatback. This stew was tepid, almost perceptibly warm from the midday heat. The coating of pork grease that had floated to the top had not congealed. Lowe Junior briefly debated making a small fire but decided against taking the time. He ate quickly, stirring the stew and scooping it into his mouth with a thin square of cornbread, biting into the gravy-soaked bread, then chewing and swallowing rapidly. Finishing his meal he drank deeply from a kerosene tin filled with water and covered with burlap (wet in the morning but now bone dry), which stood among the roots of the tree.

He stretched himself again, yawned, belched, spat, and braced himself firmly against the tree. He lay there limply, his eyes closed as though to shut out the rows and rows of small, drying-out plants that represented the work of his hands, every day, from can see to can't, since early in the spring.

"Ef hit would jes' rain some . . . seems like the mo' a man strain, hits the harder times git. Li'l rain now, an' the cotton be right up, but soon'll be too late." Weariness spread in him and the effort even of thinking was too great. He just lay there inert, more passive even than the tree, which at least stood. Even if by some miracle this cotton in the section he was "halfing" for Mr. Riley Peterson survived the drought, rains coming in August or September would turn the dust into mud and rot whatever cotton was ripening in the bolls—or else wash it into the mud.

A sudden panic came upon Lowe Junior, stretched beneath the tree. He could hardly feel his body, which was just a numbness. He felt that he could not rise, could not even begin, for his body would not obey him. For a brief moment he was terrified of making he effort lest he fail. Then he sat up suddenly, almost falling over forward from the violence of his effort. "Better study out whut t' do. No profit to layin' here scarin' m'se'f. Quarter section be a lot o' farmin' fo' a man. Sho ain't be able to keep t' grass outen the cotton by myse'f."

This was a problem for him, had been ever since he had asked Mr. Peterson to give him this quarter section. He was young but a good worker; still Mr. Peterson might not have given it to him had it not been for the fact that no other tenant would take it. Lowe Junior did not want to ask for help with the chopping because, in "halfing," the cost of the seed, fertilizer, ginning, and any hired help came out of the tenant's half. Already most of his half belonged to Mr. J. D. Odum, the merchant in Sunflower who had "furnished" him. He knew that he would have to have help with the picking, and did not want to hire any help before then, when he would at least have an idea of the crop's potential. "Man can en' up with nothin' thet way," he muttered. "Hit'll happen anyways, tho'. Figured to put in eight mebbe even nine bale fo' my share come the crop . . . now be the grace o' the good Gawd ef ah makes fo' . . . man doan feel much even t' keep on . . . Lawd, hit be better t' die, than t' live so hard." He found little comfort in those grim lines from the old Blues to which his grandmother was so partial. She was always incanting that song as though it had a special meaning for her.

After his father died, and his mother went off to the north to find work, it was the old woman, pious and accepting, who had told him the old stories, raised him in the Church, and interpreted for him the ways of their world. He remembered her story of how God had put two boxes into the world, one big and the other small. The first Negro and the first white man had seen the boxes at the same time and run towards them, but the Negro arrived first and greedily appropriated for himself the larger box. Unfortunately this box contained a plough, a hoe, a cop-axe, and a mule, while the smaller box contained a pen, paper, and a ledger book. "An' thass why," the old woman would conclude, her face serious, "the Nigger been aworkin' evah since, an' the white man he reckon up the crop; he be sittin' theah at crop time, jes' afigurin' an' areckonin'; he say

Noughts a nought
Figgers a figger,
All fo' us folks,
None fo' the Nigger."

He had been fifteen before he even began to doubt the authenticity of this explanation. Now the old lady was ailing and very old. But she had not lost her faith in the ultimate justice of the Lord or her stoic acceptance of whatever He sent. It was a joke among the neighbors that when the good sisters of the Church went in to see the old lady, now failing in sight and almost bedridden, her answer to the question, "How yo' keepin', Miz Culvah?" invariably was "Porely, thank d' Lawd." Lowe Junior chuckled, got up, dusted off his clothes, and went out into the sun.

That evening he stopped work early, just as the sun was setting, and started home, trudging slowly over the flat dusty road past fields, a few as parched and poor as his own, and large ones where elaborate machinery hurled silvery sprays over rows of tall lush plants. A wind swept the fine cool spray into the road. He felt the pleasant tickling points of coldness on his face and saw the grayish dust coating his overalls turn dark with the moisture. Minute grains of mud formed on his skin. He looked into the dazzling spray and saw a band of color where the setting sun made a rainbow.

D'Lawd give Noah d' rainbow sign,
No mo' watah, d' fiah nex' time.

"Thass whut the ol' woman would say, an tell evrahbody thet she seen d'Lawd's sign. Be jes' sun an' watah, tho'." He did not look at the green fields. Looking straight ahead into the dust of the road, he increased his pace. He wanted only to get home.

Just where the dust road meets the highway, at the very edge of a huge field, was the shack. Tin-roofed with gray clapboard sides painted only with the stain of time and weather, it had two small rooms. As Lowe Junior came up the road, it seemed to be tossed and balanced on a sea of brown stalks, the remains of last year's bean crop which came up to the back door.

In the front, the small bare yard was shaded by a pecan tree already in blossom. Small lots, well-kept and tidy, grew okra, butterbean and collard green plants on both sides of the yard. Lowe

Junior walked around the shack to a standpipe in back of the stoop. He washed the dust from his head and arms, filled his pail and drank. The water was brown, tepid, and rusty-tasting. He sprinkled the okra and bean plants, then entered the shack. The fire was out, and the huge pot hanging over the fire, from which he had taken his dinner that morning, had not been touched.

"Mam, Mam," he called softly. "Yo' awright?" There was no answer, and he went into the old woman's room. The room was stifling-hot as the tin roof radiated the day's heat. The air was heavy with the smell of stale urine, old flesh, and night sweat. The old lady lay against the wall, partially covered by an old quilt. A ray of sunlight beamed through a small knothole and lighted up the lined and creasing skin pattern on one side of her face. A single fly buzzed noisily around her open mouth and lighted on the tuft of straggling white hairs on her chin. Her eyes stared at a framed picture of the bleeding heart of Jesus, violent red and surrounded by a wreath of murderous-looking thorns and a hopeful glow, which hung on the opposite wall above the motto, "The Blood of Jesus Saves."

Lowe Junior searched his pockets slowly, almost absently, for two coins to place over her eyes. His gaze never left her face and, as he looked, the ray of sunlight gradually diminished, seeming to withdraw reluctantly from the face, finally leaving it to shadow.

Failing to find any coins, he straightened the limbs, pulled the quilt over the face, and went to tell the neighbors.

When he returned, the thick purple Delta darkness had descended with a tropical suddenness. He added more beans, fatback and water to the stew, and started the fire. Then he lit a kerosene lantern and took it into the yard to a spot beneath the pecan tree. He hung the lantern on a branch and began to dig.

The neighbors found him still digging when they began to arrive in the little yard. The first small group of women was led by Sister Beulah, a big, imposing, very black woman with a reputation for fierce holiness. She stood out from the worn and subdued group not only because of the crisp whiteness of her robe and bandanna but in her purposeful, almost aggressive manner. She led the women to the side of the hole.

"Sho sorry t' heah 'bout Sistah Culvah, but as you knows . . . ," she began.

"She inside," Lowe Junior said without looking up, "an ah thanks yo' all fo' comin'."

Interrupted in mid-benediction, Beulah stood with her mouth open. She had failed to officiate at buryings in the community only twice in the past twenty years, and then only because she had been holding revivals at the other end of the state. She had never quite forgiven the families of the deceased for not awaiting her return. She resented Lowe Junior's thanks, the first she had ever received for doing what she thought of as an indispensable service. May as well thank the grave.

"Thet boy sho actin' funny," she murmured, and swept into the shack to take charge of preparations.

More neighbors straggled into the yard. Another lantern was brought and hung in the tree, widening the chancy and uncertain perimeter of light in the otherwise enveloping blackness of the Delta night. Each man arriving offered to help Lowe Junior with the digging. Some had even brought tools, but Lowe Junior stonily refused all offers.

"Ah be finished time the box git heah," he answered without looking at the men. "Sho do thank yo', tho'."

So the men sat and smoked, speaking only in murmurs and infrequently. The women passed out steaming plates of stew and tins of coffee bitter with chicory. Lowe Junior declined all food. The plates in the shack were emptied and rotated until all were fed. After a muttered consultation, one of the men approached Lowe Junior. He was old, his hair very white against his skin. He was very neat and careful of himself, moving with great dignity. His faded overalls were clean and shiny from the iron. He stood quietly at the side of the hole until Lowe Junior stopped work and looked up at him. Then he spoke, but so softly that the other men could not make out his words. The yard was very silent.

"Brothar Culvah. The peoples ain't easy in min'. They come to he'p yo' an heah yo' takin' no he'p." Lowe Junior said nothing.

"In time o' grief, praise Jesus, folks, they wants t', an' mo'n thet, they needs, t' he'p . . . they come t' pay respeck t' the daid an' share the burden an' sarrow o' d' livin'. Thass how hits allus bin. . . . Son, when folks offer comfort an' he'p, a man mus' accep' hit, 'caus hit's mebbe all they got."

Lowe Junior looked at the old man.

"Yo' unnerstan' what ah'm asayin', son?" he asked gently.

"The peoples doan feel like as if they got anythang t' do heah, anythang thet they needs t' be adoin'."

Lowe Junior looked into the darkness. His voice was low and without inflection. "Hit ain't no he'p to give, ain't no sarrow t' share. Hits jes' thet the ol' woman was ol', an now she daid. Ain't no sarrow in thet."

They became aware of a sound. It came from the shack and at first did not seem to intrude or in any way challenge the dark silence. It began as a deep sonorous hum, close in pitch to the sound of silence. Then it grew, cadenced and inflected, gathering power and volume until it filled the yard and was present, physical and real. The men picked up the moan and it became a hymn.

hhhmmmmmmmmMMMAY THE CIRCLE . . . BE UNBROKEN BYE AN BYE, LAWD . . . BYE ANNNN BYE

"Peoples can sang," Lowe Junior said. "Praise Jesus, they can allus do thet."

The old man walked away silent. He sat on the stoop ignoring the questioning looks of the others. He hunched over, his frail body gently rocking back and forth, as though moved against his will by the throbbing cadences of the singing. He sat there in isolation, his eyes looking into the darkness as at his own approaching end, his face etched with lines of a private and unnamable old man's sorrow. Deep and low in his chest he began to hum the dirge melody.

Lowe Junior chopped viciously at the earth. The people intoned the old and troubled music that they were born to, which, along with a capacity to endure, was their only legacy from the generations that had gone before, the music that gathered around them, close, warm and personal as the physical throbbing of their natural life.

When the hole was to Lowe Junior's chin, the Haskell boys came into the yard carrying the coffin. It was of green pitchpine, the boards rough-planed so that all depressions of the surface of the boards were sticky with sap. The men also brought two boxes so that the coffin would not rest on the ground. The Haskells stood by the hole, wiping their gummy hands on their overalls.

"Yo' reckon hit'll be awright?" Ben Haskell asked.

"Sholey. Sho, hit'll be jes fine. Yo' done real good; hits a coffin, ain't hit?" Lowe Junior still had not looked at the coffin, which was surrounded by the neighbor men. The Haskells stood silent, looking at him.

"'Sides, ol' woman ... allus was right partial t' scent o' pine. Yassuh, hit'll be right fine," Lowe Junior said. Ben Haskell smiled, a diffident embarrassed stretching of his mouth. "Yo' said cedar, but see, quick as yo' needed hit, pine wuz all we could git."

"Thass right," his brother assented.

Leastwise, Lowe Junior thought, Mist' Odum wouldn' give yo' all cedar fo' credit. He repeated softly, "Yo' done good, real good." The Haskells beamed, relieved, and expressed again their sympathy before moving away.

The yard was now full, some twenty persons stood, hunkered, or sat around. Set on the boxes in the center of the group, the raw white coffin dominated the scene like an altar, filling the air with the pungent odor of crude turpentine.

Lowe Junior walked around the coffin and approached the steps of the shack. The neighbors' eyes followed him. Sister Beulah met him at the door. He saw the faces of the other women peering down at him from behind her. All conversation ceased.

"Brothah Culvah, this yer ah'm agonna say ain't strickly mah business. Some would say hit rightly ain't *none* o' mah concern atall." She paused, looking at Lowe Junior and the men in the yard. Nothing was said, and she continued. "But lookin' at hit anothah way, hit what ah'm gonna say, *is* mah business. Hits bin troublin' mah min', an hits lotsa othah folks heah, what ah *knows* feel d' same way." When she paused again, there was a faint assenting Ahmen from the people.

"So ah'm agonna say hit.... Now, yo' all knows me, bin apreachin' an aservin' the Lawd in these parts fo' thutty year, an live heah thutty year befo' thet." Murmurs of "Thass right" came from the group.

"Yas, thass the Lawd's truth, an ah knows Sistah Culvah, Miss Alice we used t' call her, from the fust come off t' plantation, an' nobody evah had a word o' bad to say 'bout her, praise Jesus. Yas, an' ah know yo' po' mothah, an yo'se'f, Brothah Culvah, from evah since." The murmurs from the neighbors were stronger now. Encouraged, Sister Beulah continued. She was now speaking louder than anyone had spoken in the yard all evening.

"She wuz a good woman, a go-o-d woman, she knowed Jesus

an' she wuz saved. Hits true, towards the las' when she wuz porely an' gittin' up in age, she couldn't git to meetin' to praise her Gawd, but yo' all knows she *lo-oved* the Church." She took a deep breath. "Now, ah knows thet back then, in slavery times, when the ol' folks could do no bettah, an' had to hol' buryin's an' Chris'nin' an' evrah-thang at night. But, thank Jesus, them days is gone. They's gone. Hit ain't fittin' an' hit ain't right an' propah t' hol' no buryin' at night, leas' hit ain't bin done herebouts. The body o' the good sistah, now called t' Glorah, ain't even bin churched. Yo' knows thet ain't right. Ah knows thet, effen she could have somepin t' say, she'd want hit done right at the las'! Ah *kno-o-ows* in mah heart she would."

"Yas, yas, ahah, praise Jesus." The neighbors agreed.

"An Brothah Culvah, yo' a young man, yo' a Gawd-fearin' man, an' ah knows yo' wants t' do right. Cause ... yo' know hit says ... the longes' road mus' ha' some endin', but a good name endureth fo'evah." On this dramatic and veiled note of warning the huge white-draped woman ended.

Everyone was quiet, but there was a faint expectant shuffling of feet as the people looked at Lowe Junior.

"'Tain't no call t' fret yo'se'f," he said. "Ol' woman wuz ol' an now she gone. Ah be aburyin' her tonight." There was a quickly-stifled murmur from the people. No one spoke, and Lowe Junior continued more softly.

"'Tain't thet whut yo' say ain't got right to hit, Sta' Beulah, 'cause hit do. But hits no law say thet effen yo' buryin' t' do, hit cain't be done in the night."

"Yas, Brothah Culvah, effen yo' *got* t' do hit. Doan seem like t' me hits no hurry ..." Beulah said.

"Yas'm, hit is a hurry. See, ah feel like ah should take care o' this thang personal. Ol' woman raise me from when ah wuz young, ah wants t' take care o' the buryin' personal."

"Whut's wrong with t'morrow? Yo' answer me thet."

"Be no tellin' jes' where ah'll be t'morrow," Lowe Junior said, lifting one end of the coffin and asking Ben Haskell to help with the other end. They took it into the shack to receive the body.

"Hey, Lowe, yo' sho nuff fixin' t' leave?" Ben could not keep the excitement out of his voice.

"Thass right." Lowe Junior's first knowledge of his decision had come when he heard himself telling Beulah, a moment before.

"Yo' mean yo' ain't even gon' stay t' make yo' crop?"

"Any one o' yo' all wants t' work hit is welcome t' my share. Ah'll sign a paper so Mist' Peterson an Mist' Odum'll know." Temptation and fear struggled in Ben's eyes, and finally he said only, "Ah'll tell d' other'ns . . . but supposin' no one wants t' take hit?"

"Yo' mean 'bout Mist' Peterson . . . well, he got mo' cotton. Fack is, he got 'bout all theah is."

"Lawd's truth," Ben agreed, and went quickly to share the news with the men in the yard. There the women were grouped around Sister Beulah who was threatening to go home. After what she judged to be sufficient entreaty to mollify her hurt dignity, she agreed to remain and conduct the burial, not only because "hits mah bounden duty to see to hit thet the pore daid woman gits a propah Christian service." She led the women into the shack to put the old lady into the coffin.

After everyone had taken a last look at the corpse, Ben Haskell nailed the lid on and the coffin was brought out and placed on the boxes. During the singing of "Leaning on the Everlasting Arms," two of the women began to cry. Lowe Junior stood a short distance off under the shadow of the pecan tree and looked out over the darkness. He took no part in the singing until the lines of "Amazing Grace,"

Ah wunst wuz lost but now ah'm Found,
Wuz blind but now ah See.

In a loud but totally uninflected voice, he repeated, "Wuz blind but now ah See."

This unexpected voice, coming as it were from behind her, distracted Sister Beulah who had begun to "line out" the succeeding lines for the benefit of any backsliders who might have forgotten them. She stopped, turned, and glared at Lowe Junior, then continued in the joyful and triumphant voice of one whose seat in the Kingdom is secure beyond all challenge.

"*'Twuz Grace thet taught mah heart t' feah,*" she exulted; *'An' Grace mah feah relieved.*" Her face was illuminated, radiant with the security of grace.

When the coffin was being lowered and was a quarter of the way down, the rope under the head slipped, and it thudded into the hole, almost upright. The people stood in momentary shocked silence. Sister Beulah at the head of the grave raised her massive white-sleeved arms to the sky as though appealing for divine vindication of this sacrilege, the result of Lowe Junior's stubbornness. Lowe Junior quickly lay flat on the edge of the grave, and shoved the high end of the coffin with all his strength. He grunted with the effort and the box slid into place with a heavy thump, followed by the rattle of dirt and pebbles from the sides.

At that moment the sky lightened. They all looked up and saw the risen moon peering from behind a wall of dark clouds that had not been there when the sun set.

"Glorah, Glorah!" a man shouted hoarsely, and the ritual resumed. Sister Beulah had thought to preach her famous "Dead Bones Arisin" sermon, capped with a few well-chosen words on the certain doom of impious children, but recent events had lessened her zeal. Almost perfunctorily she recounted the joys and glories of Salvation and the rewards awaiting the departed sister. Then they piled dirt on the coffin, patted down the pile, and departed.

Lowe Junior sat on the steps. Barely acknowledging the final murmured consolations, he watched the neighbors leave. He realized that he was not alone when the old man approached the stoop.

"Ah heah yo' is leavin', Brothah Culvah. Done any thankin' on wheah yo' goin' an' whut yo' gonna be doin'?"

Lowe Junior did not answer. He in no way acknowledged the old man's presence.

"Thass awright, yo' doan have t' answer 'cause ah knows—yo' ain't! Jes' like ah wuz when ah wuz 'bout yo' age. An ah lef' too, din' know wheah ah wuz agoin' nor whut ah wuz lookin' fo'. Effen yo' doan know whut yo' seekin', Brothah Culvah, yo' cain' know when yo' fin' hit."

Now Lowe Junior was looking at the man; he seemed interested in what he was saying. It was the first interest he had shown in anyone else that evening.

"See, Brothah Culvah, ah traveled aroun' some when ah wuz yowr age, an heah ah is now. Ah never foun' no bettah place nowheahs." He shook his head. "Fo' usses, theah wuzn't none, leastways not thet ah could fin'."

"But at leas' yo' looked," Lowe Junior said.

"Thass why ah'm asayin' t' yo' whut ah is. 'Cause ah did. Brothah Culvah, yo' a good worker, yo' knows farmin' an cotton, but whut else do yo' know? Ah disbelieves thet yo' even bin so far as Memphis."

"Well," Lowe Junior said, "t'morrow thet won' be true. But ah 'preciates yo' kin'ness."

The old man hobbled into the darkness, shrouded in his own knowledge.

Lowe Junior sat on the steps and watched him leave, until finally he was alone. He went to the tree, blew the lamp out, and sat in the darkness. . . . When the sun came up next morning he had not moved. The astringent pitchpine smell still hovered in the still air. Lowe Junior saw that the morning sky was covered by a heavy metallic-grey cloud that had come swirling up from the Gulf in the dark. He entered the shack and looked about him for something to take. In the old woman's room he found nothing. He returned, picked up his hoe, turned around in the small room, saw nothing else that he wanted, and started to leave. On the steps he changed his mind and re-entered the house. In the old woman's room he took the picture of the Sacred Heart from the frame. Then from a small wooden box he took a Bible which he held by the covers and shook. Three crumpled bills fluttered to the floor. He gave the book a final shake, tossed it into the box, then picked up the bills and carefully wrapped them in the picture. He placed the package in the long deep side-pocket of his overalls. He picked up his hoe from the steps and started out. At the dirt road he turned, not towards the highway, but east towards his section. Soon he could see the top of the oak in the thin dawning light.

"Sho nevah put no stock in all thet talk 'bout thet tree," he mused. "Burned like thet on the sides an so green t' the top, hit allus did put me in min' o' Moses an the burnin' bush. But ah wager a daid houn', ain't no Nigger agoin' t' work thisyer lan' now."

He stood for awhile looking at the tree, at the lean runted plants. "Sho do feels like ah knows yo' evrah one, evrah row an clump o' grass like hit wuz the face o' mah own han' or mah own name."

He strode up to the tree, set his feet, and swung the hoe against the trunk with all the strength of his back. The hickory handle snapped with a crack like a rifle in the early morning. The blade went whirring into the cotton-rows. He felt the shock of the blow sting the palm of his hands, and shivver up into his shoulders. He stepped away from the tree and hurled the broken handle as far as he could into the field.

"Theah," he grunted, "yo' got the las' o' me they yo' is gonna git—the natural las'."

He started back towards the highway at a dead run. There were tears in his eyes and his breath was gusty. He tired and slowed to a walk. He saw the first raindrops hitting heavy into the thick dust of the road, raising sudden explosions of dust and craters of dampness where they struck. Before he reached the cabin, torrents of water were lashing the face of the Delta. When he reached the highway, he turned once to look at the mean little house, gray and forlorn in the storm. He saw a pool already spreading around the roots of the pecan tree.

The dry earth gave off an acrid smell as the water dampened it. "Be nuff now fo' evrah one, white an black," Lowe Junior thought and laughed. "Sho doan mattah now effen they takes ovah mah fiel'. Hit be all washed out, evrah natural one."

The rain swept down with increased violence. He was completely drenched, streamlets ran down his face, washing away the dust. "Ah nevah seed the like. Sho now, be hongry folk heah this year. Even white folk be hongry in the Delta this winter." He walked steadily down the highway stretching into the distance.

The Funeral

❧ ANN ALLEN SHOCKLEY

The death of Melissa's grandmother had been expected. She had been ailing a long time, beset with the genealogical diseases of the old: arthritis, high blood pressure, and diabetes advanced by her eighty years, until these were finally laid to rest by a heart attack.

The funeral was already paid for. *Had* been paid for years ago through the fifty-cents-a-week policy taken out with the Black Brothers Burial Society. Undertaker C. B. Brown had nothing to worry about along those lines. Neither did the Reverend Thomas Cooke have reason to fret over the funeral services because all that information had been foretold to him time before time and locked in the Zion Methodist Church's metal strongbox.

The occasion had been prepared for well, and all involved rose nobly to meet it. Even the tired decrepit four-room house, whose once white frame was archaically grimy with red dust from the patch of yard surrounding it—where no grass appeared ever to be able to grow—managed to look less worn, less dull, to accommodate the throngs of people stopping by to share the grief. Helpful neighbors and friends came in hushed, sad-eyed groups, bringing plates of fried chicken, potato salad, greens, and homemade pastries to Melissa, too bereaved to bother with the mundane.

There was more food than Melissa could ever eat, since with her grandmother dead, she was left alone. If there were any other relatives, Melissa knew nothing about them, scattered here and yond up north and east and God-knows-where.

There had only been the two of them living in the house. Just the two of them facing each other in the evenings in the small living room with the shades tightly drawn: Granny rocking slowly back and forth in the ancient rocker with its high straight arrow back, and Melissa, absorbing herself in preparing for the next day which would end like the day before.

Granny sewed when the arthritic pain wasn't drawing her

284

hands, brown fingers weaving in and out, no longer swift, only halfway sure. But when the pain was there curling up the gnarled hands that had known work since thoughts could remember—cleaning up the big house for the white folks and making their children spotless—Granny would open the frayed family Bible scrawled with census records, and slowly, very slowly form the biblical words aloud with her lips. Frequently she paused to peer over at Melissa, shakily pointing to a passage she wanted read at her funeral.

Granny talked a lot to Melissa about the funeral. Especially about the clothes she wanted to be buried in—an old black satin with a lace embroidered shawl, and the black square-heel shoes kept shiny under her bed. When talking about the funeral, Granny's skinny flat chest would heave with tiny ripples like a small wind trying to press the sea into waves.

Melissa would listen sometimes, and sometimes she wouldn't. The woman was old and Melissa could smell death around her. Once in a while even see it—a dismal shadow hovering near. There were unjust moments when she wished the shadow would stay so she could make the lamps brighter and turn the tiny boxlike radio up to cheerful sounds. Now she couldn't. Bright lights hurt Granny's cataracts, and the blaring music wasn't the sound of the Lord's.

Now and then some evenings when Granny talked about the funeral, Melissa would stare blankly at her with the hand-knitted robe thrown across her lap winter and summer, focusing her eyes dreamily at the vacant corner behind the rocker where she hoped to put a secondhand television—after it was over.

"That song, Melissa. Don't forget I want Sister Smith to sing *Just a Closer Walk with Thee* right before the preaching. You hear me?" Granny's voice would rise, squeaking in the manner of a worn out reed.

"Sure, Granny, sure."

After various intervals, Melissa would get up and go through the plastic curtain door to the kitchen on the pretense of getting a glass of water. There she would turn on the faucet vigorously while reaching quickly behind the flour can for the pint of Gordon's gin. She would hurriedly gulp down the drink, choking in her haste, then return to the room, smiling a little now, able to endure the talk and the death in the chair whose cushion had long worn down with the weight and the words.

In the chair was where she died: the thin, wasted body crumpled in the rocker, head down, white hair straggling outrageously from its knot, just as if she had nodded to sleep.

Now there was no longer the quietness in the house. The door was left unlocked to admit the endless string of church members and lodge sisters, and even some of the white folks for whom Granny had scrubbed and worked and fussed over.

Granny had insisted on being laid out in the house—no funeral parlor where it was unfriendly and reeking with embalming fluid— but laid out in her satin dress with her hands crossed to show the round tarnished wedding band right in her own living room.

Since that was where she wanted to be, the living room was always the one papered each year to keep down the smoke stain ruins of the potbellied coal stove fired in the winters. The coffin was large for the room and the couch had to be moved into the bedroom to make space. Extra folding chairs were brought in by the undertaker and cardboard fans advertising C.B. Brown's Funeral Home ALWAYS THE FAMILY FIRST were distributed noticeably even though there was no need.

Melissa stayed in the bedroom, letting the visitors feel free to drift in and sign the register while Undertaker Brown stood solemnly at the door, neatly attired in his navy suit, whispering professional instructions. Across from him was stalwart Sister Mary Smith, head of the church's stewardess board, in her stiff white uniform, handling the viewers with equal aplomb.

Watching the people drift in and out, leaving behind the soft rustle of dresses and ragged shuffling of feet moving past the body, Melissa could tell the town remembered and loved Miss Eliza. That was what they all called her—Miss Eliza—young, old, white folks alike. She had been a fixture in the town like the Confederate soldier in front of the court house. A born and bred fixture claimed by time.

Melissa could hear the laments as they filed by:

"Don't she look nat-u-ral?"

"Poor Miss Eliza. God's restin' her now. Put her out of her mis-ery."

And the younger ones, impatiently: "Wonder if'n I'll live to get *that* old?"

An answering giggle. "Not at the rate you goin' now!"

"Please ..." the smooth articulate voice of the undertaker, "move on by the casket and sign the register. Others are waiting. ...."

A tray of hot food was brought to Melissa, urged upon her, heedless of her feeble sign of refusal. But finally the aroma of hot bread and chicken pressed close to her nose made her relent.

"We goin' to stay all night for the wake, honey," one of the lodge sisters murmured consolingly. "Now you lay down 'n rest. Don't cry now. The Lord giveth and the Lord taketh away."

"Give her a hot toddy ..." another voice suggested. "That *always* helps at times like these."

The undertaker thrust his head into the room. "Is Miss Melissa all right?"

"Doin' fine."

Melissa sipped the toddy, feeling a warm glow kindle within her, spreading some life into her tired body.

"Wait! Undertaker Brown ..." she called, beckoning him back. "Don't forget the expensive hearse tomorrow. The *Cad-il-lac.* Granny always said that that'd be one time she rode in style. Even if it was to her grave."

"Of course ... of course."

"And all the white folks' messages read *first.*"

"Naturally."

Melissa drank longer on the toddy, not minding the burning hot sting this time, talking excitedly now like Granny used to do. "That pretty white spray of carnations from the white folks I work for I want right in *front.*"

The undertaker nodded affirmatively, his shining bald head bobbing quickly. "Thy will be done."

A small tuneless wail suddenly rose in the outer room, coiling in a feverish pitch. "Oh Lord ... Lordy ... po' Melissa. Where's the chile?"

A stooped old woman bundled in a threadbare coat groped into the room towards Melissa. "Chile ... chile ... I knowed your grandmother *ever* since we wuz chillen. I'm goin' next. I can feel it in my bones. Death don't never stop at one. It takes more 'n more. ..."

"Sh-h-h, Miss Reva, don't cry," Melissa consoled, hugging the woman close to her. "You go on home and get a good night's sleep. You to ride with me tomorrow. You an old friend of the family. I ain't got nothing but old friends to ride with me."

Sobbing louder, the woman was aided out. "Oh, Lord, God help us all."

Melissa stretched out on the bed. Someone threw a quilt over her, persuading her to sleep. She heard the women's preparations of turning off the lamp by the bed and quietly closing the door, leaving her alone to rest. A thin shred of light shone vigilantly under the door where Granny was, and watching it, she found it hard to sleep.

The morning of the funeral was cold and gray, hanging heavily with impending rain.

"A good sign," one lodge sister said, looking out the window. "When it rains, they goin' to heaven."

Melissa sighed, fumbling with her black veil, feeling weak and worn from the four-day ordeal of death. The house reeked nauseously, emanating the sweet odors of the myriad sprays. Her arms and legs felt lifeless, debilitated by people and emotions. But inwardly she had the sensation of being alive with excitement and anticipation over the drama orbiting around her.

"Everything is in readiness," Undertaker Brown murmured gently, glancing anxiously at her. "The cars are waiting."

Melissa lowered her head in what she judged to be a proper angle, not too low or too high, but leveled to see her steps and that around her too. Sister Mary Ellen and a nurse supported her on each side as she moved falteringly on her Sunday best heels into the gray foggy mist.

The black Cadillac hearse gleamed brilliantly, and seeing it, Melissa knew how proud Granny would be. She got in the sleek family limousine whose interior was spotless. Undertaker Brown sure kept his cars up nice, she thought. Granny always said that, and Granny ought to know because she never missed a funeral. "Goin' to ever'body's. I got no folks livin' I know of 'cept you. If I go to other peoples', they'll come to mine," Granny used to say.

True to Granny's words, they were there, Melissa noticed as the car came slowly to a stop in front of the church. People were standing on the outside and in the church's doorway. Melissa furtively lifted her veil to survey the scene as the other cars came slowly to a stop behind them in the section reserved.

The sounds of sobs and moans surrounded her, reminding her of those beside her. She took a deep harsh breath, letting herself be half lifted out of the luxuriously plush seat that was better than a sofa.

"Steady ... steady," the undertaker whispered, stationing her at the head to lead the long line of lodge sisters, friends, and members of the burying order into the church. "The procession is now ready to begin ... ."

The church organist was softly playing the piece Granny wanted, *Nearer My God to Thee.* Melissa sniffled, fumbling for her handkerchief. Arms tightened around her shoulders and gently guided her through the parting crowd to the front pew by the casket.

The Reverend Cooke cleared his throat and stretched his black robed arms wide in twin hawk's wings, engulfing the congregation. "Jesus said, 'I am the resurrection, and the life: he that believeth in Me, though he were dead, yet shall he live; and whosoever liveth and believeth in Me shall never die.' Let us pray. Our Father. ... "

Melissa's fingers tightly gripped her wet handkerchief, twisting it to dabble at her eyes. Moments later, the loud resounding voice of Sister Smith filled the church with Granny's favorite hymn, *Just a Closer Walk with Thee,* punctuated by foot tapping rhythm and shouts:

"Sing it, Sister, sing it."

"She's gone ... *gone.*"

"Oh, God, have mercy."

Melissa swayed and the nurse pushed a bottle of smelling salts under her nose.

The Reverend rose again, paused, and in deep sonorous tones started his eulogy. "A good and Godly woman was Sister Eliza. Loved by all who knew her. A fine church worker has left us, who God has called to work in His heavenly church above."

"A-men."

The words of the preacher drifted around her in swelling billows that would not stop long enough for her to grasp them. So she sat still, eyes downcast, thoughts locked in nothingness.

In what seemed like a long time, the choir later began to sing softly as the minister called for the president of the Burial Society to read the obituary. The acknowledgement of cards and flowers followed, given by the head of the church's stewardess board.

"They goin' to view the body now," the nurse said softly, looking anxiously at Melissa.

Melissa heard the organist playing *Steal Away* as she half watched the long column of men, women, and children filing past to gaze one last time at Granny. A female voice shrieked hysterically, and Melissa pushed her head slightly forward to see who it was.

And last, the family. Strong capable hands clutched Melissa, and she found herself being shelteringly steeled against a large warm bosom, steadying her to look down upon Granny's sleeping face. The face was peaceful, serene, no longer complaining of the ache in her joints—especially on rainy days like this. This was one rainy day when Granny wouldn't have an ache.

Melissa reached out to touch Granny for the last time, just once more. That's what Granny had asked her to do: reach out and touch her. Melissa's hand moved slowly, hesitantly, and suddenly paused in midair, a breath away from the sunken brown cheek. She *couldn't*. A drowning siege of dizziness covered her, a temporary black cloud passing over to hover for a tiny vacuous second before going beyond.

Then poised as a tense wary bird for sudden flight, one finger extended out from the rounded mold of her hand to gently touch the cheek. And when she did, she knew that she would never forget its unyielding tough chill. Far off, she imagined hearing Granny saying, "Well done, chile, well done."

Laboriously she sat back on the bench, now aware of its hardness, and that her feet ached in the shoes she seldom wore, and the girdle was making ridges around her stomach.

The funeral had been long. Outside, rain pushed harder against the multicolored stained windows, as if to intrude with sound if nothing else. She realized by the beginning restless stirrings many of the women were listening to it and becoming angry because their hair would get wet standing in the graveyard.

There was an indistinct prayer mumbled by the minister, and through the light pressure of the protective hands beside her, she understood that it was all over. The choir rose to sing *Swing Low, Sweet Chariot,* just as Granny wanted.

They had gone. The house was the same once again, quiet, still, but not the same either. She had told them there was no need to stay with her tonight. They were being nice and polite, but the commotion was over. They had to get back to their normal routines of work and everyday living until the next funeral which would come in the manner of a charging white horse to interrupt the dull monotony of their plodding lives. Then again, they would be rejuve-

290

nated in baking their pies, caring for the living, and crying for the dead.

It was still raining, an all-night incessant dirge. She was glad everything had been carried out as Granny wished: a big expensive funeral to put her at rest in the family plot. Granny was now covered by a blanket of dirt. Ashes to ashes, dust to dust, just like the preacher said at the grave.

Melissa rose slowly and went to the kitchen, taking down a fresh bottle of gin. Pouring a drink, she started to down it quickly to keep Granny from calling and asking why she was so long in the kitchen.

Then remembering, she shrugged, picked up the bottle and glass, and went back to the living room. Wearily she sat down in the rocker which seemed still warmed by Granny's long sitting and waiting.

She began to rock slowly back and forth in Granny's rhythm with her head resting against the chair. The blinds were drawn and the room was half shadowed in illusions. She closed her eyes, listening to the measured screaks of the old rocker, a soft sound from the past, and began to wonder what would happen when she was gone someday. For everybody's got to go—someday.

Loss and Grief
Discussion Questions

1. Reread "The Lynching," noting contrasts of good and evil. How are traditional symbols of innocence reversed?

2. Even though Maumee Ruth has become a solitary and pathetic figure, what is the difference between her life and those of her children?

3. Humor is used frequently as a foil to tragic occurrences. Simple's folksy dialogue with Saint Peter and Old Governor in "Golden Gate" seems light-hearted on the surface, but in fact deals with abusive and derogatory behaviors. What does this format contribute? Is it effective?

4. In Shockley's story, "The Funeral," what relationship in life and death does Granny have with white folks? What future do you predict for Melissa, and what do you make of her drinking in terms of loss and grief?

5. Frequently, the grieving process is not as exuberantly expressed as it is in "Second Line/Cutting the Body Loose." What does a parade, such as the one described by Ferdinand, or a wake contribute to our abilities to deal with death? Compare the release of emotions in the story to your own experience of grieving.

6. What feelings did the narrator have for Willie Lee in "Requiem for Willie Lee"? Could he have been saved? Were you a sympathetic reader, or did you feel that Willie got what he deserved?

7. Countee Cullen's poem, "A Brown Girl Dead," illustrates the importance of providing the proper "laying out" for loved ones. "She'd be so proud she'd dance and sing/To see herself tonight." What is the significance of the reference to the Virgin Mary in this piece?

8. Why was Mr. Sam killed in "Cotton Alley"? Can you think of a personal experience of your own that was foolishly escalated in importance in a similar manner?

9. Discuss the relationship in "Lucielia Louise Turner" between Eugene and Ciel before the tragedy. What had Ciel come to recognize moments before the disaster occurred? Explain the circumstances leading to Ciel's abortion and the impact of that loss on the subsequent tragedy. What feelings did you have for Eugene? Eugene does not choose to attend his daughter's funeral. What reasons does he give and what other reasons might be offered? Explain Mattie's relationship to Ciel, Eugene, and Serena. What can be said about Mattie's grieving process and will she be able to provide help for the grieving Ciel?

10. In "Revelation," what does "An old woman in me walks patiently to the hospital" mean? In terms of the struggles she has endured, how will her death be different?

11. In some ways, "Mother Dear and Daddy" resembles a grotesque shopping trip. Discuss the role of irony in relation to the extended family's function in this story.

12. The death of Newt's mother in "The Learning Tree" transforms his life. How does he reconcile himself to his fears and how does the episode with Prissy suggest maturity and growth?

13. Neonatal Intensive Care Units (NICUs) are places where miracles of technology can occur for infants in distress. Michael S. Harper's poem, "We Assume: On the Death of Our Son, Reuben Masai Harper," links the realm of science with that of human feelings. Consider the richness of information about the baby's treatment in stanzas one and two, the other mother's consolation in stanza three, and the abruptness of the final two-line stanza. What does the inclusion of the child's full name contribute to the poem?

14. In June Jordan's "Poem for Granville Ivanhoe Jordan," the author grieves for her dead father. What do we learn about each of them, and do you think that the grieving is therapeutic for the author? Consider the concrete images presented by the writer, such as the coffin, the father's physical appearance, and the *National Geographic*.

15. What elements do Jordan's "Poem for Granville Ivanhoe Jordan" and "Revelation" by Carole C. Gregory share? In what ways do they differ?

APPENDIX 1

❧ ☙

THE AUTHORS

Angelou, Maya

Maya Angelou—author, poet, playwright, stage and screen performer, and singer—attended public schools in Arkansas and California. Ms. Angelou has taught at the University of California at Los Angeles, the University of Kansas, Wichita State University, and California State University at Sacramento; she is currently at Wake Forest University. Her books include *I Know Why the Caged Bird Sings* (autobiography 1970); *Just Give Me a Cool Drink of Water Before I Die* (1971); *Gather Together in My Name* (autobiography 1974); *Oh Pray My Wings Are Gonna Fit Me Well* (1975); *Singin' and Swingin' and Gettin' Merry Like Christmas* (1976); *And Still I Rise* (1978); *The Heart of a Woman* (1981); *Shaker, Why Don't You Sing?* (1983); *All God's Children Need Traveling Shoes* (1987); *Now Sheba Sings the Song* (1988); and *I Shall Not Be Moved* (1990).

Bambara, Toni Cade

Toni Cade Bambara was born in New York City and grew up in Harlem and Bedford-Stuyvesant, where she attended public and private schools.

She earned her bachelor's degree from Queen's College in 1959 and her master's degree from the City College of New York in 1963. From 1959 to 1961 she was a social investigator with the New York State Department of Welfare. She has also worked as a community organizer, youth worker, settlement house director, and freelance writer. She is editor of the anthologies *The Black Woman* (1970) and *Tales and Stories for Black Folks* (1971). Her own work includes two collections of short stories, *Gorilla, My Love* (1972) and *The Sea Birds Are Still Alive* (1977), and a novel, *The Salt Eaters* (1980).

Bontemps, Arna (1903–1973)

One of the giants of the Harlem Renaissance, Bontemps was a close friend of and collaborator with Langston Hughes. He was a novelist, poet, editor, and historian. He wrote numerous children's books, demonstrating a deep concern for the development of responsible young black people. For many years, Arna Bontemps taught at Fisk University.

Brooks, Gwendolyn

Gwendolyn Brooks has transcended the invisible ethnic line which has separated black and white American writers. Considered a major American poet, she has been the Poet Laureate of Illinois. She received the Pulitzer Prize for poetry in 1950, and in 1987 she was the guest poet at the Smithsonian Institution in Washington, D.C. She is loved and respected by the more militant young black poets of the 1960s and 1970s. She has been acclaimed for her objectivity and high degree of artistic control.

Brown, Sterling A. (1901–1989)

For over forty years Sterling A. Brown was a professor of English at Howard University. He worked on the Federal Writer's Project and the Carnegie-Myrdal Study of the Negro. His published books include *Southern Road* (1932); *The Negro in American Fiction* (1938); and *Negro Poetry and Drama* (1938); and with Arthur P. Davis and Ulysses Lee he edited the classic *Negro Caravan* (1941). Michael H. Harper has also edited a volume of his poetry, *The Collected Poems of Sterling A. Brown* (1990). Brown will be remembered as a prolific poet and a magnificent scholar and educator with tremendous abilities to inspire his students.

Clifton, Lucille

Although primarily a writer of children's books, Lucille Clifton is also the author of four books of poetry: *Good Times* (1969); *Good News about the Earth* (1972); *Next: New Poems* (1987); and *Good Woman: Poems and a Memoir* (1987). She is the mother of six children.

Collier, Eugenia

Eugenia Collier is a graduate of Howard University and Columbia University. She has published numerous articles in scholarly journals and participated in many institutes and conferences on black literature. In 1969, she won the Gwendolyn Brooks award for fiction for her short story, "Marigolds." She is the coeditor, along with Richard A. Long, of *Afro-American Writing: An Anthology of Prose and Poetry* (1985), published in 1972 by New York University Press.

Crayton, Pearl

Now residing in San Jose, California, Pearl Crayton has previously edited an Alexandria, Louisiana, newsletter. She has written numerous articles on African-Americans in Louisiana and is also published in several anthologies.

Cullen, Countee (1903–1946)

Countee Cullen attended New York University and received a master's degree from Harvard University. He dedicated his life to teaching. His first book of poetry, *Color* (1925), won the Harmon Gold Award for literature, thereby bringing him into significant regard as a black American poet.

Derricotte, Toi

Toi Derricotte currently teaches at Old Dominion University in Norfolk, Virginia, and is widely respected by her contemporaries. On the dust jacket of *Natural Birth: Poems,* poet Audre Lorde has commented that "Toi Derricotte moves us ... through worlds some black women have always known, but at times suspected might live only on the insides of our own eyelids. The pain does not exceed the power." Her volumes of poetry include the autobiographical *Natural Birth: Poems* (1983) and *Captivity* (1989).

Edwards, Junius

A native of Louisiana, Junius Edwards graduated from the University of Oslo in Norway. He was the recipient in 1958 of the Writer's Digest Award and in 1959 of a Eugene Saxton Fellowship. Mr. Edwards is now a New York City businessman.

Ferdinand, Val
a.k.a. Kalamu ya Salaam

A founder of Black Art South, a contemporary black arts movement based in New Orleans, Val Ferdinand has commented: "Our art is aimed toward building the nation. Our conclusions are drawn from our experiences and then may be put down in books. As far as we are concerned, just being literary is not and has never been sufficient" (*Black Voices*). His organization assists black writers in getting published.

Gaines, Ernest J.

All of Gaines's stories take place in unidentified Louisiana locales. His most well-known work, *The Autobiography of Miss Jane Pittman* (1972), speaks to his depth of understanding and literary skill. "The Sky Is Gray," the short story which appears in this volume, is widely anthologized. Currently, Gaines resides in the San Francisco area. He is a graduate of San Francisco State College and has studied at Stanford University. In 1959 he was the recipient of the Joseph Henry Jackson Literary Award.

Gregory, Carole C.

Carole Gregory is a graduate of Youngstown State University and is currently living and working in New York City. Her poetry has been published in numerous anthologies.

Harper, Michael S.

Michael S. Harper is a graduate of Howard University and has taught at Los Angeles City College, Contra College in California, Reed College in Oregon, and Brown University. A close friend of Sterling A. Brown's, Harper has edited a volume of Brown's poetry. Harper has been described as one of the most remarkable poets in America. Much of his early poetry is an imitation of forms that come out of black American culture, black speech, jazz structures, and the rhythms of black music.

Hodges, Frenchy

Actress and writer, Frenchy Hodges currently resides in the Atlanta area. She studied at Atlanta University, where she was the recipient of the Afro-American Studies Fellowship and the Howard Jackman Memorial Award.

Hughes, Langston (1902–1967)

Langston Hughes is the most prolific and perhaps the best known of modern African-American writers. A recent biography by Arnold Rampersad is an outstanding description not only of his life and works but of the times in which he lived. Hughes traveled widely and loved black people, especially the common man. His poetry and other writings reflect the amazing gift he had for duplicating the sounds of the Harlem ghetto. More than twelve volumes of his poems were published during his lifetime. With the possible exception of formal literary criticism, he wrote in every genre.

Hurston, Zora Neale (1903–1960)

Very much a woman before her time, Zora Neale Hurston is coming back into public view and, thanks to such writers as Alice Walker, is finally being appreciated for the multitalented genius that she was. She graduated from Barnard College in 1928 with a specialty in anthropological research. Her descriptions of black southern folklore are captured in *Mules and Men,* written in 1935. Her many novels and short stories have been republished and have gained new readership in the eighties. One of the best known is *Their Eyes Were Watching God* (1937), a sensitive love story of a black woman's search for fulfillment.

Johnson, James Weldon (1871–1938)

A native of Florida, Johnson studied at Atlanta University. In addition to his prolific writing career, he served as a public school principal, lawyer, diplomat, NAACP executive secretary, and professor of literature at Fisk University. He and his brother, J. Rosamond Johnson, wrote the words and music for the national Negro anthem, "Lift Every Voice and Sing." His works include *Fifty Years and Other Poems* (1917); *God's Trombones* (1927); and *Along This Way* (1933).

Jones, Gayl

Gayl Jones grew up in Lexington, Kentucky. She attended Connecticut College and Brown University and has taught literature and creative writing at the University of Michigan. Her works include *Corregidora* (1986); *Eva's Man* (1987); *White Rat* (1991); and *Liberating Voices: Oral Tradition in African American Literature* (1991). Gayl Jones is the third generation of black women writers in her family. Much of her work is similar in theme and content to that of her mother, Lucille Jones.

Jordan, June

A native New Yorker, June Jordan has taught at Sarah Lawrence and the City College of New York. She attended Barnard College and the University of Chicago. Her books include *Who Look at Me* (1969); *His Own Where* (1971); *Dry Victories* (1972); and *Naming Our Destiny: New and Selected Poems* (1989). She has also edited an anthology of African-American poetry for young people, *Soulscript* (1970).

Lorde, Audre

Audre Lorde was educated at Hunter College and Columbia University, and she was at one time Poet-In-Residence at Tougaloo College. Her poetry has been published widely; her works include *The Black Unicorn* (1978); *Our Dead Behind Us* (1986); and *A Burst of Light* (1988). *The Cancer Journals* (1980) is a very personal description of her bout with cancer. Lorde describes herself as a feminist lesbian poet.

Marshall, Paule

Paule Marshall is a second-generation American. Her parents immigrated to New York from Barbados, and she grew up under the influence of the "Bajan" cultural style. Her novels reflect upon problems of acculturation and racism as well as upon life in Barbados. Marshall graduated Phi Beta Kappa from Brooklyn College. She has worked as a librarian and as a journalist. Her fellowships and prizes have come from the Guggenheim and Ford foundations, the National Institute of Arts and Letters, and the National Endowment for the Arts, among others. Her novels are *Brown Girl, Brownstones* (1959); *Soul Clap Hands and Sing* (1961); *The Chosen Place, the Timeless People* (1969); *Praisesong for the Widow* (1983); and *Daughters* (forthcoming).

McMurray, Georgia L.

Georgia L. McMurray is a social worker, and private child-care and management consultant. She was recently appointed visiting professor at Fordham University. She is afflicted with Charcot-Marie-Tooth, a rare form of muscular dystrophy which has left her totally paralyzed.

McKay, Claude (1890–1948)

One of the Harlem Renaissance poets, Claude McKay was associate editor of *Liberator Magazine* during the 1920s. *Harlem Shadows,* a collection of his poetry, was published in 1922. Also a novelist, McKay's books are *Home to Harlem* (1928); *Banjo* (1929); and *A Long Way Home* (1937). He was a native Jamaican.

Naylor, Gloria

Gloria Naylor grew up in New York City in the 1950s. She received her bachelor's degree in English from Brooklyn College and her master's degree in Afro-American Studies from Yale University. She has been a writer-in-residence at George Washington University in Washington, D.C. Her first novel, *The Women of Brewster Place,* won the American Book Award for Best Fiction in 1983. "Brewster Place" was produced in 1989 by Oprah Winfrey. Ms. Naylor has written two other widely acclaimed novels, *Linden Hills* (1986) and *Mama Day* (1989).

Parks, Gordon

Gordon Parks's versatility is noted in his various accomplishments—photographer, journalist, film director, and writer. He was the recipient of the Spingarn Medal in 1972. His books include *A Choice of Weapons* (1966); *Born Black* (1971); *Moments without Proper Names* (1975); *Flavio* (1978); *To Smile in Autumn, a Memoir* (1979); and *Shannon* (1981) as well as *Voices in the Mirror: An Autobiography* (1990). He has been a photographer for both *Life* and *Vogue* magazines.

Randall, Dudley

Dudley Randall has been described as the founder, editor, and guiding spirit of Broadside Press in Detroit, a leading African-American poetry publishing house. Coauthor with Margaret Danner of *Poem Counterpoem* (1969) and coeditor with Margaret Borroughs of the anthology on Mal-

301

colm X, *Poems on the Life and Death of Malcolm X* (1969), Mr. Randall has also published several collections of his own poetry.

Shockley, Ann Allen

Ann Allen Shockley has been Special Collections Librarian at Fisk University since 1969. Although most of her writing has dealt with professional materials for librarians, she is the editor of *Afro-American Women Writers, 1746–1933: An Anthology and Critical Guide* (1989).

Thelwell, Mike

Mike Thelwell is a Jamaican writer who studied at Howard University and has taught Third-World literature at the University of Massachusetts. His short stories and literary political essays have appeared in *Partisan Review, Black Scholar,* and *The Massachusetts Review,* and he is the author of *Duties, Pleasures and Conflicts: Essays in Struggle* (1987) and *The Harder They Come* (1988). His awards include first prize in the Story Magazine Fiction Contest and fellowships from the Rockefeller Foundation and Society for the Humanities. Mr. Thelwell has also had an intimate association with Mississippi through his association with the Student Non-Violent Coordinating Committee and the Mississippi Freedom Party.

Walker, Alice

Alice Walker is a native of Georgia, and she attended both Spellman and Sarah Lawrence colleges. Although catapulted into fame for her novel, *The Color Purple* (1982), Ms. Walker is also a short-story writer and a poet. She speaks and writes from a distinctly female perspective. Other works include *Revolutionary Petunias and Other Poems* (1973); *In Love and Trouble* (1974); *Meridian* (1976); *Once: Poems* (1976); *Goodnight Willie Lee, I'll See You in the Morning* (1984); *The Third Life of Grange Copeland* (1989); *The Temple of My Familiar* (1989); and *Her Blue Body Everything We Know: Earthling Poems (1965–1990)* (1990).

SUGGESTED READINGS

Baker, Houston. *Singers of Daybreak: Studies in Black American Literature.* Washington: Howard University Press, 1983.

Bell, Roseann, Bettye Parker, and Guy Sheftall. *Sturdy Black Bridges: Visions of Black Women in Literature.* New York: Doubleday, 1979.

Evans, Mari. *Black Women Writers (1950–1980)*. New York: Doubleday, 1984.

Popkins, Michael (ed.). *Modern Black Writers*. New York: Fredrick Ungar Publishing Co., 1978.

APPENDIX 2

❧ ❧

PERMISSIONS

Hughes, Langston. "Aunt Sue's Stories" from *Selected Poems by Langston Hughes*. Reprinted by permission of Alfred A. Knopf, New York. Copyright 1959 by Langston Hughes.

SECTION I

Bambara, Toni Cade. "A Girl's Story" from *The Sea Birds Are Still Alive*. Reprinted by permission of Random House, New York, and The Women's Press, London. Copyright 1974, 1976, 1977 by Toni Cade Bambara.

Brooks, Gwendolyn. "The Mother" from *Blacks* (New York: Harper & Row, 1945). Reprinted by permission of the author. Copyright 1945 by Gwendolyn Brooks.

Brown, Sterling A. "Parish Doctor" from *The Collected Poems of Sterling Brown* by Sterling A. Brown, edited by Michael Harper. Reprinted by permission of Harper & Row Publishers, New York. Copyright 1980 by Sterling A. Brown.

Derricotte, Toi. "Delivery" and "The Presentation" from *Natural Birth: Poems* (Trumanburg, NY: Crossing Press, 1983). Reprinted by permission of the author. Copyright 1983 by Toi Derricotte.

Edwards, Junius. *If We Must Die* (excerpt) (New York: Doubleday, 1963). Reprinted by permission of the author. Copyright 1963 by Junius Edwards.

Gaines, Ernest J. "The Sky Is Gray" from *Bloodline*. Reprinted by permission of

Doubleday, a division of Bantam, Doubleday, Dell Publishing Group, New York. Copyright 1963 by Ernest J. Gaines.

Hughes, Langston. "Dr. Sidesaddle" from *Simple's Uncle Sam*. Reprinted by permission of Hill and Wang, a division of Farrar, Straus & Giroux, New York, and Harold Ober Associates, New York. Copyright 1965 by Langston Hughes.

Hurston, Zora Neale. "My Most Humiliating Jim Crow Experience" from *I Love Myself When I Am Laughing . . . and Then Again When I Am Looking Mean and Impressive: A Zora Neale Hurston Reader*, Alice Walker, ed. Reprinted by permission of the Feminist Press at City University of New York. Copyright 1979 by Alice Walker.

Jones, Gayl. "Asylum" from *White Rat*. Reprinted by permission of Random House, New York. Copyright 1977 by Gayl Jones.

Lorde, Audre. *The Cancer Journals* (excerpts). Reprinted by permission of Spinsters/Aunt Lute, San Francisco, and the Charlotte Sheedy Literary Agency, New York. Copyright 1980 by Audre Lorde.

McMurray, Georgia L. "Dreaming, I Can Dance." Reprinted by permission of the author.

Walker, Alice. "The Abortion" from *You Can't Keep A Good Woman Down*. Reprinted by permission of Harcourt Brace Jovanovich, Orlando, Florida, and David Higham Associates, London. Copyright 1980 by Alice Walker.

———. "Strong Horse Tea" from *In Love and Trouble*. Reprinted by permission of Harcourt Brace Jovanovich, Orlando, Florida, and David Higham Associates, London. Copyright 1968 by Alice Walker.

SECTION II

Angelou, Maya. "The Last Decision" from *Shaker, Why Don't You Sing*. Reprinted by permission of Random House, New York, and Virago Press, London. Copyright 1983, 1986 by Maya Angelou.

———. "On Aging" from *And Still I Rise*. Reprinted by permission of Random House, New York, and Virago Press, London. Copyright 1978, 1986 by Maya Angelou.

Bambara, Toni Cade. "Maggie of the Green Bottles" from *Gorilla, My Love*. Reprinted by permission of Random House, New York, and The Women's Press, London. Copyright 1968 by Toni Cade Bambara.

Bontemps, Arna. "A Summer Tragedy." Reprinted by permission of Harold Ober Associates, New York. Copyright 1933 by Arna Bontemps, renewed 1983.

Brooks, Gwendolyn. "The Bean Eaters" from *Blacks* (New York: Harper & Row Publishers, 1945). Reprinted by permission of the author. Copyright 1945 by Gwendolyn Brooks.

Brown, Sterling A. "Virginia Portrait" from *The Collected Poems of Sterling Brown* by Sterling A. Brown, edited by Michael Harper. Reprinted by permission of Harper & Row Publishers, New York. Copyright 1980 by Sterling A. Brown.

Clifton, Lucille. "Miss Rosie" from *Good Times*. Reprinted by permission of Random House, New York. Copyright 1969 by Lucille Clifton.

Collier, Eugenia. "Marigolds" from *Negro Digest* (November 1969). Reprinted by permission of the author. Copyright 1969 by Eugenia Collier.

Marshall, Paule. "To Da-duh, in Memoriam" from *Reena and Other Stories*. Reprinted by permission of the Feminist Press at City University of New York. Copyright 1967 by Paule Marshall.

Randall, Dudley. "George" from *Poem Counterpoem* by Margaret Danner and Dudley Randall. Reprinted by permission of Broadside Press, Detroit, and the author. Copyright 1966 by Dudley Randall.

Walker, Alice. "To Hell with Dying" from *In Love and Trouble*. Reprinted by permission of Harcourt Brace Jovanovich, Orlando, Florida, and David Higham Associates, London. Copyright 1967 by Alice Walker.

SECTION III

Brooks, Gwendolyn. "We Real Cool" from *We Real Cool*, series 6 (Detroit: Broadside Press, 1966). Reprinted by permission of the author. Copyright 1945 by Gwendolyn Brooks.

Brown, Sterling A. "Sister Lou" and "Old Lem" from *The Collected Poems of Sterling Brown* by Sterling A. Brown, edited by Michael Harper. Reprinted by permission of Harper & Row Publishers, New York. Copyright 1980 by Sterling A. Brown.

————. "Maumee Ruth" from *Southern Road* by Sterling A. Brown. Reprinted by permission of Harper & Row Publishers, New York. Copyright 1938 by Harcourt Brace Jovanovich, renewed 1968 by Sterling A. Brown.

Crayton, Pearl. "Cotton Alley" from *Negro Digest* (November 1969). Reprinted by permission of the author. Copyright 1969 by Pearl Crayton.

Cullen, Countee. "A Brown Girl Dead" from *On These I Stand*. Reprinted by permission of Harper & Row Publishers, New York. Copyright 1925 by Harper & Row Publishers, renewed 1953 by Ida M. Cullen.

Edwards, Junius. "Mother Dear and Daddy" from *The Angry Black,* edited by John A. Williams (Savage, MD: Cooper Square Publishers, 1962). Reprinted by permission of the author and Robert P. Mills, agent. Copyright 1962 by John A. Williams.

Ferdinand, Val, aka Kalamu ya Salaam. "Second Line/Cutting the Body Loose" from *What We Must See: Young Black Story Tellers,* edited by Coombs Orde (New York: Dodd Mead and Company, 1971). Revised. Reprinted by permission of the author. Copyright 1971 by Val Ferdinand.

Gregory, Carole C. "Revelation." From *Black Sisters: Poetry by Black American Women, 1746–1980* (Bloomington, IN: Indiana University Press, 1981). Reprinted by permission of the author. Copyright 1979 by Carole C. Gregory.

Harper, Michael S. "We Assume: On the Death of Our Son, Reuben Masai Harper" from *Images of Kin*. Reprinted by permission of the University of Illinois Press, Champaign, Illinois. Copyright 1977 by Michael S. Harper.

Hodges, Frenchy. "Requiem for Willie Lee." From *Midnight Birds: Stories of Contemporary Women Writers,* edited by Mary Helen Washington (New York: Doubleday, 1980). Reprinted by permission of the author. Copyright 1979 by Frenchy Hodges.

Hughes, Langston. "Golden Gate" from *Simple's Uncle Sam*. Reprinted by permission of Hill and Wang, a division of Farrar, Straus & Giroux, New York, and Harold Ober Associates, New York. Copyright 1965 by Langston Hughes.

———. "Death in Yorkville" and "Junior Addict" from *The Panther and the Lash: Poems of Our Times*. Reprinted by permission of Alfred A. Knopf, New York. Copyright 1967 by Arna Bontemps and George Houston Bass, executors of the estate of Langston Hughes.

———. "Widow Woman" and "As Befits a Man" from *Selected Poems of Langston Hughes*. Reprinted by permission of Alfred A. Knopf, New York. Copyright 1959 by Langston Hughes.

Johnson, James Weldon. "Go Down Death" from *God's Trombones*. Reprinted by permission of Viking Penguin, a division of Penguin Books, USA, New York. Copyright 1927 by Viking Press, renewed 1955 by Grace Nail Johnson.

Jordan, June. "Poem for Granville Ivanhoe Jordan" from *Things That I Do in the Dark* (Boston: Beacon Press, 1981). Reprinted by permission of the author. Copyright 1981 by June Jordan.

Lorde, Audre. "Eulogy for Alvin Frost" from *The Black Unicorn*. Reprinted by permission of W. W. Norton & Company, New York. Copyright 1978 by Audre Lorde and the Charlotte Sheedy Literary Agency, New York.

Marshall, Paule. *Praisesong for the Widow*. Reprinted by permission of the Putnam Publishing Group, New York, and Joan Daves. Copyright 1983 by Paule Marshall.

McKay, Claude. "The Lynching" from *Selected Poems of Claude McKay*. Reprinted by permission of Twayne Publishers, a division of G. K. Hall & Company, Boston. Copyright 1970 by Twayne Publishers.

Naylor, Gloria. "Lucielia Louise Turner" from *The Women of Brewster Place*. Reprinted by permission of Viking Penguin, New York. Copyright 1982 by Viking Press.

Parks, Gordon. *The Learning Tree* (excerpt). Reprinted by permission of Harper & Row Publishers, New York. Copyright 1963 by Gordon Parks.

Shockley, Ann Allen. "The Funeral." From *Out of Our Lives,* edited by Quandra Prettyman Stadler (Washington, DC: Howard University Press, 1975). Reprinted by permission of the author.

Thelwell, Mike. "Bright an' Mownin' Star" from *Massachusetts Review* 7, no. 4 (Autumn 1966). Reprinted by permission of the Massachusetts Review, Amherst, Massachusetts. Copyright 1966 by the Massachusetts Review.

Walker, Alice. "Revolutionary Petunias" from *Revolutionary Petunias and Other Poems*. Reprinted by permission of Harcourt Brace Jovanovich, Orlando, Florida, and the Wendy Weil Agency, New York. Copyright 1972 by Alice Walker.

———. "Free at Last" from *Meridian*. Reprinted by permission of Harcourt Brace Jovanovich, Orlando, Florida. Copyright 1976 by Alice Walker.